Maxim Gorky

THE LOWER DEPTHS *AND OTHER PLAYS*

Translated by Alexander Bakshy

in collaboration with

Paul S. Nathan

New Haven and London

Yale University Press

The plays in this volume originally
appeared in SEVEN PLAYS OF MAXIM GORKY,
translated by Alexander Bakshy in
collaboration with Paul S. Nathan.

Library of Congress catalog card number: 59–13678
International Standard Book Number: 0–300–00100–2

The paper in this book meets the guidelines for
permanence and durability of the Committee on
Production Guidelines for Book Longevity of the
Council on Library Resources.
Printed in the United States of America

24 23 22 21 20

CONTENTS

The Theater of Maxim Gorky
by Alexander Bakshy   vi

The Lower Depths   1

Enemies   75

The Zykovs   151

THE THEATER OF MAXIM GORKY

Maxim gorky died in 1936, at the age of sixty-eight. Many great changes had taken place in Russia during his lifetime. When Gorky was born, in 1868, serfdom, abolished seven years before, was still fresh in everyone's memory. But new political and economic forces were already at work. The landowning class, which constituted the major part of the Russian "nobility," was in the process of differentiation and economic decline. Its social exclusiveness was being undermined, its dominance in the cultural life of the country was effectively challenged. The challenge came mostly from the educated section of the middle class, the so-called intelligentsia, which was growing in numbers, thanks to the extension of educational facilities and the influx of impoverished landowning nobility. Strong as the intelligentsia was—and it had won for itself a leading place in literature and the arts and was able to wage a successful war against the characteristic class-bred ethics, esthetics, and politics of the landowning class—it was too weak to impress its predominantly radical views on the entire country. Its most ambitious effort—an attempt by terrorist means to establish a democratic regime in Russia—failed disastrously. The assassination of Tsar Alexander II in 1881 did not bring democracy to power. Instead, it ushered in a period of political and social reaction which reduced the intelligentsia to virtual impotence and put an end to all dreams of a swift transformation of Russia into a progressive country after the pattern of Western Europe. Recovery from the widespread disillusionment, frustration, and apathy did not come until the early nineties. By that time new social forces—a western-minded wealthy bourgeoisie and a growing working class, both products of the industrial development of the country—were slowly coming into play. Concurrently, the intellectual and political life of the nation began to show signs of awakening, and new, if long-distance, optimism was born.

The first short story by Gorky to attract national attention appeared in 1892, at the very opening of the new era. The young author, then twenty-four, was perhaps better versed in the realities of Russian life than most of the writing profession of his day. Brought up in the family of his grandfather, owner of a small dye works, in surroundings that were unspeakably crude and frequently brutal, he had, at an early age, been thrown on his own resources and worked hard, nearly always half starving, at one small job after another. He might well have ended as another shoemaker Alyoshka or locksmith Klestch, as he later pictured them in *The Lower Depths*, had it not been for his insatiable thirst for knowledge. Somehow he managed to educate himself sufficiently to become a copy clerk to a lawyer. The job was a "respectable" one, but it could give him little spiritual satisfaction, and eager to know the world he set out on a "grand tour" of Russia, tramping from his native Nijny Novgorod, on the upper Volga, all the way down to the southern Caucasus and back again. In those two years of vagabondage, he saw life shorn of its last vestiges of conventional culture, and shared company with the lowest derelicts of society. He returned to civilization to become a reporter on provincial newspapers, continuing on this path, with occasional intervals in jail for association with revolutionists and expressing injudiciously outspoken opinions, until the popularity of his short stories permitted him to concentrate his efforts on creative writing.

With that early experience behind him, it was natural that Gorky should grow up a rebel. His rebellion was directed as much against the conditions which condemned large sections of the population to a life of squalor and human degradation as against the intelligentsia, which had lost its larger vision of life, its sense of the heroic, and was content to bury itself in the prosaic tasks of personal well-being and professional work. In story after story Gorky pictured the world of social derelicts and outcasts whose very existence was a reproof to the existing social order, but who, surprisingly enough, were portrayed as superior beings rising above their melancholy condition to give free play to their passions, to pour contempt on the weak and the squeamish, and to glory in their personal power and their freedom from conventional restraints. These highly romanticized Russian counterparts of the American tramp struck the imagination of the Russian public. Gorky became the symbol of revolutionary protest against the existing society, and his popularity, particularly with the younger generation, bordered on idolatry.

It was at the peak of his literary fame that Gorky made his debut as a dramatist. The play was "The Smug Citizens,"* produced by the Moscow Art Theater in 1902. In retrospect, it does not seem to be an important work. But it had certain significant features which at the time insured its success with the public (if not so greatly with the critics). Its attack on the Philistine concern with comfortable living and on the lack of a clear purpose in life even among those who longed for something better than creature comforts was in line with Gorky's denunciations in his earlier stories and found a quick response in his audience. The other significant feature of the play was the portrait of a worker as a being superior to the average intellectual. This progenitor of all proletarian heroes in Russian literature possessed practical idealism, knew what he wanted, and had the will power to realize his aims. By that time Marxism had gained a large following among the intelligentsia and Gorky's glorification of the worker won him added acclaim in revolutionary circles.

Gorky himself, however, was far from pleased with his first play. He wrote to Chekhov after completing it: "Well, the play has turned out to be clamorous and bustling and, it seems, empty and dull. I dislike it very much. This very winter I will without fail write another play. And if that does not come off well, I'll write ten more until I get what I want! It has to be finely proportioned and beautiful like music."

The reference to music was no doubt a reflection of Gorky's admiration for Chekhov's plays. To a remarkable degree he achieved this quality of music in his second play, "At the Bottom" (better known in English as "The Lower Depths"), but it is music which springs from the interplay of brilliantly expressed ideas and striking characterizations, and not, as with Chekhov, from the lyrical emotion which envelops the action. Produced by the Moscow Art Theater in 1902, the play was a resounding

* "The Smug Citizens," translated by E. Hopkins, *Poet Lore*, 1906.

success with the public. The critics were far more grudging in their approval. What worried them most was the play's "message." Was old Luka, the soft-spoken dispenser of comforting lies, to be regarded as Gorky's mouthpiece, and were his ideas to be taken seriously? The heated controversy over the moral issues involved left little room for appreciation of the fact that "The Lower Depths" is a remarkable work of art, surging with a life of its own, presenting characters that are unique on the Russian stage, and distinguished by an epigrammatic brilliance that is matched in Russian drama only by Griboyedov's "Wit Works Woe" and Gogol's "The Inspector General."

It cannot be said that "The Lower Depths" is a flawless masterpiece. But only Chekhov was able to lay his finger on the flaws that really mattered. In a letter to Gorky he wrote:

"You have removed the most interesting characters (except the actor) from the fourth act, and now beware lest something happen because of that. This act may appear dull and unnecessary, particularly if with the departure of the stronger and more interesting actors, only the mediocre ones stay on.* The actor's death is terrible—it is as if you were hitting the spectator on the head all of a sudden without preparing him for it. How the Baron has got into the night lodgings and why he is a baron is not made sufficiently clear either."

Gorky did not listen to Chekhov's advice and left the fourth act as he had written it. But Chekhov was unquestionably right —in point of action the last act is anticlimactic; and it is saved from being dull mainly by Satin's speeches, the sort of rhetoric for which Chekhov, with his reverence for simplicity of writing, had little liking. A sidelight on Gorky's love of epigrammatic paradoxes, in which "The Lower Depths" is particularly rich, appears in a letter, written by Gorky to K. Chukovsky, a well-known Russian critic, some twenty years later. In that letter Gorky says:

"You are unquestionably right when you say Wilde's paradoxes are 'commonplaces turned inside out.' But don't you consider it possible that this tendency to turn all commonplaces inside out conceals a more or less conscious desire to spite Mrs. Grundy and undermine English puritanism? In my opinion such

* Reference to the proposed casting of parts at the Moscow Art Theater. A. B.

THE LOWER DEPTHS AND OTHER PLAYS

phenomena as Wilde and Bernard Shaw are most surprising for the England of the end of the nineteenth century; nevertheless they are wholly natural—English hypocrisy is the best organized hypocrisy, and I regard paradoxes in the sphere of morals as a legitimate weapon in the struggle against puritanism."

Remembering Gorky's contempt for native Russian Philistinism, one begins to understand the motive that lay behind the quips and far-fetched ridicule that he directed against it. There is a great deal of this contempt and ridicule in the portraits of various types of the intelligentsia which he painted in his next four plays: "Summer-folk" * (1903), "The Children of the Sun" † (1905), "Barbarians" (1906), and "Enemies" (1906).

The years during which these plays were written were marked by a growing political tension in Russia. The labor movement showed unexpected strength in a wave of strikes and demonstrations that swept the country in 1903, despite the government's resort to arrests and shootings. The war against Japan (1904–05) dragged on ingloriously, bringing to light the corrupt practices of the ruling clique and exposing the incompetence of the Russian military leadership. "Bloody Sunday" (January, 1905) shocked Russia as well as the rest of the world by the brutality with which the government shot hundreds of workers for presuming to march, under the leadership of a priest, to the Tsar's palace in order to submit a petition for amelioration of their lot. The mutiny in the Black Sea navy, which immortalized the battle cruiser *Potemkin*, disclosed the spread of revolutionary ideas among the very groups which were the mainstay of the Tsarist regime. The climax came with the national strike of October, 1905, which forced the Tsar to promise political freedom and a parliamentary government. That historic upheaval is better remembered today as "the abortive revolution of 1905," for the Tsar's government went back on most of his promises and continued on the path that twelve years later brought an end to the regime it headed.

Gorky did not watch this march of events from the sidelines. Busy as he was with his plays and novels, he did all he could to advance the cause of the common people. His political sym-

---

* "Summer-folk," translated by Aline Delano, *Poet Lore*, 1905.
† "The Children of the Sun," translated by A. J. Wolf, *Poet Lore*, 1906.

pathies turned more and more toward the Marxist Social Democratic party, and particularly to its Left wing which was led by Lenin. But on a few occasions his intervention was more active. He joined in a direct appeal to the leaders of the government in an attempt to prevent the butchery of Bloody Sunday and was jailed for his part in that effort. (It was while in jail, incidentally, that he wrote "The Children of the Sun.") He also gave active help to the revolutionists during the unsuccessful insurrection in Moscow in December, 1905, after which, expecting to be arrested, he hastened to leave Russia, remaining a political émigré abroad for the next eight years. (An episode in the latter period was his visit to America, where he was evicted from a hotel because he was not formally married to the lady who accompanied him as his wife.)

Gorky's political sympathies naturally found expression in the four plays he wrote during those years. In "Summer-folk" he castigated the intelligentsia for its Philistinism and futility. In "The Children of the Sun" he stressed the gulf that separated the intelligentsia from the common folk, who carried their distrust of the more privileged and educated to the point of mob violence. In "Barbarians" representatives of the intelligentsia were treated with ill-disguised sarcasm. And finally, in "Enemies" the wealthier section of the intelligentsia was bitterly assailed for the prejudice and hostility, inspired by selfish class interests, which it displayed toward the workers.

No doubt Gorky's political views are much in evidence in these four plays. But the plays, particularly "Barbarians" and "The Children of the Sun," and to a lesser degree "Enemies," have qualities of characterization that rise far above their political and moral message. In the struggle between social philosophies, which assumed great intensity during that stormy period, these qualities were largely overlooked and the majority of the intelligentsia, rising in defense of their own political and moral integrity, not only denounced the plays as libelous, but went even farther by declaring them to be utterly devoid of artistic value. In fact, after the publication of "Enemies," the cry went up that Gorky was finished as a writer. "The End of Gorky" was the title of an article by a noted liberal writer. "The coming cad" was the phrase used by another even more famous critic and novelist who branded thus the materialist, nihilist, and atheist heroes of Gorky's early stories, including "The Lower Depths."

"Summer-folk," perhaps the weakest of Gorky's plays, was condemned by the critics. But what they objected to was not so much its long-winded discussions of the meaning of life as its uncomplimentary portraits of various representatives of the intelligentsia. Among the advocates of art for art's sake the play was dismissed for other reasons. " 'Summer-folk,' " wrote one of them, "does not rise above the level of common-place mediocrity. Most unpleasantly it resembles the plays of Chekhov."

"The Children of the Sun" had a more favorable reception, probably because it did not attack the intelligentsia but rather deplored their lack of contact with the low-born and ignorant common folk who lived by their side and on whom they depended for their comforts. Yet "Barbarians," a much stronger play and one of Gorky's best, was greeted with sad shakings of the head.

Here is a characteristic comment by A. Kugel, a popular dramatic critic of the time:

"The lack of theatrical quality in Gorky's plays is explained not by his ignorance of the requirements of the stage, for these are largely technical tricks, and Gorky has a fairly good command of them. He is not a dramatist because he has no definite ethical views and because, while opposing the so-called 'smugness,' the petty Philistine morality, he has not sufficiently comprehended the realm of higher morality . . . The more Gorky reveals himself in his quest of moral truth, the poorer his plays become.

"Here, for example, is 'Barbarians'—the last but one of his plays. It had its première in St. Petersburg the other day, and it was positively painful to watch this feeble, this altogether feeble play. It is not that one cannot see any evidence of talent on the part of the author. The play has some interesting and even novel characters; a striking artistic strain breaks out here and there. Yet one is bored—it is all so trivial and uninteresting. And note how extremely confusing the moral thesis of this play is. Who the barbarians are no one can tell. It would appear the visiting engineers are the barbarians. But it is possible the barbarians are the native inhabitants of the small backwater town.

Nor can one tell what is meant by barbarism. It looks as though
barbarism is the young, bright, upcoming, untapped force
which is destined to turn everything upside down. On the other
hand, it may be that barbarism is the destruction of the elemen-
tal traditional forms without replacing them by newer ones.
. . . In 'Barbarians' the question of what is truth and where
it is to be found absolutely defies definition. After all, not a
single person in this crowd of characters commands our sympathy. And how is it possible to interest the audience in the
fate of people for whom it can find no sympathy? Thus what we
have here is precisely the result of the author's indifference to
ethical problems."

One cannot help sympathizing with the critic in his inability
to discover the moral message of the play. It is possible that
Gorky himself could not answer his questions, despite the fact
that he called the play "Barbarians" and made his characters
use the word on a few occasions. But in works of art (Tolstoy's
Anna Karenina is an outstanding example) characters have a
way of ignoring the author's message and asserting themselves
as independent entities with a life entirely their own. In such
cases, whether we sympathize with the characters or not, their
very coming to life before our eyes is the miracle that is creative
art. In "Barbarians" the characters and all their surroundings
do most vividly come to life out of the limbo of the author's
imagination, and one character in particular, the hapless, comi-
cally romantic Nadezhda, assumes such monumental proportions
that her tragedy invests the whole play with a broader and more
intense significance than the mere conflict between native "barbarism" and sophisticated "civilization."

It is to the credit of Alexander Block, the great Russian poet
of the pre-revolutionary era, that almost alone among his con-
temporaries he recognized the extraordinary tragic beauty of this
character. He wrote:

"There is one person in the play who is so remarkable that
she engraves herself on one's memory. This person is the wife of
a revenue collector, Nadezhda Polikarpovna Monakhova, a tall
woman of great beauty with enormous staring eyes. Genuine
Russian strength and freedom emanate from her being. . . .
She is strangely and beautifully whole. There is in her some
great force that both attracts one and repels. She is strong with

the power of some austere, animal fascination. I feel that the whole play was written for the sake of this character. It is possible to believe that it is she who is 'the human being,' the true heroine of the play, in the absence of a hero: 'You've killed a human being,' says her husband at the end of the play."

"Summer-folk," "The Children of the Sun," and "Barbarians" were performed on the stage, but none of them was a success. Production of "Enemies" was forbidden by the Tsarist censorship and the play did not see the footlights in Russia until 1933. Since then its exposition of the class war thesis has made it one of the classics of the Soviet repertoire.

Gorky returned to a moral-political theme in "The Last Ones" (1908). The play pictures a divided and disintegrating family faced with the moral issue of preventing or consenting to the execution of a young man accused, on questionable evidence, of a terroristic attempt on the head of the family, a debauched and callous police chief. The play's principal claim to distinction is its subtly woven, indirect dialogue. But the characterization, with a few minor exceptions, is much less impressive, and the didacticism, too heavily stressed, seems forced and unconvincing. Like "Enemies," it was forbidden to be produced in Russia and was dismissed by the book reviewers as another evidence of Gorky's declining talent.

After the revolutionary upheaval of 1905 Russian literature and drama were steadily turning away from characteristic aspects and problems of contemporary life. The new interest, shared by authors and public alike, was centered on broader generalizations stated in the form of allegory with cosmic overtones, or in terms of religious mysticism and esoteric symbolism. Gorky's deeply ingrained sense of real life, though capable of taking on romantic coloration or the fervid emotionalism of a semi-religious worship of humanity, was largely out of tune with the prevailing mood of the Russian public. It is not surprising therefore that during that era of intellectual disquiet and groping attempts to discover new gods, his works, and especially his plays, received little attention. Yet he went on writing novels, stories, and plays, concentrating more and more on lower middle-class characters buried in the depths of provincial Russia and utterly removed from the problems, interests, and ways of thought of the sophisticated intelligentsia.

Only the first one of this series of plays, "Queer People" (published in 1910), harks back to Gorky's earlier themes. The characters of "Queer People" are all intellectuals, and inevitably there is a great deal of talking concerning the problems of life. But Gorky's own attitude toward his characters has noticeably mellowed. Although he calls them queer, he presents them in a warm, sympathetic light, and he clearly admires the selfless devotion of his principal heroine, Elena, as well as forgives the indiscretions of his hero, the writer Mastakov, whom he even uses as his mouthpiece to express his own affectionately cheerful view of Russia and her people.

"Queer People" was not a success on the stage and received only condescending notices from the majority of critics. One dissenting critic, however, who is unfortunately anonymous, should be quoted here for his more penetrating appreciation of the play and of Gorky's work as a whole:

"While a certain, modernistic section of our critics have long since buried M. Gorky," he wrote, "and have, not without some malicious satisfaction, raised a big wooden cross on his grave, the writer has been confidently moving forward, with each new work revealing ever new and still untapped resources of creative power. One gains this impression of artistic growth not only from his latest short stories but also from his plays, especially 'Queer People.' Here is the same familiar yet strangely transfigured author: new ideas, new colors, new, softened tones. . . ."

" 'Queer People,' " continues the critic, "are the kind of people who do not so much live according to the demands and needs of their own inner nature, as play in their lives this or that *role* forced upon them by external circumstances."

"Vassa Zheleznova" was published in the same year as "Queer People." There is one interesting link between the two: "Vassa Zheleznova" develops an idea suggested by Mastakov, the central character of "Queer People." Speaking of an old woman, Medvedeva, who worries about her daughter, engaged to a consumptive egotist, Mastakov says to his wife, Elena: "Do you think, Lena, she's capable—out of love for her daughter—for young life—of committing a crime? . . . I *would* like her to be capable—for example—of giving poison to that Vassya. She's such a nice woman. Oh, it's a wonderful theme. Only mothers can think of the future—because they give birth to it in their children."

Critics who wrote about "Vassa Zheleznova" before the revolution could see in it nothing but a story of a sordid intrigue carried on by a collection of moral freaks. Since the revolution the play has been interpreted as demonstrating the moral disintegration of a bourgeois family that is moved by a single interest—greed for money.

Both interpretations seem far wide of the mark. Vassa Zheleznova may not be "a nice woman" of the type of old Medvedeva in "Queer People," but she is neither a freak nor a money-mad merchant's wife. She is just "a mother who thinks of the future" and for this reason "is capable of committing a crime." Nor does it seem possible that anyone today can fail to be impressed by the amazing strength, the concentrated richness and the vividness of most of the other characters who figure in the play. Yet a well-known journalist, reviewing the play in 1911, was able to write as follows:

"What do I care about the Zheleznov family? What do I care about the lop-sided Pavel and his lop-sided tragedy? What do I care about the stupid Semyon and his dream of having a jewelry store on the main street? There are many families in literature in whose fate I am intensely interested. . . . But the Zheleznov family does not interest me, and at the performance I felt as if Gorky had forced me to eavesdrop at the door of some vile lower-middle-class house. . . . Upon my word, I don't care who will get the money after the death of father Zheleznov—whether it will be his disgusting wife or his lop-eared children. I yawned at the performance, and I am yawning now as I share my dull impressions with you. After all, you don't care two pins for the Zheleznov family either.

"I don't understand why it interested Gorky. What is there in this family? A résumé of the present? A clue to the past? A source of the future? Is it that Russia is reflected in it as it is reflected in the Larin, Prozorov, and Bezsemenov families? * It is nothing of the sort. It is not even *une histoire naturelle d'une famille,* in the manner of Zola. It is simply a dull story by

* Reference to the Larins in Pushkin's "Eugene Onegin," the Prozorovs in Chekhov's "Three Sisters," and the Bezsemenovs in Gorky's "The Smug Citizens." A. B.

Mr. N. about his acquaintances, the Z. family, who live in the town NN."

One has to be reminded of this literary blindness to realize what prejudice dogged the steps of the great writer.

Twenty-six years later, a few months before Gorky's death, a new version of "Vassa Zheleznova" was published. For reasons that are not difficult to conjecture, Gorky decided to inject a "social significance" theme into his old play. The "martyrdom" of motherhood was pushed into the background, and forward came the conflict between Vassa, the property owner, and a new character, her daughter-in-law, a revolutionary socialist. Compared with the first version of "Vassa Zheleznova," which is translated in this collection, the second version is essentially a new play, and an emasculated, much weaker play at that.

Gorky's exile abroad ended in 1914. Within a few months of his return, Russia was plunged into the first World War which shook the foundations of the old regime, brought on its overthrow in the February revolution of 1917, and culminated in the cataclysm of the Bolshevik revolution. Throughout those stormy years Gorky was active in the political field. He opposed the war while it lasted, and he also opposed the Bolsheviks for letting loose forces of destruction which, he believed at the time, they were incapable of controlling. But despite the immense amount of publicist writing and the great passion with which he defended his political views, as a playwright he remained serenely aloof from politics and the problems of the day. The series of plays which followed "Vassa Zheleznova" included "The Zykovs" (1914), "The Old Man" (1919), "The Counterfeit Coin" (1926), "Yegor Bulychov" (1931), and "Dostigayev and Others" (1933). Only in the last two plays, and only retrospectively at that, did Gorky touch upon matters of politics. On the other hand, in four of these plays, "Vassa Zheleznova," "The Zykovs," "The Old Man" and "Yegor Bulychov," he is seen to be primarily interested in the study of character, which in every case is so masterly in its results that it completely overshadows the moral problems around which the plots of these plays were built. The four plays are also bound together by a revealing and significant feature—Gorky's warm, almost loving, interest in the type of self-made and strong-willed men and women who rose from the lower middle class, mostly without benefit of education, to become rich merchants and manufacturers. His semi-admiring attitude toward these low-born capitalists, of whom Antipa Zykov and Yegor Bulychov are such magnificent specimens, stands in striking contrast to the sarcasm and bitterness with which he pictures the more western-ized capitalists in "Enemies."

A place somewhat apart in Gorky's dramatic work is occupied by "The Counterfeit Coin." Its theme is the genuineness of human hearts which is put to a test by the power of counterfeit money to arouse human passions. The test, partly a psychologi-cal experiment, partly a means of exposing a crook, is conducted by a mysterious detective who has a personal interest in bringing it to a successful conclusion. The situation is complicated by the appearance of another mysterious and eccentric character, a man with a dual personality, compounded of sound common sense and lunacy, who holds out to the household he has entered the prospect of inheriting an unclaimed fortune. The play makes interesting and impressive reading, but the excess of mystery in its plot, coupled with the Pirandellian game of double identity, is rather confusing and gets in the way of direct appreciation of its characters and their individual problems.

Produced in 1918 and 1919, respectively, "The Zykovs" and "The Old Man" * attracted little attention. The same fate befell "The Counterfeit Coin," produced in 1927. In fact, not until the production of "Yegor Bulychov" in 1931 did Gorky's plays (with the exception of his two earliest, "The Smug Citizens" and "The Lower Depths") begin to come into their own in Soviet Russia. Partly this was due to Gorky's long residence abroad, mainly in Italy (1922–30) for reasons of health; partly, perhaps largely, to the wild experimentation and the keen in-terest in topical political subjects which dominated the Soviet theater during the first ten years after the revolution. The trend toward realism which became marked in the early thirties re-vived interest in Gorky's work. "Dostigayev and Others," a rather plotless play describing the confusion, conflicting sympa-thies, and final break-up of a bourgeois family under the impact of the Bolshevik revolution, was produced in 1933, and like "Yegor Bulychov," of which it is vaguely a sequel, without equaling

---

* The play appeared in an English translation by Marie Zakrevsky and Barrett H. Clark under the title "The Judge" (McBride, 1924).

it either in power or color, has since established itself firmly in the Soviet repertoire. So has "Enemies," the reason, again, being its political message. Since Gorky's death, however, all his plays have come to be regarded as "classics" and as such are included in "the classic repertoire" which in Soviet Russia is an obligatory part of repertoire in all theaters. The great stature of Gorky as a dramatist still awaits full recognition in Russia where he is appreciated mostly as a critic of bourgeois society. Nevertheless, a number of his plays, including "The Lower Depths," "Yegor Bulychov," "Enemies," "Barbarians," and "The Zykovs" have already achieved a large measure of popularity with the Russian public, while several others are gaining steadily in public favor.

Besides the fifteen major plays that have been discussed here, Gorky wrote two one-act comedies which were produced in his lifetime, and two other plays which were published posthumously. There is little to be said of the comedies. One of them, "The Welcome" (1910), has amusing dialogue and characters, rather in the manner of Chekhov's "The Wedding," but very little action. The other, "The Hardworking Man Slovotyokov" (1920), a satire on Soviet officialdom, is a brief vaudeville sketch with more pantomime than dialogue.

Far more important are the two plays that appeared after Gorky's death. "Somov and Others," a play in four acts, must have been written, according to its editors, in 1930–31. It represents Gorky's only serious attempt to picture Soviet life and reflects the popular interest of the time in the so-called "wrecking activities" of the anti-Soviet elements. The story concerns a group of engineers and their families who are plotting to undermine the Soviet economy. The characters are motivated variously by a thirst for power, or hatred of the new regime, a desire to avenge themselves for past humiliations, or sheer greed. The all-knowing agents of the government appear at the exact psychological moment and arrest all the conspirators. Despite some felicities in the dialogue and one or two interesting characters, the play lacks balance, thanks to a sub-plot that leads nowhere, and is disappointing in its conventional and mechanical ending.

The other posthumously published play, "Yakov Bogomolov," dated 1926–27 by the editors (who also supply its title), is unfortunately incomplete, lacking its last act. It bears an elusive but unmistakable resemblance to "Queer People," its central theme, as in the earlier play, being the problem of love. Only this time it is a woman who inspires different kinds of love and who confounds all her admirers by a paradoxical return to her husband, a practical dreamer of grandiose schemes, whose idealism and selfless devotion to her convince her of his superiority over his rivals. The subtlety of characterization and dialogue in this play makes Gorky's failure to complete it a particularly regrettable loss to all lovers of the theater.

This sketch could be ended with a summary of Gorky's contribution to the Russian drama—his extraordinary sense of character, his scintillating dialogue, his deep sincerity, his moral earnestness, his questing spirit. But a broader appreciation of him as a writer, which the poet Alexander Block expressed with such power and insight, seems to be more fitting at this point:

"Gorky is bigger than he wants to be and than he always wanted to be, because his intuition is deeper than his intellect: inscrutably, by the fatal force of his talent, his blood, the nobility of his strivings, the infinity of his ideal, and the scope of his spiritual suffering, Gorky is *a Russian writer* . . . I will even go as far as to say that if there exists in reality what is called 'Russia,' or, better still, 'Russ,' beyond territory, state authority, state church, social hierarchy, and so forth—that is, if there exists that great, boundless, spacious, melancholy and felicitous something which we are accustomed to combine under the name of 'Russ,' then we have to recognize Gorky as the man who expresses all this to a very high degree."

ALEXANDER BAKSHY

THE LOWER DEPTHS

GORKY's original title for this play was "At the Bottom of Life."
On the advice of a friend he soon shortened it to "At the Bottom," under which name the play was given its first production on the stage of the Moscow Art Theater. The play has been translated into English under a variety of titles, but "The Lower Depths" is the one best known in English-speaking countries.

The action of the play is laid in a Volga town at the turn of the century. The characters inhabiting Kostylyov's lodging house are representatives of the type known in Russia as *bosyák*, the name, literally meaning "a barefoot," having come to be applied to the whole class of people who did occasional odd jobs but lived mostly by their wits. They formed a motley, shiftless, and often criminal fringe of the population of most Russian towns and used to be particularly numerous in port towns.

Three of the characters in "The Lower Depths" (the Baron, Satin, and Peppel), are former jailbirds, and Luka (judging by Gorky's film scenario based on the play) is one of them, too, though obviously reformed. Three other characters, the locksmith Klestch and the two longshoremen, the Tartar and the Goiter, typify the conscientious, upright working man. Even the cynical capmaker, Bubnov, is honest in his own way. The contrast is significant. But it is Satin, Luka, and Peppel through whom the moral message of the play is mostly conveyed. The translator must own to inconsistency in retaining the Russian nickname "Kvashnya" (which means "a tub for leavening dough") for one of the characters, while translating the nickname of another character, "Goiter" (which is "Krivoy Zob" in Russian, meaning "a lopsided Adam's apple"). His main excuse, aside from reasons of convenience, is that as used in the play "Kvashnya" takes on almost the quality of a proper name.

A. B.

THE LOWER DEPTHS

Characters

The Baron, age 33

Kvashnya, peddles dumplings in the market, age close to 40

Bubnov, a capmaker, age 45

Andrey Dmitrich Klestch, a locksmith, age 40

Nastya, a girl of the streets, age 24

Anna, Klestch's wife, age 30

Satin, age close to 40

The Actor, age close to 40

Mikhail Ivanovich Kostylyov, keeper of the lodgings, age 54

Vassily (Vassya) Peppel, age 28

Natasha, sister of *Vassilissa Kostylyova,* age 20

Luka, a pilgrim, age 60

Alyoshka, a cobbler, age 20

Vassilissa Karpovna Kostylyova, wife of *Mikhail Kostylyov,* age 26

Abram Ivanych Medvedev, a policeman, *Vassilissa's and Natasha's* uncle, age 50

The Tartar ⎫
⎬ longshoremen
The Goiter ⎭

ACT I

A cavelike basement. A heavy vaulted ceiling, blackened with smoke, with patches where the plaster has fallen off. The light comes from the direction of the audience and from a square window high up the wall, right. The right corner is cut off by a thin partition behind which is PEPPEL's *room. Near the door leading into it is* BUBNOV's *plank bed.* In the left corner is a big Russian stove. In the stone wall, left, is a door to the kitchen, where* KVASHNYA, *the* BARON, *and* NASTYA *live. By the wall between the stove and the door stands a wide bed screened off by a dirty cotton-print curtain. Everywhere along the walls are plank beds. Near the left wall, downstage, stands a block of wood with a vise and a small anvil mounted upon it. Sitting before it, on a smaller block of wood, is* KLESTCH, *who is busy trying keys in old locks. On the floor lie two bunches of keys strung on wire rings, a battered tin samovar, a hammer, and some files. In the center of the basement stand a big table with a samovar, two benches, and a square stool—all unpainted and dirty. At the table* KVASHNYA *is serving tea, the* BARON *is munching black bread, and* NASTYA, *seated on the stool and leaning on the table, is reading a battered book.* ANNA, *lying on the bed behind the curtain, is heard coughing. On his plank bed the capmaker* BUBNOV, *holding a hat block between his legs, is fitting a ripped pair of pants over it, figuring out the best way to cut the cloth. Scattered about him are a torn hatbox containing cap visors, scraps of oilcloth, and cast-off clothing.* SATIN, *just awake, lies on a plank bed emitting loud guttural sounds. On top of the stove, unseen by the audience, the* ACTOR *is puttering around and coughing.*

It is morning in early spring.

* A plank bed is a low wooden platform, which was used in Russian prisons and cheap lodging houses to provide sleeping accommodations, generally for several persons lying alongside one another. In the play Bubnov has a small plank bed to himself—TRANSLATOR.

Baron. Go on.

Kvashnya. Oh, no, my friend, says I, keep away from me with that. I went through all that before, says I, and now you won't make me go to the altar even if you give me a hundred boiled crawfish.

Bubnov (*to Satin*). What are you snorting about?

Satin continues to grunt.

Kvashnya. That I, a free woman and my own mistress, says I —that I should enter myself in somebody else's passport and make myself a man's slave—never! I wouldn't marry him even if he were an American prince.

Klestch. Liar.

Kvashnya. What's that?

Klestch. You're lying. You'll marry Abram all right.

Baron (*snatches Nastya's book and reads the title*). *Fatal Love.* (*He laughs.*)

Nastya (*stretching out her hand*). Oh, give it back. Don't be childish.   *The Baron gazes at her, waving the book in the air.*

Kvashnya (*to Klestch*). You red-haired goat! I'm lying, am I? How dare you speak to me like that?

Baron (*hitting Nastya on the head with the book*). You *are* a fool, Nastya—

Nastya (*wresting the book from him*). Let me have it.

Klestch. Ha! A great lady. And you *will* marry Abram all the same—that's all you've been waiting for.

Kvashnya. Oh, of course! I haven't got anything better to do. You've driven your wife till she's nearly dead—

Klestch. Shut up, you old sow! It's none of your business!

Kvashnya. Oh, you don't like to hear the truth!

Baron. There it goes! What's doing, Nastya?

Nastya (*without lifting her head*). Go away!

Anna (*thrusting her head out from behind the curtain*). Another day starting! For heaven's sake, stop shouting and quarreling!

Klestch. Now she's whining again.

Anna. Every day it's the same thing. Won't you let me die in peace?

Bubnov. Noise never stopped anybody from dying.

Kvashnya (*walking up to Anna*). How could you live with such a brute?

Anna. Leave me alone—

Kvashnya. Well, you *are* a patient sufferer, poor soul. How does your chest feel? Any easier?

Baron. Kvashnya! It's time to go to market!

Kvashnya. I'm coming. (*To Anna.*) Would you like some hot meat dumplings?

Anna. No, thank you. Why should I bother to eat?

Kvashnya. Never you mind. Heat softens your innards. I'll put some in a cup and leave it for you—eat them when you feel like it. Come on, nobleman— (*To Klestch.*) You devil, you! (*Goes off to the kitchen.*)

Anna (coughing). Oh, Lord—

Baron (giving Nastya a nudge on the back of the neck). Drop it, silly!

Nastya (in a loud voice). Go away—I'm not keeping you.

                The Baron follows Kvashnya off, whistling.

Satin (half rising from his plank bed). Who beat me up last night?

Bubnov. Does it make any difference?

Satin. You're right, I suppose. But why did they beat me?

Bubnov. Did you have a card game?

Satin. I did.

Bubnov. That's why they beat you up.

Satin. The dirty swine!

Actor (poking his head down from the stove). They'll beat you to death one time—

Satin. You're a blockhead.

Actor. Why?

Satin. Because you can't kill a man two times.

Actor (after a pause). I don't understand—why not.

Klestch. You'd better come down off the stove and clean the place up— You've been loafing up there long enough.

Actor. That's none of your business.

Klestch. Wait till Vassilissa comes in—she'll show you whose business it is.

Actor. To hell with Vassilissa! Today it's the Baron's turn to clean. Baron!

Baron (coming in from the kitchen). I've no time for cleaning —I'm going to market with Kvashnya.

Actor. That has nothing to do with me—you can go **to jail** for all I care, but it's your turn to sweep the floor—I'm not going to do other people's work.

Baron. Oh, the devil with it! Nastya will sweep up. Hey, you, fatal love! Wake up! (*Snatches Nastya's book from her.*)

Nastya (*rising*). What do you want? Give it back, you boor. Call yourself a nobleman.

Baron (*returning the book*). Nastya, sweep the floor for me, will you?

Nastya (*going off to the kitchen*). No, thank you!

                    Kvashnya appears at the door.

Kvashnya (*to the Baron*). Come along with me. They can clean up without you. You've been asked, Actor, and you should do it. It won't break your back.

Actor. It's always me—I don't get it.

Baron (*coming in with a yoke over his shoulders, two baskets containing large cloth-covered pots hanging from the ends*). It's rather heavy today.

Satin. Hardly worth your while to have been born a baron.

Kvashnya (*to the Actor*). Now, mind you sweep the floor.

                    Preceded by the Baron, Kvashnya goes off.

Actor (*coming down from the stove*). It's hard for me to breathe dust. (*Speaking with pride.*) My organism is poisoned with alcohol. (*He sits on a plank bed, sunk in thought.*)

Satin. Organism—organon—

Anna. Andrey Dmitrich—

Klestch. What is it now?

Anna. Kvashyna has left me some dumplings in there—you eat them.

Klestch (*walking up to her*). Aren't you going to?

Anna. No, I don't want any. Why should I eat? You work—you need it.

Klestch. Are you afraid? Don't be. You may pull through—

Anna. Go eat the dumplings. I feel all in. Seems as though it's coming soon—

Klestch (*moving away*). Never mind—you may get up yet—that happens sometimes. (*Goes off into the kitchen.*)

Actor (*in a loud voice, as if waking up suddenly*). Yesterday, in the hospital, the doctor said to me: Your organism, he said, is completely poisoned with alcohol—

Satin (*smiling*). Organon—

Actor (*insistently*). Not organon, but or-gan-ism—

Satin. Sycamore—

Actor (*waving his hand at him*). You and your nonsense. I'm speaking seriously—I am. If my organism is poisoned, then it's bad for me to sweep the floor—to breathe dust—

Satin. Macrobiotics— Ha!

Bubnov. What are you mumbling about?

Satin. Words— Here's another—transit-dental—

Bubnov. What does that mean?

Satin. Don't know—I can't remember.

Bubnov. Why do you say them then?

Satin. Because. I'm tired, my friend, of all human words, our words. I'm fed up with them. I've heard every one of them a thousand times, if I've heard them once.

Actor. There's a line in the play *Hamlet:* "Words—words— words!" A fine piece of work. I played the gravedigger.

Klestch (*coming in from the kitchen*). How soon are you going to play with the broom?

Actor. None of your business. (*Striking himself on the chest.*) The fair Ophelia! Nymph, in thy orisons be all my sins remembered!

> *From off stage, somewhere in the distance, can be heard a muffled noise—followed by shouts and a policeman's whistle. Klestch resumes his work, rasping with a file.*

Satin. I love rare words I can't understand. When I was a boy I had a job in a telegraph office—used to read lots of books—

Bubnov. So you were a telegrapher too?

Satin. I was. There are some fine books—with lots of odd words. I was an educated man, you know.

Bubnov. I've heard that a hundred times. So you were. So what? I was a fur-dresser at one time—had my own shop. My hands and arms got so yellow from dyeing furs—oh, so yellow —up to the elbow, I tell you. I thought I'd never wash it off —even go to my grave with yellow arms. Well, look at them now—they're just dirty. Yes.

Satin. And so?

Bubnov. Nothing. That's all.

Satin. Well, what are you driving at?

Bubnov. Oh, just something to think over. It comes to this—

no matter how you paint yourself up, it'll all rub off—yes, it'll all rub off.

Satin. Oh—my bones are sore.

Actor (sitting with his arms around his knees). Education is rubbish. The main thing is talent. I knew an actor—he could scarcely read—but when he played his part the theater shook and rattled with the audience's raptures.

Satin. Bubnov, give me five kopecks.

Bubnov. All I've got is two kopecks.

Actor. Talent, I say, is what an actor needs. And talent is faith in oneself, in one's own powers.

Satin. Give me five kopecks and I'll believe you're a talent, a hero, a crocodile, a bailiff— Klestch, give me five kopecks.

Klestch. Go to hell! There are too many of your kind around here.

Satin. What are you cursing for? I know you haven't a kopeck.

Anna. Andrey Dmitrich—I'm suffocating, I feel awful—

Klestch. What can I do?

Bubnov. Open the door to the front hall.

Klestch. Thank you. You sit there on a plank bed, and I'm on the floor. Let me have your place, and you can open the door all you want. I have a cold as it is.

Bubnov (calmly). There's no reason for me to open the door. It's your own wife asking.

Klestch (sullenly). People will ask for anything.

Satin. Wow, my head's ringing! Why, I'd like to know, do people punch each other in the head?

Bubnov. Not only heads—they do it to the rest of the body too. *(Rising.)* Got to go buy myself some thread. Funny, our landlord and his lady haven't shown up today—maybe they've dropped in their tracks. *(Goes off.)*

Anna coughs. Satin lies motionless, his arms under his head.

Actor (looks around with sad eyes and walks up to Anna). Feeling bad?

Anna. It's too stuffy in here.

Actor. If you like, I'll take you out into the hallway. Here, get up. *(He helps Anna to rise, throws some old garment over her shoulders, and, holding her under the arm, leads her out to the hallway.)* Come, come—step out. I'm sick myself—poisoned with alcohol. *Kostylyov appears in the doorway.*

Kostylyov. Going out for a walk? A fine couple—a ram and a lamb.

Actor. Make way—you see invalids are going out, don't you?

Kostylyov. Pass on, if you please. (*Humming some hymn, he looks the place over suspiciously and inclines his head to the left as if trying to hear something in Peppel's room. Klestch tinkles his keys and rasps his file with great firmness, meanwhile watching his landlord from under his brows.*) Grating away, are you?

Klestch. What?

Kostylyov. You're grating, I say. (*After a pause.*) Oh—yes—what is it I wanted to ask you? (*Quickly, in a low voice.*) Has my wife been here?

Klestch. I haven't seen her.

Kostylyov (*moving cautiously toward Peppel's room*). What a lot of space you get from me for two rubles a month! A bed—a place to sit—h'm—it's worth all of five rubles, I swear! I think I'll raise you half a ruble.

Klestch. Raise me by the neck and strangle me while you're at it. You'll be dead soon, but all you think about is half rubles.

Kostylyov. Why should I strangle you? What good will it do anybody? God be with you, my good man, live to your heart's content. But I *will* raise your rent a half ruble. That'll buy me more oil for my icon lamp—and my sacrifice will burn before the holy icon. That sacrifice will be reckoned for me as amends for my sins, and for yours too. You never think of your sins, do you? So there it is. Oh, Andrey! You're such a spiteful man. Your wife has withered away because of your spitefulness. Nobody likes or respects you—and your work grates on people's ears, disturbs everybody—

Klestch (*shouting*). Have you come to plague me?

Satin emits a loud roar.

Kostylyov (*startled*). My goodness!   *Enter the Actor.*

Actor. I've seated the lady in the hallway, wrapped her up—

Kostylyov. You have a kind heart, my friend. That's fine—that'll be credited to you.

Actor. When?

Kostylyov. In the next world, my friend. Every deed, everything, is entered in a man's account there.

Actor. That's there. You ought to reward me for my kindness here.

Kostylyov. Now, how could I do that?

Actor. Slash my debt in half.

Kostylyov. Hee-hee! You will have your little joke, my dear fellow, you will keep play acting. Why, is kindness of heart comparable to money? Kindness stands above all benefits. And your debt to me is just what it is—a debt. Therefore you have to pay it back. To me who am an old man you must show kindness without looking for rewards—

Actor. Old man, you're a rogue.

The Actor goes off to the kitchen. Klestch rises and exits to the hallway.

Kostylyov (to Satin). He's run away, the grater—hee-hee! He doesn't like me.

Satin. Who does like you, outside the devil?

Kostylyov (laughingly). You *are* sharp. For myself, I like all of you—I understand you, my wretched, worthless, ruined brethren. (*Suddenly, quickly.*) Is Vassily in?

Satin. Go look.

Kostylyov (walks up to Peppel's door and knocks). Vassya!

The Actor appears at the kitchen door, munching.

Peppel (off stage). Who's there?

Kostylyov. It's me, Vassya.

Peppel (from his room). What do you want?

Kostylyov (moving back from the door). Open the door—

Satin (without looking at Kostylyov). He'll open, and she's there.   *The Actor laughs.*

Kostylyov (alarmed, in a low voice). What's that? Who's there? What do you mean?

Satin. Are you speaking to me?

Kostylyov. What was it you just said?

Satin. I was talking to myself.

Kostylyov. Look out, my friend. Know when to stop with your jokes—yes! (*Knocks loudly on Peppel's door.*) Vassily!

Peppel opens his door.

Peppel. Well? What's the idea of disturbing me?

Kostylyov (peeking into the room). You see, I have—

Peppel. Have you brought the money?

Kostylyov. I have some business to talk over with you.

Peppel. Have you brought the money?

Kostylyov. What money? Wait—

Peppel. I say the money, the seven rubles for the watch. Come on.

Kostylyov. What watch? Oh, Vassya—

Peppel. Now look! Yesterday, before witnesses, I sold you a watch for ten rubles. I received three rubles, now hand over the other seven. Why are you blinking at me like that? You wander around here, disturb other people's sleep, but don't know your business.

Kostylyov. Sh-sh! Don't lose your temper, Vassya. The watch —that's—

Satin. Stolen goods—

Kostylyov (sternly). I don't take stolen goods—how can you say—

Peppel (seizing Kostylyov by the shoulder). Why did you wake me up? What do you want?

Kostylyov. I don't want anything—I'll go—if you feel that way.

Peppel. Go bring the money.

Kostylyov. Such rude people! I must say! (*Goes off.*)

Actor. A regular comedy!

Satin. Wonderful! I love it!

Peppel. What brought him here?

Satin. Don't you understand? He's looking for his wife. Why don't you finish him off, Vassily?

Peppel. It's not worth spoiling my life over trash like him.

Satin. You ought to make a neat job of it. Then you can marry Vassilissa—become our landlord—

Peppel. I can hardly wait! With your kind hearts you'll drink up all my property in a barroom, and me too. (*He sits down on a plank bed.*) The old pest—woke me up! And I had such a fine dream. I was fishing some place and caught a huge perch. It was such a size, it could only happen in a dream. Well, I pull it along on the hook and all the time I'm afraid the line will snap. I keep the bag ready hoping to get the perch in any minute—

Satin. It wasn't a perch—it was Vassilissa.

Actor. He caught Vassilissa a long time ago.

Peppel. Go to hell, all of you—you *and* Vassilissa!

                    Klestch enters from the front hall.

Klestch. Damn cold out!

Actor. Why didn't you bring Anna in? She'll freeze to death.

Klestch. Natasha took her into her kitchen.

Actor. The old man will throw her out.

Klestch (sitting down to resume his work). Well, then Natasha will bring her here.

Satin. Let me have five kopecks, Vassily.

Actor (to Satin). Five kopecks! Look, Vassya! Give us a quarter of a ruble.

Peppel. I'd better give it to you quick—before you ask for a ruble. Here!

Satin. Gibraltar! There are no better people in the world than thieves.

Klestch. Money comes easy to them—they don't have to work.

Satin. Money comes easy to many people, but it doesn't come so easy to let it go. As for work, just you make it pleasant for me and I'll probably work— Yes, I probably will. When work is a pleasure, life is a joy! When work is a duty, life is slavery. *(To Actor.)* Let's go, Sardanapalus.

Actor. Let's go, Nebuchadnezzar. I'm going to get boiled— like forty thousand sots.   *Satin and the Actor go off.*

Peppel (yawning). Well, how's your wife?

Klestch (after a pause). Looks like it'll be pretty soon now.

Peppel. You know, looking at you—I can't see any sense to your grating.

Klestch. What else can I do?

Peppel. Do nothing.

Klestch. How am I supposed to eat?

Peppel. Other people manage to live.

Klestch. You mean the ones here? They're not people. Scum, hoodlums—that's all they are. I'm a worker—I feel ashamed to set eyes on them—I've been working since I was a kid. You think I won't get out of here? I'll wriggle out of this hole even if it tears my skin off. Just wait till my wife dies— I've lived six months here, but it feels more like six years—

Peppel. Nobody here is any worse than you are—you're wrong about that.

Klestch. They're not! These men with no honor or conscience—

Peppel (indifferently). What good are honor and conscience?

You can't put them on your feet instead of boots. Honor and conscience are only important to those who have power—force—   *Enter Bubnov.*

Bubnov. Whew, I'm shivering!

Peppel. Bubnov, have you got a conscience?

Bubnov. What? Conscience?

Peppel. That's what I said.

Bubnov. What do I want a conscience for? I'm no moneybags.

Peppel. That's just what I say. Only rich people need honor and conscience. And Klestch here criticizes us, says we have no conscience.

Bubnov. Why, does he want to borrow some?

Peppel. He has plenty of his own.

Bubnov (to Klestch). Then you're selling it? Well, you'll have a tough time finding customers here. There's one thing I would buy—marked cards—but even those would have to be on credit.

Peppel (lecturing him). You're a fool, Andrey. You ought to listen to Satin—or the Baron about conscience.

Klestch. I have nothing to talk to them about.

Peppel. They've got more brains than you have—even if they are drunks.

Bubnov. Be both drunk and smart—you've got a good start.

Peppel. Satin says—everybody wants his neighbor to have a conscience, but it turns out nobody can afford one. And it's the truth.

> *Enter Natasha. She is followed by Luka who has a stick in his hand, a peasant knapsack on his back, and a kettle and teapot hanging from his waist.*

Luka. Good health to you, honest people.

Peppel (smoothing down his mustache). Ah, Natasha!

Bubnov (to Luka). We were honest, you bet—so far back we forget.

Natasha. This is a new lodger.

Luka. It's all the same to me. I have just as much respect for crooks. To my way of thinking, every flea is a good flea—they're all dark and all good jumpers. Where do I accommodate myself here, my dear?

Natasha (pointing to the kitchen door). Step in there, grandpa.

Luka. Thank you, girlie. Anywhere you say. To an old man any place that's warm is homeland. (*Luka goes off.*)

Peppel. What an interesting old man you've brought, Natasha.

Natasha. More interesting than you are. Your wife's in our kitchen. Andrey. Come get her in a little while.

Klestch. All right, I will.

Natasha. You ought to treat her more kindly, Andrey. It won't be long now—

Klestch. I know.

Natasha. You know. It's not enough to know—you have to understand. It's a frightening thing to die.

Peppel. I'm not afraid of death.

Natasha. You *are* a brave man.

Bubnov (*whistles*). This thread is rotten.

Peppel. Really, I'm not afraid. I'll accept my death any time —right now. Take a knife and stab me to the heart, I'll die without a sigh of regret. Even with joy, because it comes from a pure hand.

Natasha (*as she turns to go off*). Well—you'd better pull the wool over somebody else's eyes.

Bubnov (*drawling*). The thread is rotten, it's a fact.

Natasha (*at the door*). Don't forget about your wife, Andrey.

Klestch. All right.   *Natasha goes off.*

Peppel. A fine girl.

Bubnov. Not bad.

Peppel. Why is she so uppity with me—turning me down? She'll get ruined here anyway.

Bubnov. She will—through you.

Peppel. Why through me? I feel sorry for her.

Bubnov. Like a wolf for a sheep.

Peppel. That's a lie. I feel very sorry for her. She has a hard time of it here—I see it.

Klestch. Wait till Vassilissa catches you talking to her.

Bubnov. Vassilissa? Y-yes, that one doesn't make anybody a present of what's hers.

Peppel (*lying down on a plank bed*). Go to hell, both of you — Prophets, too!

Klestch. You'll see—just wait.

Luka (*in the kitchen, singing*). In the darkness of the night you can't see the road aright—

Klestch. Listen to that howling. New lodger! Hmph! (*Goes off into the hall.*)

Peppel. God, I'm bored. What is it makes me feel bored? You go on living, everything is fine. Suddenly, as if you'd caught a chill—you feel bored.

Bubnov. Bored? H'm!

Peppel. Up to here.

Luka (*singing in the kitchen*). No, sir, you can't see your road aright—

Peppel. Hey, there, old man!

Luka (*peeping out of the kitchen*). You mean me?

Peppel. Yes, you. Stop singing.

Luka (*coming in*). Don't you like it?

Peppel. I do when the singing's good.

Luka. Then mine is bad?

Peppel. It seems so.

Luka. Imagine! And I thought I sang well. It's always like that. A man thinks to himself: I'm doing a good job. Then bang —everybody is displeased.

Peppel (*laughing*). That's true!

Bubnov. You say you're bored, and there you're laughing.

Peppel. What's that to you? The croaking raven.

Luka. Who's bored around here?

Peppel. I am.   *Enter the Baron.*

Luka. Imagine that! In the kitchen there a girl is sitting. She's reading a book and crying—yes, crying! Tears roll down from her eyes. I say to her, What's the matter, my dear? And she answers, I feel so sorry for him. For who? I ask her. And she says—the man here, in this book. Some people find strange things to bother them, don't they? Must be from boredom too.

Baron. That one is a fool.

Peppel. Baron, have you had tea?

Baron. Yes. Go on.

Peppel. Would you like me to treat you to half a bottle?

Baron. Of course I would. Go on.

Peppel. Get down on all fours and bark like a dog.

Baron. Idiot! Who are you—a wealthy merchant? Or are you drunk?

Peppel. Oh, come on—do some barking. It'll amuse me. You're one of the high and mighty. Time was when you looked upon the common folk like me as if we weren't human beings and all that sort of thing—

Baron. Go on.

Peppel. Well, today I'll make you bark like a dog, and you will bark. You know you will.

Baron. So I will. Fathead! What sort of pleasure can you derive from that, when I know myself I've grown perhaps even worse than you. You should have tried to make me walk on all fours when you weren't my equal.

Bubnov. That's true.

Luka. Very good, if you ask me.

Bubnov. What's gone is gone, and what's left isn't worth talking about. We have no high and mighty gentlemen here—everything has washed off—only the naked man remains.

Luka. Therefore all are equal. Were you a baron, dear fellow?

Baron. What is this? Who are you, you old goblin?

Luka. I've met a count, and a prince too—but this is the first time I've ever seen a baron, and a damaged one at that.

Peppel (laughs). You know, Baron, you've made me feel a bit ashamed of myself.

Baron. It's time you showed more intelligence, Vassily.

Luka. Oh-ho-ho! Just to look at you, my good friends, one can see what kind of a life—

Bubnov. Every morning's so foul we wake up with a howl.

Baron. We knew better times too. I used to wake up in the morning and drink coffee in bed—yes, coffee with cream!

Luka. Yet all of you are just human beings. Yes, put on as much as you like, wriggle as much as you can, but just as you were born a man, so you'll die a man. And as I look on I see everybody getting cleverer and more interesting. They all live worse, it's true, but they all want something better—a stubborn lot.

Baron. Who are you, old man? Where do you come from?

Luka. Who, me?

Baron. Are you a pilgrim?

Luka. All of us are pilgrims on this earth. I've even heard people say that the earth itself is a pilgrim in the heavens.

Baron (sternly). That may be, but how about a passport? Have you got one?

Luka. And who are you, a detective?

Peppel (*delightedly*). That's the ticket, old man. Got it in the neck, eh, Baron?

Bubnov. Y-yes, our gentleman got it good and proper.

Baron (*embarrassed*). What's the matter? I'm only joking, old man. Why, my friend, I have no papers myself.

Bubnov. Liar.

Baron. That is, I have papers, but they're no good for anything.

Luka. All papers are like that—no good for anything.

Peppel. Baron, let's go have a drink.

Baron. I'm ready. Good-by, old man. You are a rogue, though.

Luka. All's possible, my friend.

Peppel (*at the hallway door*). Well, come on.

            Peppel goes off, the Baron hurrying after him.

Luka. The fellow actually was a baron?

Bubnov. God knows! But he's an aristocrat all right. Even now it breaks out all of a sudden. Seems it never got completely rubbed off.

Luka. Maybe aristocracy is just like smallpox. A man gets well, but the pock marks remain.

Bubnov. He's not bad, though. Only sometimes he's got to kick up a fuss—like about your passport today.

            *Enter Alyoshka. He is tipsy, carries an accordion, and is
            whistling as he comes in.*

Alyoshka. Hey, inhabitants!

Bubnov. What are you yelling for?

Alyoshka. Excuse me. Pardon me. I'm a polite man—

Bubnov. Off on a binge again?

Alyoshka. All I can hold! Just a minute ago subinspector Medyakin threw me out of the police station. Don't let me even get the smell of you in the streets, says he, ever! And I'm a man of character. My boss spits at me like a cat. And what's a boss? Pooh! He's a drunkard, my boss is. And I'm a man—who wants nothing. Nothing—and that's that! You can have me for a ruble twenty! But I want nothing! Give me a million—I don't want it. And to let my fellow worker who's a drunkard order me around—I won't have it. I won't, no, I won't!

            Nastya appears in the kitchen doorway and shakes her

head as she watches Alyoshka.

Luka (good-humoredly). You *have* got yourself in a tangle, young man—

Bubnov. Just human foolishness.

Alyoshka (stretching himself out on the floor). There, you can eat me up for all I care. But I want nothing. I'm a reckless man. Explain to me—why am I worse than other people, and who are they? Medyakin says: Keep off the street or I'll knock your block off. But I will go out. I'll lie in the middle of the street—let them run over me! I want nothing!

Nastya. Poor thing! So young, and already—makes a fool of himself.

Alyoshka (noticing Nastya, raises himself to his knees). Mamsel! Parlez français? Prix-fixe? I'm painting the town red—

Nastya (in a loud whisper). Vassilissa!

> *Flinging open the hallway door, Vassilissa enters.*

Vassilissa (to Alyoshka). You here again?

Alyoshka. Good morning—please step right in—

Vassilissa. I told you, dog, not to show your face around here, didn't I? And you're here again?

Alyoshka. Vassilissa Karpovna— I'll play you a funeral march, shall I?

Vassilissa (pushing him by the shoulder). Get out!

Alyoshka (moving toward the door). Now wait—you can't do that. A funeral march—I've just learned it—fresh music. No, wait—you can't do that.

Vassilissa. I'll show you what I can't do. I'll set the whole street on you, you dirty prattler. You're too young to go around yapping about me.

Alyoshka. All right, I'm going. *(Runs out.)*

Vassilissa. Don't let him set foot in here ever again. You hear me?

Bubnov. I'm not your watchman.

Vassilissa. I don't care who you are. You're living here on charity, remember that. How much do you owe me?

Bubnov (calmly). I haven't counted it.

Vassilissa. Look out, or I will!   *Alyoshka opens the door.*

Alyoshka (shouting). Vassilissa Karpovna! I'm not afraid of you—not that much!   *He sneaks into the kitchen. Luka laughs.*

Vassilissa. Who are you?

Luka. A wayfarer—a pilgrim.

Vassilissa. For a night or to stay?

Luka. That depends.

Vassilissa. Your passport.

Luka. You shall have it.

Vassilissa. Let me see.

Luka. I'll bring it to you—drag it up to your very own door.

Vassilissa. Wayfarer indeed! You should have called yourself a tramp—that would have been nearer the truth.

Luka (*with a sigh*). Not much kindliness in you, woman.

Vassilissa moves toward Peppel's room. Alyoshka peeps out of the kitchen.

Alyoshka (*in a whisper*). Has she gone?

Vassilissa (*turning toward him*). You still here?

Alyoshka disappears, whistling. Nastya and Luka laugh.

Bubnov (*to Vassilissa*). He's out.

Vassilissa. Who is?

Bubnov. Vassily.

Vassilissa. Have I asked you about him?

Bubnov. I see you're looking in everywhere.

Vassilissa. I'm looking to see that things are in order—understand? And why hasn't the floor been swept at this hour? How many times have I ordered you to keep the place clean?

Bubnov. It's the Actor's turn—

Vassilissa. I don't care whose it is. But if the sanitation inspectors come and I'm fined, I'll throw the whole damn lot of you out!

Bubnov (*calmly*). What will you live on then?

Vassilissa. Don't let me see a speck of dust here! (*Walks toward the kitchen and stops before Nastya.*) What are you sticking around for? And your face all swollen up too. Don't stand there like a stump. Sweep the floor. Have you seen—Natasha? Has she been here?

Nastya. I don't know— I haven't seen her.

Vassilissa. Bubnov! Has my sister been here?

Bubnov (*pointing at Luka*). She brought him in.

Vassilissa. And that one—was he in?

Bubnov. Vassily? Yes, he was. She talked to Klestch here, your Natasha.

Vassilissa. I'm not asking you who she talked to. Dirt—filth everywhere! Oh, pigs! See that this place is clean, hear me? (*She goes off quickly.*)

Bubnov. God, what a brute that woman is!

Luka. A peppery madam.

Nastya. Anybody would be a brute leading such a life. Tie any live human being to a husband like hers—

Bubnov. Well, she's not tied too fast—

Luka. Does she always act up like this?

Bubnov. Always. You see, she came to see her lover, and he's out.

Luka. So she felt hurt— I see. Oh-ho! So many different people order others around on this earth—and try to throw all sorts of scares into each other, but still there's no order in life—nor cleanliness.

Bubnov. Everybody wants order, but their brains are in disorder. Anyway—somebody's got to sweep the floor. Nastya, you take care of it.

Nastya. Oh, of course! I'm not your maid here. (*After a pause.*) I'm going to get drunk today—gloriously drunk!

Bubnov. That's an idea.

Luka. Why do you want to get drunk, girlie? Just a while ago you were crying—now you say you want to get drunk.

Nastya (*challengingly*). And when I'm drunk I'll cry again— that's all.

Bubnov. All—that isn't much.

Luka. But what's the reason, tell me? Even a pimple doesn't just spring up, without a reason. (*Nastya makes no answer, only shakes her head.*) I see— Oh-ho-ho! You human beings! What's going to happen to you? Well, let me sweep up here then. Where's your broom?

Bubnov. Behind the door, in the hallway. (*Luka goes into the hallway.*) Nastya!

Nastya. Yes?

Bubnov. Why did Vassilissa jump on Alyoshka?

Nastya. He's been telling everybody Vassily's sick of her and wants to drop her for Natasha. I'm going to get out of here and move to other lodgings.

Bubnov. What for? And where?

Nastya. I'm fed up— I'm not needed here.

Bubnov (calmly). You're not needed anywhere. For that matter all humans on this earth are not needed.

Nastya shakes her head, rises, and goes out into the hallway. Enter Medvedev, a policeman, followed by Luka carrying a broom.

Medvedev. I don't think I know you.

Luka. Do you know everybody else?

Medvedev. On my beat I have to know everybody. But I don't know you.

Luka. That's because the earth couldn't squeeze all of itself into your beat, uncle—a bit of it has remained outside. (*He goes off to the kitchen.*)

Medvedev (walking up to Bubnov). He's right, mine is a small beat—though it's worse than any big one. Just a while ago, before going off duty, I took the cobbler Alyoshka to the station. He stretched himself out in the middle of the street, began playing his accordion, and yelled—I don't want anything —I don't want anything. There were horses in the street and all sorts of traffic—he could have been crushed to death and all that. A wild fellow. Well, I took him in—he's too fond of disorder.

Bubnov. Coming for a game of checkers tonight?

Medvedev. I am. Y-yes. And how is—Vassily?

Bubnov. He's all right. The same as always.

Medvedev. Then he's still carrying on?

Bubnov. Why shouldn't he? He can carry on—

Medvedev (doubtfully). Can he? (*Luka, carrying a bucket, crosses the room to the hallway.*) Y-yes— There's been some talk about Vassily around here—have you heard it?

Bubnov. I hear all sorts of talk—

Medvedev. About him and Vassilissa— Have you noticed anything?

Bubnov. Noticed what?

Medvedev. Just in general— Or maybe you know and are lying to me? Everybody knows it— (*Severely.*) One mustn't lie, my friend.

Bubnov. Why should I lie?

Medvedev. Glad you see it my way. Oh, the swine! They say Peppel and Vassilissa—are like that— What's that got to do with

me? I'm not her father—only her uncle. Why should they make fun of me?   *Enter Kvashnya.*
God knows what people are coming to—they laugh at everything. Ah! It's you!

Kvashnya. It's me, my precious uniform! Bubnov, he pestered me again at the market to marry him—

Bubnov. Why not? Go to it! He's got money, and still makes a presentable swain.

Medvedev. Me? Ho! Ho!

Kvashnya. Ah, so? Don't touch my sore spot, policeman. I went through it once before, dear man. When a woman gets married it's like jumping into a hole in the ice in the middle of winter: you do it once, and you remember it the rest of your days.

Medvedev. Wait a minute. Husbands aren't all alike.

Kvashnya. But I'm always the same. When my darling husband—God blast his soul—gave up the ghost, I was so happy I stayed in alone the whole day— I sat and couldn't believe my good luck.

Medvedev. If your husband beat you—for no good reason, you should have complained to the police.

Kvashnya. I kept complaining to God for eight years—he never helped.

Medvedev. Today wife-beating is forbidden. Today there's law and order in everything. You can't beat anybody for nothing. If you do beat anyone, it's got to be for the sake of order.
                    Enter Luka, leading Anna.

Luka. Here, we've made it. Don't you know you mustn't walk around alone with your weak constitution? Where's your place?

Anna (pointing to her bed). Thank you, grandpa!

Kvashnya. There's a married one. Look at her.

Luka. The little woman has a very weak constitution. She was walking along the hallway, clinging to the walls, and moaning. Why do you let her walk by herself?

Kvashnya. It was careless of us, sir, please forgive us. And her chambermaid must have gone out for a stroll.

Luka. You're making a joke of it—but how can anybody cast off a human being? Whatever condition he's in, a human being is always worth something.

Medvedev. You have to keep your eye on a person. What if she dies? There'll be a lot of complications. Yes, you have to keep an eye open.

Luka. Very true, master sergeant.

Medvedev. Y-yes—though I'm not quite a master sergeant yet—

Luka. Ain't you? You look like a hero.

There is noise and a stamping of feet in the hallway. Muffled sounds of shouting are heard.

Medvedev. Must be a brawl?

Bubnov. Sounds like it.

Kvashnya. I'm going to take a look.

Medvedev. I'll have to be going too. Duty is duty! I wish when people started a fight other people would leave them alone. They'd stop fighting themselves—when they got tired. They should be allowed to knock each other around without interference, for all they're worth. They wouldn't be so keen to get into scrapes again—they'd remember their bruises—

Bubnov (getting up from his plank bed). You ought to tell that to the Chief of Police—

The door bursts wide open, revealing Kostylyov on the threshold.

Kostylyov (shouting). Abram! Come quick! Vassilissa's—killing—Natasha! Quick!

Kvashnya, Medvedev, and Bubnov rush out into the hallway. Luka gazes after them, shaking his head.

Anna. Oh, God! Poor little Natasha!

Luka. Who's fighting out there?

Anna. Our landladies—sisters—

Luka (walking up to Anna). What are they dividing up?

Anna. They've nothing better to do—they're well fed and strong—

Luka. What's your name?

Anna. Anna. You know, as I look at you, you remind me of my father—just as kind—and soft.

Luka. I've been through the wringer—that's why I'm soft. (*He laughs with a cracked senile laugh.*)

CURTAIN

ACT II

The same basement. On the plank bed near the stove SATIN, *the* BARON, *the* GOITER, *and the* TARTAR *are playing cards.* KLESTCH *and the* ACTOR *are watching the game. On his plank bed* BUBNOV *is playing checkers with* MEDVEDEV. LUKA *is sitting on a square stool by* ANNA's *bed.*

It is evening. The place is lighted by two lamps: one hanging from the wall near the cardplayers, the other on BUBNOV's *plank bed.*

Tartar. I play one more game—then I play no more—

Bubnov. Goiter, sing! (*Striking up.*) The sun comes up, the sun goes down again—

Goiter (*continuing*). But in my cell it's never light—

Tartar (*to Satin*). Mix cards—mix 'em good! I know good what you are.

Bubnov and Goiter (*singing together*). The guards are watching my barred window—e-eh! Watching closely day and night—

Anna. Beatings—harsh words, that's all I've ever known in my life. Nothing but that—

Luka. Forget it, my good woman. Don't upset yourself.

Medvedev. Where are you moving your man? Are you blind?

Bubnov. A-ah! I see—I see—

Tartar (*threatening Satin with his fist*). Why you try hide a card? I see it— Oh!

Goiter. Don't bother, Assan! They'll clean up on us anyway! Bubnov, sing.

Anna. I don't remember a time I didn't feel hungry. I counted every piece of bread. All my life I've trembled and worried that I might eat more than my share. All my life I've been wearing rags—all my miserable life. What have I done to deserve this?

Luka. Poor child! You are worn out. Never mind.

Actor (to the Goiter). Play the jack—the jack, you fool!

Baron. And we have a king.

Klestch. They'll always beat your card.

Satin. Such is our habit.

Medvedev. King!

Bubnov. Mine too. Well—

Anna. I'm dying now—

Klestch. Oh, oh! Stop playing, Assan, take a tip from me and get out of the game.

Actor. He can't do without your advice, can he?

Baron. Watch out, Andrey, or I'll send you packing to hell!

Tartar. Deal again. The jug went for water—broke himself— and me too!   *Shaking his head, Klestch moves over to Bubnov.*

Anna. I keep thinking: O God! Am I to be punished with suffering in the next world too? Even there, O God?

Luka. You won't be. Don't worry. Nothing will happen to you. You'll have a good rest there. Just bear up a little more. Everybody bears his life, my dear, each in his own way. (*He rises and walks quickly to the kitchen.*)

Bubnov (singing). You guards can watch my window closely—

Goiter (singing). I will not try my leave to take—

Bubnov and Goiter (together). I'd surely like to get my freedom—e-eh! But no—my chains I cannot break.

Tartar (shouting). Ah! You push a card up your sleeve.

Baron (embarrassed). Well—where do you want me to push it—up your nose?

Actor. You're wrong, Assan—nobody would do that—never.

Tartar. I saw it. Crook. I no play.

Satin (gathering the cards). Leave off, Assan. You knew we were crooks. If so, why did you play with us?

Baron. You've lost two quarter rubles, but make three rubles' worth of noise. Ah!

Tartar (heatedly). You must play honest.

Satin. What for?

Tartar. What you mean, what for?

Satin. Just that—what for?

Tartar. You not know?

Satin. I don't. Do you?

The Tartar spits in bitter disgust. The others laugh at him.

Goiter (*good-humoredly*). You're a funny man, Assan. Can't you understand? If they're going to start living honestly, they'll die of hunger in three days.

Tartar. That no my business. People must live honest.

Goiter. There he goes—like a parrot. We'll do better to go have tea. Bubnov! (*Singing.*) O chains, you heavy chains that bind me—

Bubnov. You are my iron guards in truth—

Goiter. Come on, Assan. (*Goes off, singing.*) I know I cannot break you ever—e-eh!

> *The Tartar shakes his fist at the Baron and follows his friend.*

Satin (*to the Baron*). Your Excellency, you made a magnificent fool of yourself once again. You're an educated man, and still you can't do a proper job of cheating at cards—

Baron (*spreading his hands*). Devil knows how I muffed it.

Actor. You lack talent—faith in yourself—and without that a man can do nothing—ever.

Medvedev. I have one king, and you have two. H'mm!

Bubnov. Even one is all right if he's clever and bright. Your move.

Klestch. Your game is lost, Abram Ivanych.

Medvedev. Mind your own business, understand? Hold your tongue.

Satin. Winnings—fifty-three kopecks.

Actor. Three kopecks go to me. Though what do I want three kopecks for?   *Enter Luka from the kitchen.*

Luka. Well, you've cleaned up the Tartar. Now you'll go drink some vodka, I take it?

Baron. Come with us.

Satin. I'd like to see what sort of a man you are when drunk.

Luka. No better than when I'm sober.

Actor. Come along, grandpa—I'll recite some verses to you.

Luka. What are those?

Actor. You know—poems.

Luka. Oh, poems! And what do I want poems for?

Actor. They make one laugh—or sometimes sad.

Satin. Are you coming, reciter? (*Satin and the Baron go off.*)

Actor. In a minute. I'll catch up with you. Here, grandpa, is something from a poem—I forget how it begins— H'm, I forget— (*He rubs his forehead.*)

Bubnov. There! It's good-by to your king. Your move.

Medvedev. Damn it—I made the wrong move.

Actor. In the old days, old man, when my organism wasn't yet poisoned with alcohol, I had a good memory. Now it's all over with me—it's all over. I always read that poem with great success—it brought the house down. You don't know what applause is— It's like vodka, my friend. I would come on the stage, stand like this— (*Assumes a pose.*) Yes, stand like this and— (*A long pause.*) I can't remember a thing—not a single word! And it's the poem I loved best of all— That's bad, old man, isn't it?

Luka. It can't be good if you've forgotten something you loved best. All our soul is in what we love.

Actor. I've drunk up my soul, old man. I'm lost. And why am I lost? Because I had no faith in myself. I'm finished.

Luka. Why finished? You get yourself treated. They treat for drunkenness today, so I hear. Free of charge, too. There's a special hospital for drunkards—so they can be treated for nothing. They've decided, you see, that a drunkard is a human being like everybody else, and they're even glad when he wants to be treated. There's a chance for you—go there right away.

Actor (*reflectively*). Go where? Where is it?

Luka. It's—in a town—what's its name? It's called— Never mind, I'll give you the name! Only you know what—you prepare yourself in the meantime. Keep away from vodka. Pull yourself together and bear up! Then later you'll be cured—and you'll start your life all over again. Yes, all over again—wouldn't it be fine, my friend? Well, make up your mind—and be quick about it!

Actor (*smiling*). All over again—from the start— That'll be fine— Yes, yes. Again. (*He laughs.*) Of course. I can do that. Surely I can, don't you think?

Luka. Why, certainly. A man can do anything, if he only wants to.

Actor (*as if suddenly awakened*). You're a queer fellow. So long! (*Whistles.*) So long, old man. (*Goes off.*)

Anna. Grandpa!

Luka. What is it, my dear?

Anna. Talk to me.

Luka (*coming up to her*). All right, let's talk.

> *Klestch looks about, walks up to his wife, gazes at her, and gesticulates as if wishing to say something.*

What is it, my friend?

Klestch (*in a low voice*). Nothing. (*He walks slowly toward the hallway, stops for a few seconds at the threshold, and goes off.*)

Luka (*after following Klestch with his eyes*). Your husband finds it hard to bear.

Anna. I have other things than him to think of now.

Luka. Did he beat you?

Anna. Didn't he though! It's through him, I think, that I took sick—

Bubnov. My wife—had a lover. The rascal was awfully good at checkers—

Medvedev. H'm—

Anna. Talk to me, grandpa dear. I feel sick—

Luka. It's all right. It's before death, dear. It's all right. You keep hoping. You'll die, you see, and then you'll have peace. You'll have nothing to fear—nothing at all. There'll be peace and quiet—and you'll have nothing to do but lie. Death quiets everything. It's kind to us humans. When you die you'll have rest, folks say. It's true, my dear. For where can a human being find rest in this world?

> *Enter Peppel. He is slightly tipsy, and looks disheveled and sullen. He sits down on a plank bed near the door and remains silent and motionless.*

Anna. But has one to suffer there too?

Luka. There'll be nothing there, nothing. Believe me. Peace and nothing more. They'll call you before the Lord and say: Look, O Lord, here's your servant Anna—

Medvedev (*sharply*). How do you know what they'll say there?

> *At the sound of Medvedev's voice Peppel raises his head and listens.*

Luka. It must be I do, master sergeant—

Medvedev (*in a conciliatory tone*). I—see. Well, it's your business. Though I'm not quite a master sergeant yet—

Bubnov. I take two.

Medvedev. Drat it.

Luka. And the Lord will look at you gently and caressingly and will say: I know this Anna. Well, he'll say, conduct Anna to heaven. Let her rest—I know she's had a very hard life and is very tired. Give Anna rest—

Anna (gasping). Oh, grandpa dear—if it were only like that! If I could only have rest—feel nothing—

Luka. You won't, I tell you. You have to believe. You have to die with joy, without fear. To us, I tell you, death is like a mother to little children.

Anna. But maybe—I'll get better?

Luka (ironically). What for? For more suffering?

Anna. Well—just to live a little longer—just a little. If there isn't going to be any suffering there, I can bear it here—yes, I can.

Luka. There'll be nothing there. Just—

Peppel (rising). That's true— Or maybe it isn't.

Anna (in a frightened voice). O God—

Luka. Hello, handsome—

Medvedev. Who's hollering?

Peppel (walking up to him). I am. Why?

Medvedev. There's no call for your hollering—that's why. Every man must behave himself quietly.

Peppel. Blockhead! Call yourself an uncle— Ho! Ho!

Luka (to Peppel, in a low voice). You there—don't shout. There's a woman dying here—her lips are already brushed with earth—don't interfere.

Peppel. For you, grandfather, I'll be glad to do it. You're a smart fellow. You tell lies and pleasant tales mighty well. That's all right with me. Go on lying. There's damn little in this world that's pleasant.

Bubnov. Is the woman really dying?

Luka. She doesn't look like she's joking—

Bubnov. Well, then she'll stop coughing. Her coughing's been disturbing everybody. I take two.

Medvedev. Ah, blast your hide!

Peppel. Abram.

Medvedev. I'm no Abram to you.

Peppel. Abrashka, is Natasha ill?

Medvedev. What business is that of yours?

Peppel. Come on, tell me: did Vassilissa beat her up badly?

Medvedev. That has nothing to do with you either. It's a family affair. And who are you, anyway?

Peppel. Never mind who I am. But if I decide so, you'll never see Natasha again.

Medvedev (interrupting his game). What's that? Do you know who you're talking about? That my niece should ever become— You thief!

Peppel. I may be a thief, but you never caught me—

Medvedev. You wait. I'll catch you yet—it won't be long!

Peppel. If you catch me, it will be so much the worse for your whole brood. Do you think I'm going to keep mum before the court examiner? Expect good deeds from a wolf! Who kept after me to start thieving and who showed me the places? Mishka Kostylyov and his wife. Who took in what I stole? Mishka Kostylyov and his wife.

Medvedev. Liar. They won't believe you.

Peppel. They will—because it's the truth. I'll drag you into it too—ha! I'll ruin all of you, you scoundrel, you'll see.

Medvedev (taken aback). You're lying. Just lying. And when have I done you any harm? A mad dog, that's what you are.

Peppel. And when have you done me any good?

Luka. Aha—

Medvedev (to Luka). What are you croaking about? You have no business here. This is a family affair.

Bubnov (to Luka). Leave off. They're not tying nooses for you and me.

Luka (meekly). I know. I only say if a man hasn't done somebody good, he's done him ill.

Medvedev (missing Luka's point). That's better. Around here we all know one another. And who are you? (*Spitting like an angry cat, he goes off quickly.*)

Luka. The gentleman lost his temper. Oh-ho-ho! You *have* got yourselves into all sorts of mix-ups, my friends—

Peppel. He's run to complain to Vassilissa.

Bubnov. You're playing the fool, Vassily. What's all this showing off how brave you are? Bravery is all right when you go picking mushrooms in the woods. It's not much use in these parts. They'll wring your neck in no time here.

Peppel. Oh, no. We folks from Yaroslavl don't knuckle down without a fight. And if it's going to be a fight, I'm ready for it.

Luka. Really, young man, why don't you go away from here?

Peppel. Where to? Can you tell me?

Luka. Go to—Siberia.

Peppel. Oh, yes? No, I'll wait until I'm sent there at government expense.

Luka. You listen to me—go to Siberia. New paths will open up for you there. Men like you are needed there.

Peppel. My life is cut out for me. My father spent all his life in prisons and taught me to do the same. I was only a tyke when everybody already called me a thief, a thief's son—

Luka. Well, Siberia's a fine place—a golden land. For a man who's strong and has a good head on his shoulders it's like a hothouse for a cucumber.

Peppel. Why do you tell lies, old man?

Luka. What?

Peppel. Gone deaf suddenly. Why do you lie, I say?

Luka. Where do you see me lying?

Peppel. Everywhere. You keep saying it's fine here and it's fine there, but you know you're lying. What for?

Luka. Well, take my word for it and go look it over for yourself. You'll thank me for it. What's the good of sticking around here? Anyway, what do you want the truth for? The truth might come down on you like an ax.

Peppel. I don't care. An ax is all right with me.

Luka. You're a queer fellow. Why be your own killer?

Bubnov. I don't understand what all this silly talk is about. What truth do you want, Vassily? And what for? You know the truth about yourself—everybody knows it.

Peppel. Shut up, Bubnov, don't croak. I want him to tell me— Listen, old man: Does God exist?

Luka smiles, making no answer.

Bubnov. People live like chips floating down the river. The house is built, but the chips are thrown away to take care of themselves.

Peppel. Well? Does he? Answer me.

Luka (*in a low voice*). If you believe in him, he exists. If you don't, he doesn't. Whatever you believe in exists.

Peppel, puzzled, stares at Luka in silence.

Bubnov. I'm going to have some tea. Come along, you two!

Luka. Why are you looking at me?

Peppel. Well—wait. So you say—

Bubnov. I'll go alone then— (*He walks toward the door as Vassilissa enters.*)

Peppel. So you mean to say—

Vassilissa (*to Bubnov*). Is Nastya in?

Bubnov. No. (*He goes off.*)

Peppel. Oh, it's you.

Vassilissa (*going up to Anna*). Still alive?

Luka. Don't disturb her.

Vassilissa. Why are you hanging around here?

Luka. I can leave, if necessary.

Vassilissa (*walking toward Peppel's room*). I want to talk over some business with you, Vassily. (*She enters Peppel's room, while Luka moves to the hallway door, opens it, slams it loudly, and cautiously climbs over a plank bed onto the stove.*) Come here, Vassya.

Peppel. I don't want to.

Vassilissa (*coming out*). Why not? What makes you cross with me?

Peppel. I'm bored—fed up with all this business.

Vassilissa. Fed up with me too?

Peppel. Yes, with you too. (*Vassilissa pulls her shoulder kerchief tight, pressing her hands to her breast, then walks to Anna's bed, peeps silently behind the curtain, and returns to Peppel.*) Well, if you have anything to say—

Vassilissa. What is there to say? You can't force one to like you—and it's not in my character to beg for alms. Thank you for speaking the truth.

Peppel. What truth?

Vassilissa. That you're fed up with me. Or isn't it true? (*Peppel gazes at her in silence. She moves up to him.*) Why are you staring at me? Don't you recognize me?

Peppel (*with a sigh*). You *are* beautiful to look at, Vassilissa — (*Vassilissa puts an arm around his neck, but he shakes it off with a shrug of his shoulders.*) But you never touched my heart. I lived with you and all that sort of thing—but I never really cared for you—

Vassilissa (*in a low voice*). I see— Well?

Peppel. Well—there's nothing we can talk about—nothing at all! Just leave me.

Vassilissa. You've taken a fancy to somebody else?

Peppel. That's none of your business. If I have, I won't ask you to be my matchmaker.

Vassilissa (significantly). That's a pity. I could probably get you the right party.

Peppel (suspiciously). Who do you mean?

Vassilissa. You know who—why pretend? Vassily, I'm a straightforward person— *(Lowering her voice.)* I won't hide it—you've hurt me. For no reason whatever you struck me as if with a whip. You were telling me you loved me and then all of a sudden—

Peppel. It wasn't sudden at all. I've felt like that for a long time. There's no soul in you, Vassilissa. A woman must have a soul. We men are brutes. We should be—we have to be tamed and trained. And what kind of training have you been giving me?

Vassilissa. What's gone is gone. I know we're not masters of our feelings. If you don't love me any more—all right—so be it.

Peppel. Well, then, that's that. We'll each go our own way, quietly, without any fuss, and that's fine.

Vassilissa. No, wait. That's not all. When I lived with you I was always counting on you to help me get out of this mess— free me from my husband, my uncle—this whole life. Maybe it wasn't you I loved, Vassya, but this hope, this constant thought on my mind, that I loved in you. You understand? I was waiting for you to pull me out of here—

Peppel. You're no nail, and I'm no pair of pliers. I thought myself that with your brains—you *are* clever—and smart too— aren't you?

Vassilissa (bending closer to him). Vassya, let's—help each other.

Peppel. How?

Vassilissa (quietly, but strongly). I know you like—my sister.

Peppel. That's why you're so brutal—always beating her. Look out, Vassilissa. Keep your hands off her.

Vassilissa. Wait. Don't excite yourself. It can all be done quietly—arranged in a friendly way. You want to marry Natasha? All right—marry her. I'll even give you some money—

say three hundred rubles. When I've saved more, I'll give you more.

Peppel (*moving away from Vassilissa*). Now just a minute— What's that for? What's the idea?

Vassilissa. Free me from my husband— Take that noose off my neck.

Peppel (*whistles quietly*). So that's it! I see. Very neat on your part—the husband packed off into the grave, the lover to Siberia, and you yourself—

Vassilissa. No, Vassya—why Siberia? You don't have to do it yourself—you can get others. And even if you do it, who'll know? Think of Natasha. And you'll have money—you'll go away somewhere—you'll free me for life—and as far as my sister's concerned, it'll be better for her, too, to be away from me. It's hard for me to see her— I get bitter because of you— and I can't restrain myself. I torment her, beat her—beat her so hard I cry myself for pity of her. But I keep beating her and will go right on doing it.

Peppel. A demon—that's what you are. And you're boasting about it.

Vassilissa. I'm not boasting—I'm speaking the truth. Think, Vassya. Twice you did time on account of my husband—because of his greed. He's sucking my blood like a bedbug—been doing it for four years. What sort of a husband is that? And he's harsh with Natasha, taunts her, calls her a beggar. He's poison to everybody.

Peppel. There's something too clever in all this.

Vassilissa. My meaning is clear—only a fool can fail to understand what I want.

   Kostylyov enters cautiously and moves stealthily forward.
Peppel (*to Vassilissa*). Well, you'd better go now.

Vassilissa. Think it over. (*Noticing her husband.*) What brings you here? Looking for me?

   Peppel jumps to his feet and stares wildly at Kostylyov.
Kostylyov. It's me—it's me. And you're alone here? Ah—you have been having a chat? (*Suddenly stamps his feet and squeals at Vassilissa.*) You slut! You dirty trash! (*He is frightened by his own voice, as the other two look at him silently without moving.*) God forgive me—you've led me into sin again, Vassilissa. I've been looking for you everywhere. (*Squealing*

again.) Time to go to bed! You've forgotten to put oil in the icon lamps! You—miserable swine.

He shakes his trembling hands at Vassilissa. She walks slowly to the hallway, looking back at Peppel.

Peppel (to Kostylyov). Get out of here!

Kostylyov (shouting). It's my house! You get out of here! Thief!

Peppel (in a low voice). Get out, Mishka!

Kostylyov. Don't you dare! I'll—I'll—

Peppel grabs him by the collar and shakes him. A loud shuffling and a long animal-like yawn are heard from the top of the stove. Peppel releases Kostylyov, who runs into the hallway screaming.

Peppel (jumping onto the plank bed). Who's up there—on the stove?

Luka (popping out). What?

Peppel. You?

Luka (calmly). Yes—it's me—none other— O Lord Jesus Christ!

Peppel (closes the hallway door and looks for the bolt, but cannot find it). Ah, those devils! Come down, old man!

Luka. I'm coming—right away. (*He comes down.*)

Peppel (roughly). Why did you get up on top of the stove?

Luka. Was there somewhere else I should have gone?

Peppel. But you went into the hall?

Luka. It's too cold out there for an old man like me.

Peppel. Did you—hear?

Luka. I heard. How could I help hearing? I ain't deaf. Ah, what luck has come to you, my boy—what luck!

Peppel (suspiciously). What sort of luck?

Luka. That I got up on the stove.

Peppel. And why did you start shuffling around up there?

Luka. Because I felt hot—fortunately for you, my boy. Besides, I figured the fellow can make a mistake and squeeze the old man to death.

Peppel. Yes—I could've done that— I hate him—

Luka. Nothing easier. Anybody could do it. People often make that mistake.

Peppel (smiling). Say, maybe you made it yourself once?

Luka. Listen to what I'm going to tell you, my boy. You've got to cut yourself off from that woman. Don't let her come near you—ever. She'll drive her husband into the grave herself, and she'll do a neater job of it than you can—believe me! Don't listen to that witch. Look at my head. Bald, isn't it? And why? Because of these same women. I've known more of them maybe than I had hair on my head. And this Vassilissa woman is worse than a savage.

Peppel. I don't understand. Am I supposed to say thank you, or are you just another—

Luka. Don't say anything. You can't improve on what I said. Better listen to me—whoever she is, the girl you like around here, take her by the arm and be off with you! Get away from here—as fast as you can!

Peppel (somberly). I can't make people out—which are kind and which are out to get you—I can't understand anything.

Luka. What is there to understand? A man can live any which way—however his heart tells him—kind today, mean tomorrow. If that girl here has touched your heart real strong, go away with her and that's all there is to that. Or you can go away alone. You're still young—you have plenty of time to settle down with a woman.

Peppel (taking Luka by the shoulder). No, tell me what are you getting out of all this?

Luka. Now wait—let go. I want to have a look at Anna—there's been too much rattle in her breathing. (*Walks up to Anna's bed, draws the curtain, looks, touches her with his hand. Peppel watches him attentively, with a puzzled air.*) Jesus Christ, the all-merciful. Receive the soul of thy newly departed servant, Anna, with peace.

Peppel (quietly). Is she dead? (*Staying where he is, he straightens up and gazes at the bed.*)

Luka (quietly). Her suffering has ended. Where's her man?

Peppel. Over at the inn, most likely.

Luka. I must go tell him.

Peppel (with a shudder). I don't like dead people.

Luka (walking toward the hall door). What's there to like them for? It's the living people we should like—yes, the living ones.

Peppel. I'll go along with you.

Luka. Are you afraid?

Peppel. I don't like—
They hurry out. The place is deserted and quiet. After a time a noise is heard beyond the hallway door—it is indistinct, uneven, and unintelligible. Then the Actor enters.
Actor (stops just across the threshold without closing the door, and, holding onto the jamb with both hands, shouts). Hey, old man! Where are you? It's come back to me—listen. (*Staggering, takes two steps forward and, assuming a stage pose, recites.*)

If the world, my friends, is unable to find
The road to justice and truth,
Honor be to the madman who weaves golden dreams
Giving mankind surcease.

   Natasha appears at the door behind the Actor.
Old man, listen.

If tomorrow the sun should forget to light up
Our planet's eternal path,
A thought of some madman will instantly flash
To illumine the darkened earth.

Natasha (laughing). You loon! Been out getting crocked?
Actor (turning to Natasha). Ah! It's you? And where's the old man, the darling little old man? There's nobody here, it seems. Well, farewell Natasha—yes, farewell!
Natasha (stepping forward). You never said good evening, and now you're saying farewell.
Actor (barring her way). I'm leaving, going away. Spring will come, but I'll be here no more.
Natasha. Let me pass. Where are you off to?
Actor. I'm going to look for a town—to get treatment. You should go too. Ophelia—get thee to a nunnery. You see, there's a hospital for organisms—for drunkards. A splendid hospital—marble everywhere—marble floors—bright, clean rooms—food —everything free! And yes, marble floors! I'll find this hospital, get cured, and once again I'll—act. I'm on the road to rebirth, as King—Lear said. My stage name is Sverchkov-Zavolzhsky— nobody knows that—nobody. I have no name here. Do you realize how it hurts to lose one's name? Even dogs have names.

   Natasha quietly moves around the Actor, stops at Anna's bed, and looks.
Without a name there's no man.

Natasha. Look—but she's dead!

Actor (*shaking his head*). That can't be.

Natasha (*stepping back*). Really—look.

> *Bubnov appears at the door.*

Bubnov. Look at what?

Natasha. Anna's—dead.

Bubnov. That means the end of her coughing. (*Walks up to Anna's bed, looks at her, and proceeds to his own place.*) Somebody should tell Klestch about it—it's his business.

Actor. I'm going—I'll tell him— She's lost her name! (*He goes off.*)

Natasha (*standing in the center of the room*). Some day I will end like that—in a basement—forgotten by everybody—

Bubnov (*spreading some tattered clothes on his plank bed*). What? What are you mumbling there?

Natasha. Nothing—I was talking to myself.

Bubnov. Waiting for Vassily? Look out! He'll break your neck for you.

Natasha. What's the difference who breaks it? I'd rather it's him.

Bubnov (*lying down*). Well, it's up to you.

Natasha. It's a good thing she died—but I can't help feeling sorry for her. God! What did she live for?

Bubnov. It's like that with everybody—a man is born, lives a while, and dies. I'll die too—and so will you. Nothing to be sorry about.

> *Enter Luka, the Tartar, the Goiter, and Klestch. Klestch walks slowly behind the others, stooped over.*

Natasha. Sh-sh! Anna—

Goiter. We know— God rest her soul, if she's dead.

Tartar (*to Klestch*). You must pull her out! Pull her out hallway! Here no dead people. Here live people will sleep.

Klestch (*in a low voice*). I'll pull her out.

> *They all walk up to the bed. Klestch gazes at his wife over the shoulders of the others.*

Goiter (*to the Tartar*). You think there'll be a bad smell from her? No! She dried up while she was still alive.

Natasha. God! Not one to feel sorry for her—not a single kind word from anybody— Shame on you!

Luka. Don't take it that way, girlie— It's all right. How can we feel sorry for the dead? Why, girlie, we don't feel sorry for the living—even for ourselves. So what can you expect?

Bubnov (*yawning*). And another thing—death isn't afraid of words— Sickness is, but not death.

Tartar (*moving away*). Must call police.

Goiter. The police? Positively. Did you report to the police, Klestch?

Klestch. No. I have to bury her—and all I have is forty kopecks.

Goiter. Well, in a case like that borrow somewhere. Or we can take up a collection—five kopecks from this one, as much as he can spare from that. But you have to report to the police—and do it quick—or they'll think you've killed the woman—or something— (*Walks to his plank bed and prepares to lie down alongside the Tartar.*)

Natasha (*moving away toward Bubnov's plank bed*). Now I'll be seeing her in my dreams. I always see dead people in my dreams—I'm afraid to go back alone—it's dark in the hall.

Luka (*following her*). The people to fear are the living ones —take it from me—

Natasha. Come with me to the door, grandpa.

Luka. All right—let's go.   *The two exit. There is a pause.*

Goiter. Oh-ho-ho! Assan! Spring is coming, friend—life will be warm again! In the villages the peasants are already mending their plows, harrows—getting ready to turn the earth—y-yes! And we? Assan! The cursed Mohammed, he's dead to the world.

Bubnov. Tartars love to sleep.

Klestch (*standing in the center of the room and gazing dully into space*). What am I to do now?

Goiter. Lie down and sleep—that's all.

Klestch (*in a low voice*). And how—about her?

          Nobody answers him. Enter Satin and the Actor.

Actor (*shouts*). Old man! Come here, my faithful Kent!

Satin. Behold the great explorer! Ho-ho!

Actor. It's all settled and done with! Where's the town, old man? Where are you?

Satin. Fata-morgana! The old man lied to you. There's nothing! No town, no people—nothing!

Actor. You're lying!

Tartar (jumping up from his bed). Where's landlord? I go see landlord. I not sleep, I not pay money. Dead people— drunken people— (*He rushes out. Satin whistles after him.*)

Bubnov (in a sleepy voice). Come to bed, fellows, stop making so much noise. People are supposed to sleep at night.

Actor. Oh, yes—there's a dead body here. "Daddy, Daddy, have you heard? Our nets have caught a corpse"—a poem by— Shakespeare.

Satin (shouts). Corpses don't hear! Corpses don't feel! Shout —yell—corpses don't hear!   *Luka appears at the door.*

CURTAIN

ACT III

A vacant plot of ground littered with junk and overgrown with weeds. At the rear a high red-brick wall cuts off the sky. Near the wall is a cluster of elder. To the right of it runs a dark log wall which is part of some kind of shed or stables. To the left is a gray wall with patches of plaster. This belongs to the KOSTYLYOV *lodging house and stands at an angle, its far corner jutting out almost to the center of the plot, and a narrow passage showing between it and the red-brick wall. In the gray wall are two windows, one at ground level, the other up about five feet and nearer the corner. Alongside this wall lie a country sledge, turned upside down, and a log about ten feet long. Piled against the wall on the right are some beams and old wooden planks.*
It is early spring, and the snow has already melted away. The black twigs of the elder bush have not yet budded. The setting sun casts a red glow on the brick wall, rear.

Sitting on the log, side by side, are NATASHA *and* NASTYA. LUKA *and the* BARON *are seated on the sledge.* KLESTCH *is lying on the heap of wood across from them.* BUBNOV'S *head is visible in the lower window.*

Nastya (speaking in a singsong voice, her eyes closed and her head beating time to her words). So one night he comes to the garden, to the arbor, as we arranged—and I'm already there waiting for him a long time, trembling with fear and grief. He too is trembling all over, his face white as chalk, and a revolver in his hand—

Natasha (cracking sunflower seeds). Imagine that! It seems to be true what people say about students being desperate—

Nastya. And he says to me in a ghastly voice: My dearest, my precious love—

Bubnov. Ho-ho! Precious?

Baron. Just a minute. Don't like it, don't listen—but don't spoil a good lie. Go on.

Nastya. My adorable one, says he. My parents refuse to give their consent, says he, to my taking you for my spouse and threaten to put an eternal curse on me for my love of you. On account of this, says he, I'm obliged to take my life. And the revolver in his hand is ever so big and has ten bullets in it. Farewell, dear heart, says he, nothing can make me change my mind, for I could never live without you—never! And I answered him: My never-to-be-forgotten friend—Marcel—

Bubnov (with surprise). Morsel? What's that? Something to eat?

Baron (laughing). But listen, Nastya—last time it was Gaston!

Nastya (jumping to her feet). Keep quiet, you miserable things! You're nothing but stray dogs! How can you understand what love—real love is? And I did have real love! (*To the Baron.*) You pitiful wretch! You're an educated man. You drank coffee in bed, you say—

Luka. Now wait, folks! You mustn't interrupt her. Oblige the girl, let her have her way. It doesn't matter what's said, but why it's said. Never mind them, girlie, go on with your story.

Bubnov. Paint your feathers, crow. Fire away!

Baron. Well, go on.

Natasha. Take no notice of them. Who are they? They're just envious—they have nothing to say about themselves.

Nastya (resuming her seat). I don't want to talk any more. No, I won't. If they don't believe me—if they laugh at me— (*She stops abruptly, pauses for a few seconds, then, closing her eyes again, continues in a fervent, loud voice, waving her hand to the beat of her speech as if listening to distant music.*) And so I reply to him: Joy of my life! My bright star! For me too it's positively impossible to live in this world—because I love you madly and will go on loving you as long as my heart beats in my breast. But, says I, you mustn't destroy your young life —as it's needed by your dear parents for whom you are their only joy— Forget me! Better that I suffer—the heartache of missing you— For I have nobody—my kind never has! Better let me be destroyed—it won't matter now! I'm not fit for anything and I've nothing—nothing— (*She covers her face with her hands and weeps silently.*)

Natasha (*turning away from Nastya, in a low voice*). Don't cry—don't!   *A smile on his face, Luka strokes Nastya's head.*

Bubnov (*roars with laughter*). Damn fool!

Baron (*laughing*). Do you think this true, grandpa? She took it all from the book *Fatal Love*— It's all bunk! Don't bother with her!

Natasha. What's that to you? Better hold your tongue—if you have no heart left in you.

Nastya (*fiercely*). You godforsaken, empty man! Where's your soul?

Luka (*taking Nastya by the arm*). Come along, dear. Don't mind them—calm yourself. I know—I believe you. Yours is the truth, not theirs. If you believe you had a real love, then you did have it—you certainly did. And don't be angry with your Baron. Maybe he does laugh from plain envy—maybe he never knew anything true and real in his life. Come along.

Nastya (*pressing her hands to her breast*). Honest, grandpa, it's true, it did happen. He was a student, a Frenchman—Gaston was his name— He had a small black beard—and wore patent leather boots—may lightning strike me dead! And he loved me so dearly—so dearly!

Luka. I know. I believe you. You say he wore patent leather boots? My goodness! And you loved him too?

The two go off around the corner.

Baron. That girl is so stupid—kind, but so unbearably stupid.

Bubnov. What is it that makes human beings so fond of lying? As if they were always facing a court examiner—

Natasha. Lies must be more pleasant than the truth, it seems. I too—

Baron. Well—go on.

Natasha. I too like to imagine things. I imagine them and— wait.

Baron. For what?

Natasha (*smiling embarrassedly*). Oh, I don't know. Maybe tomorrow, I think, somebody will come—somebody—quite different— Or maybe something will happen—something that's never happened before. I wait and wait—I'm always waiting. But really, come to think of it, what have I to wait for?

A pause.

Baron (*ironically*). There's nothing to wait for. I don't expect anything. Everything has already happened. It's over—and done with! Go on.

Natasha. Or sometimes I imagine that tomorrow—I'll suddenly die. It gives you such a creepy feeling. Summer is a fine time for imagining death— All those thunderstorms in summer —it's easy to get killed by lightning.

Baron. You have a hard life. That sister of yours has a devilish character.

Natasha. And who has a good life? Nobody. I see it all around me.

Klestch (*until this moment motionless and indifferent, suddenly springing to his feet*). Nobody? That's a lie! Some people have it! If everybody suffered, it'd be all right. You wouldn't feel then that life's been unfair to you.

Bubnov. What's got into you? The devil? Howling like that! Huh!

> *Klestch lies down on the heap, as before, mumbling to himself.*

Baron. I suppose I have to go and make up with Nastya—or she won't give me anything for a drink.

Bubnov. H'mm— People do love telling lies. With Nastya, I can understand it. She's used to painting her face—so she wants to paint her soul too—put rouge on it. But why do others do it? Take Luka for instance—he lies an awful lot—gets nothing out of it. And he's already an old man. What does he do it for?

Baron (*moving away, with a smile*). All human beings have gray little souls—and they all want to rouge them up.

Luka (*returning from around the corner*). Look, my dear man, why do you upset the girl? You should leave her alone. Let her amuse herself by crying. You know she cries for her own pleasure—what harm does it do you?

Baron. The whole thing is stupid, old man. I'm tired of it. Today it's Marcel, tomorrow Gaston—and every day it's the same story! However, I'm off to make up with her. (*He goes.*)

Luka. Go and be gentle with her. It never does any harm to be gentle to a human being.

Natasha. You're a kind man, grandpa. What makes you that way?

Luka. Kind, you say? That's all right, if it's true. (*Soft sounds of an accordion and a song drift on from behind the red wall.*) Somebody has to be kind, my girl—we have to feel sorry for people. Christ felt sorry for everybody and bid us do the same. Believe me—feeling sorry for a man at the right moment can do a lot of good. One time, for instance, I was a watchman in a country house in Siberia, near Tomsk, working for an engineer, you know. Well, the house stood in the woods, all by itself—no other homes around. It was winter and I was all alone in the house. I felt fine. One day I hear noises at a window!

Natasha. Burglars?

Luka. That's right. Trying to break in. Well, I picked up my rifle and went out. I look around and there I see—two men trying to open the window—and working so hard at it they didn't even notice me. I shout at them: Hey, you! Get out of here! And what do they do?— They turn around and rush at me with an ax. I warn them, Keep away, I say, or I'll shoot, and at the same time I cover them with my rifle, now one, now the other. Down on their knees they went as if begging me to let them go. But by now I felt very cross with them—for the ax, you know. You devils wouldn't go away when I told you, says I, now, says I, break off some twigs from a tree, one of you. That was done. And now, I order, one of you lie down and let the other lash him with the twigs. So by my order they gave each other a fine lashing. And after they did it they say to me, Grandpa, they say, for mercy's sake give us some bread. We've been tramping around on an empty belly. So there are your

burglars, my dear— (*Laughing.*) And with an ax too! Yes, fine
fellows they were, both of them. I say to them: You devils
should have asked for bread right away. And they answer me—
We're tired of asking. You keep asking people—and nobody
gives you anything—it makes you feel pretty sore. And so they
stayed with me right through the winter. One of them, Stepan,
would take a rifle sometimes and go into the woods for days.
The other, Yakov, was poorly, coughed all the time. And so the
three of us kept watch over that country house. When spring
came they said, good-by, grandpa! and left—to tramp their way
to Russia.

Natasha. Were they runaway convicts?

Luka. They were—they ran away from a convict camp. Fine
fellows! If I hadn't felt sorry for them, they might have killed
me—or something. And then they would have been tried, sent
to jail, to Siberia—what sense in that? Jail doesn't teach anyone
to do good, nor Siberia, but a man—yes! A man can teach another man to do good—believe me!   *A pause.*

Bubnov. Y-yes! Now *I* don't know how to tell lies. What good
are they? What I say is—give 'em the whole truth just as it is.
Why feel shy about it?

Klestch (*again jumping suddenly to his feet, as if burned,
and shouting*). What truth? Where's the truth? (*Running his
hands through his tatters.*) Here's the truth! No work, no
strength, not even a place to live. The only thing left is to die
like a dog! This is the truth! Good God! What do I want the
truth for? I want to breathe more freely—that's all I ask. What
have I done wrong? Why should I have been given the truth?
No chance to live—Christ Almighty—not a chance—that's the
truth!

Bubnov. Whew! It certainly got him!

Luka. Lord Jesus— Look, my friend, you should—

Klestch (*shaking with emotion*). You keep saying, The truth
—the truth! And you, old man, keep comforting everybody. So
I tell you—I hate you all—and this truth too—to hell with it.
Understand? To hell with it! (*Rushes off around the corner,
glancing back as he goes.*)

Luka. My, my! How upset he got! And where is he off to?

Natasha. He acted as if he suddenly went off his nut.

Bubnov. A fine show, I call it. Just like on the stage— That kind of thing happens, though, every once in a while. The man hasn't got used to life yet—

> *Peppel enters slowly from around the corner.*

Peppel. Peace to you honest people! Well, Luka, you sly old man—still telling stories?

Luka. You should have been here—a man was screaming his lungs out.

Peppel. Was it Klestch? What got into him? I saw him running as if he was on fire.

Luka. Who won't run when it gets you right in the heart?

Peppel. I don't like him—he's too bitter and proud. (*Imitating Klestch.*) "I'm a working man"—and everybody's below him, he'll have you think. Well, work if you like it—what's there to be proud of? If we're supposed to judge people by their work, the horse is better than any man—you drive it—and it doesn't speak. Are your folks at home, Natasha?

Natasha. They've gone to the cemetery—said they'd go to the evening mass afterward.

Peppel. And I've been wondering why you're free. It's a rare sight.

Luka (*to Bubnov, reflectively*). You've been saying we need the truth. But it isn't always that truth is good for what ails a man—you can't always cure the soul with truth. I remember this case, for instance. I knew a man who believed in the true and just land—

Bubnov. Believed in what?

Luka. In the true and just land. There must be such a land in the world, he'd say. The people in that land, says he, are of a special kind—a fine people. They respect one another, help one another, and everything they do is decent and fine. And so every day this man was thinking of going to look for that true and just land. He was a poor man, and had a hard life. But whenever things were so bad he was ready to lie down and die, he didn't let himself lose heart; he just smiled and said: It's all right—I can bear it. I'll wait a while, and then I'll give up this life and go to the true and just land. He had only one joy in life—that land—

Peppel. Did he go?

Bubnov. Where? Ho! Ho!

Luka. Then there came to that place—all this happened in Siberia—a man exiled by the government, a learned man, with books, maps, and all sorts of things like that. So our man says to the scientist: Do me a favor, please, show me where the true and just land lies and how to get there. The scientist at once opens his books, spreads his maps—looks here, looks there—there's no true and just land anywhere. Everything is right, all the lands are shown—but the true and just land is just not there.

Peppel (in a low voice). Not there? Really? *Bubnov laughs.*

Natasha. Don't interrupt. Go on, grandpa.

Luka. My man doesn't believe him. It must be there, says he, look harder for it. Otherwise your books and maps, says he—they're all worthless if they fail to show the true and just land. The scientist is sore at that. My maps, says he, are the truest of all, and the true and just land doesn't exist anywhere. Hearing that, my man too gets angry. What? says he. I've lived and suffered all these years believing it exists, and your maps make out it doesn't? It's robbery! And he says to the scientist: You dirty swine. You're a crook, not a scientist. And bang! he punches him in the nose, and bang! again! *(He pauses.)* After that he went home—and hung himself.

All are silent. Luka looks at Peppel and Natasha with a smile.

Peppel (in a low voice). What the devil! That's not what I'd call a gay story—

Natasha. He couldn't bear having been deceived.

Bubnov (somberly). It's all tales.

Peppel. Y-yes. There is the true and just land for you. None such, it turns out.

Natasha. I feel sorry for the man.

Bubnov. It's all make-believe. Ho! Ho! The true and just land! How do you like that? Ho! Ho! Ho! *(He vanishes from his window.)*

Luka (nodding in the direction of Bubnov's window). He's laughing. Hee-hee! *(He pauses.)* Well, friends, may you come to good ends. I'm leaving you soon.

Peppel. Where are you off to now?

Luka. To the Ukrainians. I've heard they've discovered a new faith down there—I must have a look at it. Yes, people keep looking—keep wishing for something better. God give them patience!

Peppel. What's your opinion? Will they find it?

Luka. Who, people? They'll find it. Look for something—want something with all your heart—you'll find it.

Natasha. If they would only find something—think up something good—

Luka. They'll think it up. Only we have to help them, girlie— make it easier for them.

Natasha. How can I help? I get no help myself.

Peppel (resolutely). I'm going to—I will talk to you again, Natasha— Let him hear it too—he knows all about it. Come— with me!

Natasha. Where? From one jail to another?

Peppel. I said I'd give up thieving. I swear I will. And I mean it. I'm not an illiterate—I'll work. Luka here says one ought to go to Siberia of his own free will. Let's go there. Don't you think I'm sick of my life? I know, Natasha, I see it all. I try to make myself feel better thinking others steal much more than I do and have honors heaped on them—but that doesn't help me—it's no answer. I'm not letting conscience prick me into saying this—I don't believe in conscience. But one thing I do know—this is not the way to live. I must live a better life. I must live—in such a way that I can respect myself—

Luka. You're right, my boy. May the Lord Jesus Christ help you. You're right—a man must respect himself.

Peppel. I've been a thief from the time I was a kid. Everybody called me Vasska the thief! Vasska the thief's son! Ah, so? Then have it your way. Here I am—a thief! You must understand— I'm a thief maybe only out of spite—only because nobody ever thought of calling me by any other name. You'll call me something else, Natasha, won't you?

Natasha (in a melancholy tone). I can't believe any words— somehow. And I feel uneasy today—my heart aches—as if I were expecting something to happen. I'm sorry you've started this conversation, Vassily—

Peppel. How long should I have waited? This isn't the first time I've brought it up.

Natasha. Well, I don't know how I could go with you. Frankly, I can't say I love you very much. Sometimes I seem

to like you. Other times it makes me sick to look at you. It must
be I don't really love you. When you love somebody you don't
see anything wrong with them. I do.

Peppel. You'll love me all right—don't worry. I'll see you get
to like me—if you'll only say yes. I've been watching you for
over a year—I can see you're a good girl—strict with yourself
—dependable—and I've fallen in love with you—deeply.

*Vassilissa, in her best finery, appears at the higher window
and listens, standing by the jamb.*

Natasha. I see. You say you love me—and what about my
sister?

Peppel (embarrassed). Oh, she's nothing to me. There are
lots of her kind—

Luka. Don't mind that, girlie. When there's no bread, you
eat grass—

Peppel (somberly). I ask you to bear with me. Mine is a bitter life—a hungry wolf's life—there's no joy in it. I feel as if
I'm sinking in a bog—whatever I lay hold of is rotten, nothing
can keep me from going down. Your sister—I thought she was
different. If she weren't so greedy for money—I'd have done
anything for her. Only she had to be all mine. But she's after
something else—she wants money—and freedom too—freedom
to play around with men. She can't help me. But you—you're
like a young fir tree—prickly to touch, but strong to hold on
to—

Luka. My advice too, girlie—marry him. He's all right—he's
a good fellow. Only you have to remind him as often as you
can that he's a good fellow—so he doesn't forget it. He'll believe you. Just keep telling him—you're a good man, Vassya,
remember that! And besides, my dear, where else can you go?
Your sister is a wicked wild beast, and as for her husband—
well, nothing you can say about him can be as bad as he is.
Then, all this life around here—it can take you nowhere. And
Vassily—he's substantial, there's something to him.

Natasha. I know I have nowhere else to go—I've thought of
that myself. Only—I have no faith in anybody. But you're
right, I've nowhere to go—

Peppel. There's one road for you here—but I won't let you
go that way—I'd rather kill you.

Natasha. There! I'm not your wife yet, and you already want to kill me.

Peppel (putting his arms around her). Stop it, Natasha. Let's not say any more!

Natasha (pressing close to him). I'll say one thing, Vassily—and let God be my witness—the very first time you strike me—or wrong me in some other way—I won't spare my life—I'll either hang myself or—

Peppel. May my hand wither away, if I ever touch you!

Luka. Have no doubts, dear. He needs you more than you need him.

Vassilissa (from the window). Congratulations on the happy ending!

Natasha. They're back! God, they've seen us. Oh, Vassily!

Peppel. What are you scared of? Nobody will dare touch you now.

Vassilissa. Don't be afraid, Natasha. He won't beat you. He can neither beat nor love—I know.

Luka (in a low voice). Oh, what a woman—a regular viper—

Vassilissa. He's brave mostly with words—

Enter Kostylyov.

Kostylyov. Natashka! What are you doing here, loafer? Scandal-mongering? Complaining about your family? And all this time the samovar hasn't been prepared, the table hasn't been cleared—ah?

Natasha. But you said you wanted to go to church.

Kostylyov. What we wanted to do is none of your business! You have to see to your own work—do what you're told!

Peppel. You shut up! She's not your servant any more. Don't go, Natasha—don't do anything!

Natasha. Don't you give orders—it's too early for you. (*She goes off.*)

Peppel (to Kostylyov). Enough! You've bullied the girl all you're going to. Now she's mine.

Kostylyov. Yours? When did you buy her? How much did you pay?   *Vassilissa laughs loudly.*

Luka. Go away, Vassya.

Peppel. Watch out you—laughers! See you don't have to cry!

Vassilissa. Oh, how frightening! Oh, I'm so scared!

Luka. Go away, Vassily. Don't you see she's egging you on, trying to get you worked up?

Peppel. Oh, so? Not me! I'll be damned if you have your own way!

Vassilissa. And I'll be damned if I don't, Vassya!

Peppel (shaking his fist at her). We'll see about that! (*He goes off.*)

Vassilissa (disappearing from the window). I'll fix you a nice wedding!

Kostylyov (walking up to Luka). What's doing, old man?

Luka. Nothing doing, old man.

Kostylyov. Really. I hear you're leaving?

Luka. It's time to go.

Kostylyov. Where to?

Luka. Where my nose leads me.

Kostylyov. I see, tramping about. Seems you find it uncomfortable to stay in one place?

Luka. That's for stones. And they say even water won't flow under a stone.

Kostylyov. We're not talking about stones. A man must live in one place. You can't let people live like cockroaches—crawling every which way. A man ought to stick to his place—not wander about the earth for nothing.

Luka. What if a man's place is everywhere?

Kostylyov. Then he's a tramp, a useless man. A man must be useful, he must work—

Luka. You don't say.

Kostylyov. Yes—certainly. What's a pilgrim? A pilgrim, I've heard tell, means a foreigner, a stranger. He's a strange man, not like other people. If he's really strange—if he knows something—has learned something that's of no use to anybody—it may even be some truth—but not every truth is useful—not by a long shot— Well, let him keep what he knows to himself—and hold his tongue. If he's a real pilgrim he doesn't talk—or talks so nobody understands him. He doesn't want anything, minds his own business, and doesn't stir up trouble for nothing. It's none of his business how people live. Let him follow a righteous life—live in the woods—in the thickets—out of everybody's sight. It's not for him to interfere or criticize, but to pray

for everybody—for all worldly sins—mine and yours—for everything. That's why he puts worldly vanity behind him—just so
he can pray. Exactly! (*He pauses.*) And what sort of pilgrim
are you? You have no passport. A good man must have a passport. All good people have passports—yes.

Luka. There are people, and there are also just plain men.

Kostylyov. Don't try to be funny. And don't talk to me in
riddles. I'm no more stupid than you are. What do you mean
by people and men?

Luka. This is no riddle. I say there's soil unfit for sowing,
and there's fertile soil—whatever you sow on it grows— That's
all the difference.

Kostylyov. Well? What do you mean by that?

Luka. Take yourself, for instance. If the Lord God himself
says to you: Mikhail, be a man!—he'll be wasting his breath—
as you are, so you'll stay—

Kostylyov. And do you know my wife has an uncle who's a
policeman? And if I—   *Enter Vassilissa.*

Vassilissa. Come have tea, Mikhail Ivanovich.

Kostylyov (to Luka). Listen, you—get out of here! Clear out
of the house!

Vassilissa. Yes, old man, be off with you. Your tongue is much
too sharp. And who knows—maybe you're a fugitive—

Kostylyov. If I see hide or hair of you after today—I'll take
steps!

Luka. Call your uncle? Call him. Tell him you've caught a
fugitive. He may get a reward—about three kopecks—

                          Bubnov reappears in the lower window.

Bubnov. What's up? What's being sold for three kopecks?

Luka. He's threatening to sell me.

Vassilissa (to Kostylyov). Come on.

Bubnov. For three kopecks? Watch out, old man, they'll sell
you for one kopeck.

Kostylyov (to Bubnov). You would pop your head out like
a devil in an oven!

Vassilissa (as she goes). The world seems to be full of suspicious characters—and all sorts of crooks.

Luka. Hope you'll enjoy your tea.

Vassilissa (glancing back). Hold your tongue—you dirty

toadstool!   *She and Kostylyov disappear around the corner.*
Luka. Tonight I'll be out of here.
Bubnov. The best thing you can do. It's always better to go away while there's still time.
Luka. You're right.
Bubnov. I know what I'm talking about. I probably saved myself from Siberia by going away in time.
Luka. Did you?
Bubnov. That's the truth. It was this way. My wife got mixed up with a furrier. He was a fine worker—I must say—very clever in dyeing dog skins to look like raccoon—also turning cat skins into kangaroo fur—muskrat—and all sorts of other furs. He *was* clever. Well, my wife got mixed up with him, and the two of them were so close I began to be afraid they'd poison me any minute or think up some other way to get rid of me. I started beating my wife, and the furrier beat me. He was a fierce fighter. Once he pulled half my beard out and broke a rib. I got angry too—one day I whacked my wife on the head with a poker—and all in all it was quite a war going on. Well, I realized I couldn't get any place that way—they were getting the best of me. So I made up my mind to kill my wife—I was in dead earnest about it. But I woke up in time and went away instead.
Luka. That was a better idea. Let them make dogs into raccoons.
Bubnov. Only, my workshop was in my wife's name—and I was left—as you see me now. Though, to tell the truth, I'd have drunk up my shop anyway. You see, I have spells of heavy drinking—
Luka. Have you? A-ah!
Bubnov. Terrific spells. When it comes over me I drink up every little thing I have—about all I end up with is my skin. And another thing—I'm lazy. You can't imagine how I hate work.   *Satin and the Actor enter, arguing.*
Satin. Bunk! You'll go nowhere. It's nothing but a damn pipe dream. Look here, old man. What sort of ideas have you been giving this broken-down old windbag?
Actor. You lie. Grandpa, tell him he's lying. I'm going. I had work today, I swept the street—but I haven't touched vodka. How's that? Here are the thirty kopecks, but I'm sober.

Satin. It's crazy, that's all. Give them to me—I'll drink them up for you—or gamble them away—

Actor. Go away! It's for the trip.

Luka (*to Satin*). Now why do you discourage the poor fellow?

Satin. Tell me, O wizard, belov'd by the gods, what fate do my stars hold in store? I lost every kopeck I had, brother. The world hasn't entirely gone to the dogs, grandpa—there are still cardsharpers cleverer than I am.

Luka. You're a jolly fellow, Konstantin, and a real pleasant one.

Bubnov. Come here, Actor.

The Actor walks over to the window and squats before Bubnov. They talk in low voices.

Satin. In my young days I was quite amusing, old man. It's pleasant to think back to those days. I was a happy-go-lucky sort of fellow—danced beautifully, performed on the stage, liked to make people laugh—it was a fine time.

Luka. What made you stray from the path then?

Satin. You're very curious, old man. You want to know everything— What for?

Luka. To understand the affairs of human beings, my man. Now I look at you and can't make you out. You're so manly, Konstantin, and you've got brains too. Why, then, suddenly—

Satin. It's jail, old man. I was four year and seven months in jail—and after jail a man can go nowhere.

Luka. So. And what did you do time for?

Satin. For a dirty swine—I killed him in a fit of temper. It was in jail that I learned to play cards too.

Luka. Did you kill because of a woman?

Satin. Because of my sister. But don't bother me. I don't like being questioned. Besides, it was all long ago—my sister's dead —nine years since. A fine little person my sister was.

Luka. I must say you take life lightly. Now the locksmith here let out such a scream a while ago, it was something frightful.

Satin. Who, Klestch?

Luka. That's the one. No work, he shouts, no nothing!

Satin. He'll get used to it. What shall I do with myself now, I wonder?

Luka (*quietly*). Look, here he comes.

His head bent low, Klestch enters slowly.

Satin. Hey, widower! Why so down in the dumps? What's on your mind?

Klestch. I'm trying to think what to do. I've no tools. The funeral swallowed up everything.

Satin. I'll give you a word of advice—don't do anything. Just let yourself be a burden on the world at large!

Klestch. You with your talk. I have some shame before other people.

Satin. Forget it. People aren't ashamed at your living worse than a dog. Think this over—you stop working—I stop—hundreds and thousands of others—everybody—understand?—everybody stops working. Nobody wants to do any work—what'll happen then?

Klestch. Everybody will drop dead from hunger.

Luka (to Satin). You ought to join the Wanderers with your ideas. There are such people, called Wanderers.*

Satin. I know—they're no fools, grandpa.

From the Kostylyovs' window come Natasha's cries: "What have I done wrong? Please, what have I done?"

Luka (with alarm). Sounds like Natasha. Oh, God!

Noise, uproar, the sound of dishes being smashed in the Kostylyovs' apartment.

Kostylyov (off stage). You heathen—you slut—

Vassilissa (off). Wait, I'll fix her—

Natasha (off). They're beating me! They're killing me!

Satin (shouting through the window). Hey, you there!

Luka (fidgeting). We ought to call Vassily— Oh, God! Boys, friends—

Actor (running off). I'll get him—

Bubnov. They do beat her an awful lot now.

Satin. Come on, old man—we'll be witnesses.

Luka (following Satin). I'm no good as a witness—no! If only Vassily would come quick— (*The two go off.*)

Natasha (off stage). Vassilissa! Sister! Vassi—

Bubnov. They've gagged her—I'll go look—

* A Russian religious sect dating from the time of Peter the Great and called Wanderers (or sometimes Runners) because they preached running away from places where the government-instituted religious reforms were being enforced—TRANSLATOR.

The disturbance in the Kostylyov apartment dies down, apparently moving out of the room into the hall. Luka's shout, "Stop!" is heard. A door is slammed loudly, chopping off the noise as with a hatchet. All is quiet on the stage. Twilight.

Klestch (he is sitting indifferently on the upturned sleigh, rubbing his hands hard. Then he begins muttering something—at first indistinctly). How now? I have to live— (*Raising his voice.*) I have to have a place to live in—don't I? I haven't one. I have nothing. Only myself. Just one solitary being. No help from anybody.

Hunching over, he goes off slowly. There are a few seconds of sinister silence. Then a low, confused din rises somewhere in the passage. It swells and draws nearer. Individual voices can be distinguished off stage.

Vassilissa. I'm her sister! Let go!

Kostylyov. What right have you?

Vassilissa. Jailbird!

Satin. Call Vassya, quick! Lay into him, Goiter!

A police whistle is heard. The Tartar, his right arm in a sling, rushes on.

Tartar. What such law is there—kill in daytime?

The Goiter enters, followed by Medvedev.

Goiter. Ah, what a wallop I gave him!

Medvedev. How dare you strike people?

Tartar. And you? What's your duty?

Medvedev (running after the Goiter). Stop. Give me my whistle.   *Kostylyov runs on.*

Kostylyov. Abram! Catch him—arrest him!

Kvashnya and Nastya come on from around the corner, supporting a disheveled Natasha under the arms. They are followed by Satin, stepping backward as he fends off Vassilissa, who, arms waving, tries to reach out and hit Natasha. Alyoshka skips madly around Vassilissa, blowing a whistle into her ears, shouting, and yelling. A few tattered figures, men and women, drift on to join the others.

Satin (to Vassilissa). Where are you pushing? You damned hoot owl—

Vassilissa. Keep away, jailbird! I'll tear her to pieces if it kills me too!

Kvashnya (moving Natasha away). Come, Vassilissa. You ought to be ashamed. Stop acting like a wild animal.

Medvedev (catching hold of Satin). Now I've got you!

Satin. Goiter! Give it to them! Vasska! Vasska!

Natasha is led to the pile of wood, right, where she can sit down. The rest are bunched together near the passage, against the red wall. Peppel, rushing out of the passage, elbows his way through the crowd silently and vigorously.

Peppel. Where's Natasha? Ah, it's you—

> *Kostylyov slips around the corner.*

Kostylyov (off stage). Abram! Get hold of Vasska! Boys, help him catch Vasska! He's a robber, a thief!

Peppel. Ah, you old goat!

Swinging his fist, he belabors Kostylyov. The latter falls to the ground, only the upper part of his body showing around the corner. Peppel dashes over to Natasha.

Vassilissa. Do something to Vasska! All you good people, beat him up—the dirty thief!

Medvedev (shouting to Satin). Keep out of this! This is a family affair! They're relations—and who are you?

Peppel. What did she do to you? Stab you?

Kvashnya. Just look what the brutes did—scalded the girl's feet with boiling water.

Nastya. Toppled the samovar on her.

Tartar. Maybe accident— You must know certain—you mustn't talk if you not know—

Natasha (almost fainting). Take me away, Vassily—hide me—

Vassilissa. My God! Look! He's dead. They've killed him—

> *Everybody crowds around Kostylyov in the passage. Bubnov comes out of the crowd and walks up to Peppel.*

Bubnov (in a low voice). Look, Vasska. The old man is—you know what—finished.

Peppel (looking at Bubnov without understanding a word). Go call somebody—to take her to a hospital— Well, I'll get even with them!

Bubnov. I was saying—somebody has flattened the old man—

> *The noise on the stage dies down like a campfire doused with water. Random exclamations uttered in undertones can be heard: "Is it really?" "What do you know!" "Well?"*

"Let's get away from here." "Oh, hell!" "Now look out!"
*The crowd dwindles. Bubnov, the Tartar, Nastya, and
Kvashnya rush over to Kostylyov's body.*

Vassilissa (rises from the ground and shouts). They've killed
him! They've killed my husband! (*In a triumphant voice.*)
Here's the murderer. Vasska did it. I saw it. Good people, I
saw it with my own eyes. Well, Vassya? What'll you say to the
police now?

Peppel (leaving Natasha). Get out of the way! (*Gazes at the
dead man. To Vassilissa.*) Well? You're glad? (*Touches the
body with his foot.*) The old pig has popped off! You've had
your way. Well, I'd better finish you off too!

*He makes a dash for her, but Satin and the Goiter stop him
quickly. Vassilissa flees into the passage.*

Satin. Come to your senses!

Goiter. Whoa! Where are you galloping?   *Vassilissa returns.*

Vassilissa. Now what, my dear friend Vassya? One can't escape his fate. Call the police inspector, Abram! Blow your
whistle!

Medvedev. They've swiped my whistle, those bastards!

Alyoshka. Here it is— (*He blows the whistle. Medvedev runs
after him.*)

Satin (leading Peppel to Natasha). Don't be afraid, Vasska!
Killing a man in a fight is nothing serious. It doesn't cost
much—

Vassilissa. Hold Vasska! He killed him—I saw him do it!

Satin. I punched the old man a few times myself. He didn't
need much to keel over. Call me as a witness, Vasska.

Peppel. I need no alibis. What I need is to get Vassilissa into
it, and that I will do. It was she who wanted all this—egged me
on to kill her husband!

Natasha (suddenly, in a loud voice). Oh, now I understand!
So that's it, Vassily? Kind people! They're in this together! My
sister and him—they're together! They've plotted all this. Isn't
that so, Vassily? You talked to me today the way you did—so
she'd hear everything? Kind people! She's his mistress—you
know that—everybody knows it—they're both guilty! It was
she who got him to kill her husband— He was in their way—
and I was too. So they've maimed me—

Peppel. Natasha—what are you saying?

Satin. What the hell.

Vassilissa. Liar! She lies—I—it was he, Vasska—he killed him!

Natasha. They're in it together! I curse you! I curse you both!

Satin. Such goings on! Watch out, Vassily! They'll be the death of you.

Goiter. This is more than I can understand. Good God, what a business!

Peppel. Do you really mean it, Natasha? Do you really believe that I and she—

Satin. Honest, Natasha, think—

Vassilissa (*in the passage*). My husband has been killed, sir. Vasska Peppel, the thief—he killed him, Inspector. I saw it— everybody saw it—

Natasha (*tossing about, almost unconscious*). Kind people! My sister and Vasska killed him. Listen to me, police! That one, my sister, taught—got him—her lover—there he is, damn him —they killed the man! Arrest them—try them. Take me too— to jail! For Christ's sake, take me to jail!

CURTAIN

ACT IV

The same setting as the first act. The partitions forming PEP-PEL's room have been removed, and the room no longer exists. Lying in that corner now is the TARTAR; he is restless and groans occasionally. The wood block with anvil, at which KLESTCH used to work, is also gone. KLESTCH himself is sitting at the table tinkering with an accordion and trying the scales. At the other end of the table are SATIN, the BARON, and NASTYA. In front of them they have a bottle of vodka, three bottles of beer, and a big chunk of black bread. The ACTOR is on the stove, and can be heard moving about and coughing.

It is night. The place is lit by a lamp standing in the center of the table. Outside a wind is blowing.

Klestch. Y-yes—it was during all that mix-up that he disappeared.

Baron. Vanished from the police—like unto smoke fleeing from the face of fire.

Satin. Thus do sinners vanish from the sight of the righteous.

Nastya. He was a good old man. And you—you're not men, you're just rust.

Baron (*drinking*). Here's to you, your ladyship!

Satin. Yes, he was an interesting old gaffer. Nastya fell plumb in love with him.

Nastya. I did fall in love with him. I won't deny it. He saw —he understood everything—

Satin (*laughing*). And, all in all, to quite a few people he was like soft bread to the toothless.

Baron (*laughing*). Like plaster to an abscess.

Klestch. He had pity for other people. You haven't.

Satin. What good will it do you if I pity you?

Klestch. You know—well, if not how to pity a man—you know how not to hurt him.

Tartar (*sitting up on his plank bed and rocking his wounded arm, as if it were a baby*). Old man was good. He had the law in his soul. Who has the law in his soul—he is good. Who lost the law, he is lost.

Baron. What kind of law, Assan?

Tartar. Different kind. You know what kind.

Baron. Go on.

Tartar. Not hurt a man—this is the law!

Satin. It's called "The code of criminal and reformatory penalties."

Baron. Also "The code of penalties imposed by Justices of the Peace."

Tartar. Is called Koran. Your Koran called the law. In every soul must be Koran—yes.

Klestch (*trying the accordion*). Damn it, listen to it hiss. Assan is right. We must live according to the law—according to the Gospels—

Satin. Do that.

Baron. Yes, try it.

Tartar. Mohammed gave Koran, said: Here is law! Do as written here. Then time come—Koran is not enough—time will give new law. Every new time will give its law.

Satin. That's right. Time came, and it gave us the Penal Code. A strong law—not to be worn out in a hurry.

Nastya (banging on the table with her glass). Why do I go on living with you—here? I'm going away—anywhere—to the world's end!

Baron. Without shoes, your ladyship?

Nastya. Stark naked! Even if I have to crawl on all fours!

Baron. It'll make a delightful picture, your ladyship—particularly on all fours.

Nastya. Yes, I'm willing to crawl—just so long as I don't have to see your pan any more. Oh, I'm so disgusted with everything —with all life—all people!

Satin. When you leave, take the Actor with you. He's about ready to go there too. It's come to his knowledge that half a mile from the world's end there is a hospital for organons—

Actor (peeping out from the top of the stove). For organisms, you fool!

Satin. For organons poisoned by alcohol—

Actor. And he will go! Yes, he will. Just wait!

Baron. Who's he, sir?

Actor. I!

Baron. Thank you, servant of the goddess—what's her name? —the goddess of drama, of tragedy—what was she called?

Actor. A muse, fathead! A muse, not a goddess.

Satin. Lachesis—Hera—Aphrodite—Atropos—devil knows which. Do you see what the old man did, Baron? It was he who worked the Actor up to this state.

Baron. The old man is a fool—

Actor. Savages! Ignoramuses! Mel-po-me-ne! Clods! He'll go, you'll see. "Guzzle ye, O somber minds"—a poem by Béranger —yes! He'll find himself a place where there's no—no—

Baron. Where there's nothing, sir?

Actor. Yes, nothing! "This hole—my grave will be—I die of sickness and infirmity!" Why do you live? Why?

Baron. You, Edmund Kean or Genius and Dissipation! Stop yelling!

Actor. Not on your life! I will yell!

Nastya (lifts her head from the table and flings her arms out). Yell! Let 'em hear you!

Baron. What's the sense, your ladyship?

Satin. Leave them alone, Baron! To hell with them! Let them holler! Let them split their heads wide open! There's sense enough in that! Keep out of people's way, as the old man used to say. Yes, he was like yeast, leavening our crowd here—

Klestch. He beckoned them to go somewhere, but he didn't show them the road.

Baron. The old man is a faker.

Nastya. Liar! You're a faker yourself.

Baron. Shush, your ladyship.

Klestch. The old man didn't like the truth—dead set against it, he was— And he was right. I say too—what can we do with the truth when even without it we can't breathe? There's Assan —had his arm crushed on the job—it'll have to be cut off, I suppose—that's truth for you.

Satin (banging on the table with his fist). Shut up, you brutes, numskulls! That's enough about the old man! (*In a calmer tone.*) You're the worst of all, Baron. You understand nothing—and lie. The old man is not a faker. What's truth? Man —that's the truth! He understood this—you don't. You're dull, like a brick. I understand the old man—I do. Certainly he lied —but it was out of pity for you, the devil take you! There are lots of people who lie out of pity for others—I know it—I've read about it. They lie beautifully, excitingly, with a kind of inspiration. There are lies that soothe, that reconcile one to his lot. There are lies that justify the load that crushed a worker's arm—and hold a man to blame for dying of starvation—I know lies! People weak in spirit—and those who live on the sweat of others—these need lies—the weak find support in them, the exploiters use them as a screen. But a man who is his own master, who is independent and doesn't batten on others—he can get along without lies. Lies are the religion of slaves and bosses. Truth is the god of the free man.

Baron. Bravo! Splendid! I agree with you. You speak—like a decent man.

Satin. Why shouldn't a cheat speak well sometimes, when the decent people—speak like cheats? Yes, I've forgotten a lot, but

I still know some things. The old man had a head on his shoulders. He had the same effect on me as acid on an old, dirty coin. Let's drink to his health! Fill the glasses—

Nastya pours a glass of beer and hands it to Satin, who continues with a smile.

The old man lives from within—he looks at everything through his own eyes. I asked him once: Grandpa, what do people live for? (*Trying to imitate Luka's voice and manner.*) "They live for something better to come, my friend. Let's say, there are cabinetmakers. They live on, and all of them are just trash. But one day a cabinetmaker is born—such a cabinetmaker as has never been seen on this earth—there's no equal to him—he outshines everybody. The whole cabinetmaking trade is changed by him—and in one jump it moves twenty years ahead. Likewise, all the rest—locksmiths, say—cobblers and other working people—and peasants, too—and even the masters—they all live for something better to come. They live a hundred—and maybe more years for a better man."

Nastya regards Satin fixedly. Klestch stops work on the accordion and listens. The Baron, his head bowed low, drums quietly with his fingers on the table. The Actor, leaning over from the stove, cautiously tries to lower himself onto the plank bed.

"Everybody, my friend, everybody lives for something better to come. That's why we have to be considerate of every man— Who knows what's in him, why he was born and what he can do? Maybe he was born for our good fortune—for our greater benefit. And most especially we have to be considerate of youngsters. Kids need plenty of elbowroom. Don't interfere with their life. Be kind to them."

Baron (*reflectively*). H'm—for something better to come? That reminds me of our family. An old family—goes back to the time of Catherine the Great—noblemen—warriors! The founders came from France. They served the government, kept rising higher and higher. In the reign of Nicholas I my grandfather, Gustave Debil, held a high post— There was wealth—hundreds of serfs—horses—cooks—

Nastya. Liar! There was not!

Baron (*jumping to his feet*). What? Well, go on.

Nastya. There wasn't.

Baron (shouting). A house in Moscow! A house in St. Petersburg! Carriages—with the coat of arms!

    Klestch picks up the accordion and, moving to one side, watches the scene.

Nastya. There wasn't!

Baron. Shut up! I say dozens of flunkies!

Nastya (with relish). There wasn't.

Baron. I'll kill you.

Nastya (ready to run off). There weren't any carriages!

Satin. Chuck it, Nastya! Don't tease him.

Baron. Just wait—you scum! My grandfather—

Nastya. There was no grandfather! There was nothing!

                                 Satin laughs.

Baron (exhausted by his outburst, sits down on the bench). Satin, tell this slut— You're laughing too? You don't believe me either? *(Shouts in despair, banging the table.)* There was, the devil take you!

Nastya (triumphantly). A-ah, you scream? You understand now how it feels when somebody doesn't believe you?

Klestch (returning to the table). I thought there was going to be a fight—

Tartar. A-ah, people are stupid. Very bad.

Baron. I can't permit anybody to insult me! I have proofs—documents, damn it!

Satin. Chuck them! And forget about your grandfather's carriages. In the carriages of the past you can't go anywhere.

Baron. But how dare she?

Nastya. Imagine! How dare I!

Satin. You see, she dares. Is she any worse than you? Although, in her past—she certainly didn't have not only carriages and a grandfather, but even a father and mother—

Baron (calming down). Damn you—you can reason calmly. I don't seem to have any character—

Satin. Get yourself one. They're useful. *(A pause.)* Have you been visiting the hospital, Nastya?

Nastya. What for?

Satin. To see Natasha.

Nastya. A little late, aren't you? She left the hospital a long time ago. She came out—and vanished. Nobody's seen her anywhere.

Satin. She must have evaporated—fizzed out.

Klestch. It'll be interesting to see which one does the most to ruin the other one—whether Vasska drags Vassilissa down, or the other way around.

Nastya. Vassilissa will wriggle out of it—she's clever. And Vasska will go to Siberia.

Satin. The penalty for killing in a fight is only jail.

Nastya. That's a pity. Siberia's more his style. I wish you'd all be packed off to Siberia—or swept off like dirt—into some pit.

Satin (startled). Have you gone raving mad?

Baron. I'll bloody her nose—for her impertinence.

Nastya. You try—just touch me.

Baron. I certainly will.

Satin. Drop it. Don't touch her. Don't hurt another human being. I can't get that old man out of my head. (*Laughs.*) Don't hurt another human being! But I was hurt once—hurt for the rest of my life with a single blow. What am I supposed to do? Forgive it? Not on your life! Never!

Baron (to Nastya). You have to understand once and for all, you're not my equal. You're—dirt under my feet!

Nastya. You good-for-nothing! Why, you're living off me like a worm off an apple.   *The men all burst into laughter.*

Klestch. A sweet little apple! Ah, what a crackbrain!

Baron. You can't be cross with this idiot!

Nastya. You're laughing? You faker! You don't think it's funny.

Actor (somberly). Give it to them good!

Nastya. If I had the power—I'd smash you all like this! (*She picks up a cup from the table and smashes it on the floor.*)

Tartar. Why break cup? Such—pighead!

Baron (rising). I'll teach her good manners!

Nastya (running toward the hall door). You go to hell!

Satin (after her). Hey! Stop it! Who are you scaring? And what's it all about, anyway?

Nastya. Beasts! I hope you'll be struck dead! Beasts! (*She disappears into the hallway.*)

Actor (somberly). Amen.

Tartar. Oh! Russian woman, spiteful woman! Too free! Tartar woman—no! She know the law! Nothing stop her!

Klestch. She needs a good beating.

Baron. What a bitch!

Klestch (*trying the accordion*). It's finished. But no sign of the owner. The boy is on a binge again.

Satin. Have a drink.

Klestch. Thanks! It's time to turn in too.

Satin. Getting used to us?

Klestch (*downs his drink and moves to his plank bed in the corner*). It's all right. It's the same human beings everywhere. At first, you don't see it. Then, you get a good look at them, and it turns out they're all human beings—they're all right.

> *The Tartar spreads out some garment on his plank bed, kneels down, and begins to pray.*

Baron (*to Satin, pointing at the Tartar*). Look.

Satin. Leave him alone. He's a good fellow. (*Laughs.*) I'm in a kind mood today—the devil knows why.

Baron. You're always kind when you're oiled—kind and brainy.

Satin. When I'm drunk I like everything. Yes, sir. He's praying? Fine. A man can believe or not believe—it's his own affair. A man is free—he pays for everything himself—for belief and disbelief, for love, for intelligence, and that makes him free. Man—that's the truth. What is man? It's not you, nor I, nor they— No, it's you, I, they, the old man, Napoleon, Mohammed —all in one. (*Outlines the figure of a man in the air.*) You understand? It's tremendous! In this are all the beginnings and all the ends. Everything in man, everything for man. Only man exists, the rest is the work of his hands and his brain. Man! It's magnificent! It has a proud ring! Man! We have to respect man, not pity him, not demean him— Respect him, that's what we have to do. Let's drink to man, Baron! (*Rises.*) It's good to feel oneself a man! I'm a jailbird, a murderer, a cheat—granted! When I walk down the street, people look at me as at a crook —they side-step and glance back at me—and often say to me: Scoundrel! Charlatan! Work! Work? For what? So that I have what my body needs and feel satisfied? (*Laughs.*) I've always despised people whose main thought in life is to feel satisfied. That's not important, Baron—no! Man is above that! Man is above satisfaction!

Baron (shaking his head). You can reason. It's a fine thing—
it must warm your heart. I haven't got that—I can't reason.
(*Looks around and speaks in a low voice, cautiously.*) I feel
scared sometimes, old fellow. You know? I get panicky. Because,
what's to become of me?

Satin (walking up and down). Nonsense! What can a man
fear?

Baron. You know, ever since I can remember myself I've always felt a sort of fog in my head. I could never understand anything. I have an awkward feeling as if all my life I've done
nothing but change clothes— But to what end? I can't figure it
out. I was given education, wore the uniform of a college for the
nobility—but what did I study? I don't remember. I got married
—to a woman who was no good, wore tails, then a dressing
gown—why? I don't know. I went through my fortune—came
to wear an old gray jacket and faded pants— But how did I go
broke? I didn't notice. I got a job on a government board—
wore a uniform, a cap with a badge—then embezzled government money, had prison clothes put on me, and later changed
into this. And all that as if in a dream. It's funny.

Satin. Not very. Stupid, rather.

Baron. Yes—I too think it's stupid. Yet there must have been
some purpose that I was born for—don't you think?

Satin (laughing). Probably. A man is born for something
better to come. (*Nods his head.*)

Baron. That Nastya! Where did she run off to? I'd better go
look. After all, she's— (*He goes out. There is a pause.*)

Actor. Tartar! (*A pause.*) Assan! (*The Tartar turns his head.*)
Pray—for me.

Tartar. What?

Actor (in a lower voice). Pray—for me.

Tartar (after a pause). Pray yourself.

*Actor (coming down hurriedly from the stove, walks up to
the table, pours himself some vodka with a trembling hand,
downs it, and almost runs into the hallway).* I'm gone.

Satin. Hey you, sycamore! Where are you going? (*He whistles.*)

> *Enter Medvedev, wearing a woman's quilted jacket, and
> Bubnov. They are both slightly drunk. Bubnov carries a*

string of pretzels in one hand and a few small smoked fishes in the other, with a bottle of vodka under his arm and another sticking out of his pocket.

Medvedev. The camel is a kind of—donkey, only without ears.

Bubnov. Forget it. You're kind of a donkey yourself.

Medvedev. The camel has no ears at all—he hears with his nostrils.

Bubnov (to Satin). Friend! I've been looking for you in all the barrooms. Take a bottle, my hands are full.

Satin. Put the pretzels on the table and that'll free your hand.

Bubnov. You're right, by God! Look, policeman—here's a clever fellow, isn't he?

Medvedev. Crooks are all clever—I know. They can't do without brains. A good man can be stupid and still be good. But a bad man must have brains—absolutely. As for the camel, you're wrong. He's a beast of burden, and has no horns—nor teeth—

Bubnov. Where is everybody? Why isn't there anybody here? Hey you! Come out! I'm treating everybody! Who's over in the corner?

Satin. How soon are you going to drink up your money? Scarecrow!

Bubnov. It'll be soon. This time I've saved up only a little capital. Goiter! Where's Goiter?

Klestch (walking up to the table). He's out.

Bubnov. B-rr! Fido! Brlyn—brlyn—brlyn! Turkey! Don't bark, don't cackle! Drink! Enjoy yourselves! Get out of the dumps! I'm treating everybody. I love treating people. If I was rich—I'd have a free barroom—you bet I would. With music—and a choir singing too. Everybody could come, drink, eat, listen to songs—ease their hearts! You're a poor man? Step right in—into my free barroom! Satin! I'd make you—I'd give you half of all my capital! There!

Satin. Give me all you have now.

Bubnov. My whole capital? Now? Take it. Here's a ruble—here's a quarter—here are the coppers—everything!

Satin. That's fine. They'll be safer in my hands—I'll have a game with them—

Medvedev. I'm witness—the money's been given for safe-keeping—to what amount?

Bubnov. You? You're a camel. We don't need witnesses.

Enter Alyoshka, barefoot.

Alyoshka. Folks! I got my feet wet.

Bubnov. Come! Wet your whistle! That'll set you right. My dear fellow—you sing and play—that's fine. But you shouldn't drink. Drinking's bad for a person, my friend. It certainly is.

Alyoshka. I can tell that by looking at you. The only time you look like a man is when you're drunk. Klestch, have you fixed my accordion? (*Sings, dancing.*)

> If this here phiz
> Weren't so fair to see,
> My girl wouldn't be
> So sweet on me.

I'm shivering, boys. It's cold.

Medvedev. H'mm!—And may I ask who the girl friend is?

Bubnov. Leave him alone. You're off the police force now, my friend. It's all over, finished. You're neither a policeman nor an uncle any more.

Alyoshka. Just Aunt Kvashnya's husband.

Bubnov. One of your nieces is in jail, the other is dying.

Medvedev (*haughtily*). Liar! She's not dying—she's missing!

Satin laughs.

Bubnov. It's all the same, brother. A man without nieces is no uncle.

Alyoshka. Your Excellency! (*Sings.*)

> My girl friend has money,
> I haven't a soul!
> But I'm a gay lad,
> And the girls think so too!

Damn, it's cold.

Enter the Goiter. From time to time, up till the end of the act, other figures, men and women, come in. They undress for sleep and take their places on the plank beds, muttering to themselves.

Goiter. Bubnov! Why did you run away?

Bubnov. Come here! sit down. Now let's sing—you know, my favorite—eh?

Tartar. Night all must sleep. Sing song daytime.

Satin. It's all right, Assan! Come over here!

Tartar. How is all right? Will be noise. When you sing song, is noise.

Bubnov (*walking up to the Tartar*). How's your hand, Assan? Have they cut it off?

Tartar. Why cut off? I wait. Maybe they no have cut it off. Hand is not iron, you cut it off quick.

Goiter. You're in a rotten way, Assan. Without a hand you're no good for anything. The likes of us are valued for their hands and their backs. No hand, no man. Yes, yours is a bad case. Come have some vodka—and to hell with it all!

Enter Kvashnya.

Kvashnya. Ah, my dear lodgers! And isn't it terrible outdoors? Cold—wet! Is my policeman here? Policeman!

Medvedev. Here I am.

Kvashnya. Wearing my blouse again? And from the looks of it—a bit under the influence, ain't you? How does that happen?

Medvedev. It's on account of his birthday—Bubnov's— And it's cold and wet.

Kvashnya. Wet! Look out! Don't give me any of that! Go to bed.

Medvedev (*going off to the kitchen*). To bed—that I can—I want to go to bed—it's time.

Satin. You *are* strict with him. Why?

Kvashnya. You can't be otherwise, my friend. A man like him has to be kept in line. I took him on for a companion thinking I'd benefit by it—after all, he's a military man, and you're wild people, while I'm only a woman— And right off the bat he takes to drink! That's of no use to me.

Satin. You didn't choose your assistant very well.

Kvashnya. No, you're wrong. You wouldn't want to live with me—you wouldn't have me. And even if you did, within a week you'd gamble me away at cards—me and my tripe!

Satin (*laughing*). You're right there, landlady. I certainly would.

Kvashnya. There you are. Alyoshka!

Alyoshka. Here he is—that's me.

Kvashnya. What sort of tales are you telling about me?

Alyoshka. Me? I tell everything—just as it is, honestly.

There's a woman, says I. A remarkable woman. In flesh, fat, and bones she's a heavyweight twice over. But she hasn't an ounce of brains!

Kvashnya. Now, that's a lie. I have plenty of brains. But why do you say I beat my policeman?

Alyoshka. I thought you were beating him when you pulled his hair.

Kvashnya (laughing). You're a fool! As if you didn't see. Why carry dirt out of the house? Besides, it hurt his pride. He took to drink because of your tales.

Alyoshka. Then it's true what they say—hens drink too.

Satin and Klestch laugh.

Kvashnya. You do have a wicked tongue! I can't make out what sort of man you are, Alyoshka.

Alyoshka. The very finest sort of man! Can do anything. Something catches my eye, and off I fly.

Bubnov (near the Tartar's plank bed). Come along. We'll keep you awake anyway. We'll be singing—all night. Goiter!

Goiter. Want a song? All right.

Alyoshka. I'll play the accompaniment.

Satin. I'm all ears.

Tartar (smiling). Well, devil Bubnov—now we have some your vodka. Drink we will, play we will, death will come, die we will!

Bubnov. Fill his glass, Satin. Sit down, Goiter. Ah, friends! A man doesn't need much, does he? Here am I—I've had some drink—and I'm happy. Goiter, start my favorite one. I'll sing and weep!

Goiter (sings). The sun comes up, the sun goes down again—

Bubnov (picking it up). But in my cell it's never light—

The hallway door is flung open. The Baron, standing on the threshold, shouts.

Baron. Hey, you! Come—come here! Out there—in the vacant lot the Actor—has hanged himself!

There is a general silence. Everybody gazes at the Baron. Nastya appears from behind the Baron's back and slowly, her eyes wide open, walks up to the table.

Satin (in a low voice). Ah, spoiled the song—the fool!

CURTAIN

ENEMIES

UNDER the old regime,˙ strikes of workers were forbidden by
law, and were suppressed by the authorities whenever they oc-
curred. The method of suppression was that of house-to-house
searches to obtain evidence of "subversive ideas," and rounding
up of "ringleaders," both operations performed by the police or
the *gendarmerie* (the political secret police) and assisted by
troops when the situation assumed "an ugly aspect." In "Enemies" the strike situation is complicated by the murder of the
director of the factory at an early stage of the conflict. Taking
part in a strike and particularly agitating for and organizing a
strike was regarded as a political offense which was handled by
the gendarmerie and other agencies of the government without
recourse to court procedure. Murder cases however were usually
tried in court. This is why in the play the preliminary investigation is conducted not only by Captain Boboyedov, of the gendarmerie, but also by Assistant District Attorney Skrobotov.

In the early years of this century in which the action of the
play is laid, "socialism" was a forbidden and dangerous word
which could only be whispered. It was preached secretly, mainly
among students and workers, by various groups which differed
among themselves in the formulation of their aims and the meth-
ods of achieving them. All socialists supported and often organized strikes, although some were interested in their political
effects while others were concerned with the immediate economic benefits for the workers. In the play the actual role played
by socialists in provoking the strike seems to be negligible, and
among the workers themselves, as in the case of Levshin, ideas
have currency which have more in common with the moral concepts of Leo Tolstoy than with the economic concepts of socialism. The attitude toward strikes and socialism among the
well-to-do, the bourgeoisie, followed the familiar pattern. It was

either violently belligerent, denouncing them as a menace to society and culture, or it was more yielding, ready to make concessions on minor points, for reasons of humanity, but equally uncompromising when it came to defending the employers as a class and denying the rights of the workers to demand social and economic equality. Both points of view, the strictly conservative and the liberal, have their spokesmen in the play.

A. B.

ENEMIES

Characters

Bogdan Denisovich Pologhy, an office clerk

Kon, a former soldier

Agrafena, the housekeeper in the *Bardins'* home

Yakov Ivanovich Bardin, brother of *Zakhar Bardin,* age 40

General Pechenegov, uncle of the *Bardins*

Mikhail Vassilyevich Skrobotov, Zakhar Bardin's partner, age 40

Matvey Nikolayevich Sintsov, an office clerk

Polina Dmitriyevna, wife of *Zakhar Bardin,* age close to 40

Zakhar Ivanovich Bardin, age 45

Nikolay Vassilyevich Skrobotov, an assistant district attorney, brother of *Mikhail Skrobotov*

Tatyana, wife of *Yakov Bardin,* age 28, an actress (stage name *Tatyana Lugovaya*)

Nadya, Polina's niece, age 18

Cleopatra Petrovna, wife of *Mikhail Skrobotov,* age 30

Alexey Grekov, a worker

Levshin, an elderly worker

Police Sergeant

Police Inspector

Yagodin, a worker

Pavel Ryabtsov, a worker

Captain Boboyedov

Corporal Kvach

A Lieutenant

ACT I

A garden. Tall old linden trees. Downstage, under the trees, a soldier's white tent. Right, under the trees, a wide bench made of turf, with a table in front. Left, in the shade of the lindens, a long table laid for breakfast with a small samovar boiling on it. Around this table are several wicker chairs.

AGRAFENA *is making coffee.* KON, *smoking a pipe, and* POLOGHY *are standing under a tree.*

Pologhy (talking with absurd gesticulations). Of course, what you say is right—I'm a small man and my life is a trivial one. But I've grown every cucumber with my own hands, and I cannot permit anybody to rip them off without recompense to me.

Kon (gloomily). Nobody's asking for your permission.

Pologhy (pressing his hand to his heart). But excuse me! If your property is being destroyed, haven't you the right to ask for the protection of the law?

Kon. Ask for it. Today it's cucumbers that are ripped off, tomorrow it'll be heads. There's the law for you.

Pologhy. It's strange and even dangerous, I must say, to hear such opinions. How can you, a soldier, disregard the law?

Kon. There is no such thing as the law. There's the command. Left face—forward march! And you march. You're told: Halt! and you halt.

Agrafena. You shouldn't smoke your shag here, Kon. Even the leaves on the trees wither from it.

Pologhy. I could understand it if they did it from hunger. Hunger can explain many acts. It can be said that all vile acts are done to satisfy hunger. When a man wants to eat, then of course—

Kon. Angels don't eat. Yet Satan rose against God—

Pologhy (joyfully). It's just that sort of thing that I call mischief-making—

Yakov Bardin comes on. He speaks in a low voice and with an air of listening closely to his own words. Pologhy bows to him. Kon greets him casually with a military salute.

Yakov. Good morning. What is it, Pologhy?

Pologhy. I want to make a request of Zakhar Ivanovich.

Agrafena. He's come to make a complaint. The factory boys stole some of his cucumbers last night.

Yakov. Oh! My brother should be told of that.

Pologhy. Very true. That's just why I'm going to him.

Kon (in a querulous tone). You're not going anywhere—you just stand here and whine.

Pologhy. I don't think I'm in your way or disturbing you. Of course, I might be, if you were reading a newspaper or doing something—

Yakov. Kon, come here.

Kon (walking up to Yakov). You're a niggard, Pologhy, a pettifogger.

Pologhy. You have no reason at all to say such things. The tongue is given to human beings for lodging complaints.

Agrafena. Do stop it, Pologhy—you talk as if you weren't a human being but a mosquito.

Yakov (to Kon). What does he want here? I wish he'd go—

Pologhy (to Agrafena). If my words disturb your ears, but don't touch your heart, I'll keep silent. (*He moves off down a path and strolls leisurely back and forth, putting out his hand to feel the trees.*)

Yakov (with embarrassment). Well, Kon, I seem to have— offended somebody again last night?

Kon (smiling). You did—that you did.

Yakov (moving about). H'm! It's extraordinary. Why do I always say offensive things when I'm drunk?

Kon. That happens to people. Sometimes, when he's drunk, a man is better than when he's sober, has more courage in him. He's afraid of nobody, and doesn't go too easy on himself either. We had a sergeant in our company. Sober, he was a lickspittle, a tattler, liked to use his fists. But when he was drunk, he would cry. Boys, says he, I'm a man too—spit in my face, he begs us. And some did spit.

Yakov. And who did I talk to last night?

Kon. The district attorney. You called him a wooden head. Then you told him the director's wife has a lot of lovers.

Yakov. I see. What business is that of mine?

Kon. I don't know. You also—

Yakov. Fine, Kon, that'll do. Or I may discover that I said something nasty to everybody. Yes, what a misfortune it is—this vodka. (*He walks up to the table, gazes at the bottles, then fills a glass with vodka and sips it. Agrafena, watching him out of the corner of her eye, sighs.*) You're a bit sorry for me, are you?

Agrafena. I am, very much. You act so simple with everybody, as if you weren't a master.

Yakov. Now Kon doesn't feel sorry for anybody. He only philosophizes. To make a man think, you have to wrong him, isn't that so, Kon? (*In the tent the General is heard shouting:* "Hey, Kon!") You've been taking it on the chin a lot—is that why you're so intelligent?

Kon (*walking off*). The moment I lay eyes on the General I turn into a fool.   *The General comes out of the tent.*

General. Kon! Time for my swim!

Yakov (*sitting down and rocking in a chair*). Is my wife still asleep?

Agrafena. No, she's up. She's already been for a swim.

Yakov. So you're sorry for me?

Agrafena. You ought to get yourself treated.

Yakov. Well, pour me a drop of cognac.

Agrafena. Perhaps you shouldn't, Yakov Ivanovich?

Yakov. Why not? If I don't have one drink, it won't help me any.

> *With a sigh Agrafena pours Yakov some cognac. Enter Mikhail Skrobotov, with hurried steps. He is excited, fingers his pointed little black beard, and keeps squeezing the hat he carries.*

Mikhail. Is Zakhar Ivanovich up? Not yet? Naturally. Give me—have you some cold milk? Thanks. Good morning, Yakov Ivanovich. Have you heard the news? Those scoundrels demand that I fire the foreman Dichkov, no less! They threaten to stop working—the devil take them!

Yakov. Well, dismiss the foreman.

Mikhail. That's simple enough, but that's not the question.

The thing that matters is that concessions spoil them. Today they demand dismissal of the foreman, tomorrow I'll have to hang myself to satisfy them.

Yakov (*softly*). You think they'll want that tomorrow?

Mikhail. You think it's funny. You should try to handle these grimy gentlemen—nearly a thousand strong—their heads turned by your brother with his liberal notions and by those idiots who go around passing out illicit handbills. (*Glances at his watch.*) It's almost ten, and they've promised to start their fireworks right after dinner. Yes, Yakov Ivanovich, during my leave of absence your worthy brother has ruined our factory—corrupted the men by his lack of firmness—

    Enter, from right, Sintsov. He looks about thirty. There is something calm and impressive about his figure and face.

Sintsov. Mikhail Vassilyevich! Delegates representing the workers have come to the office. They demand to see the head.

Mikhail. Demand? Tell them to go to hell!

              Polina comes on from left.

I beg your pardon, Polina Dmitriyevna.

Polina (*amiably*). You're always swearing. What is it this time?

Mikhail. It's that proletariat. It demands. Formerly, it begged of me humbly.

Polina. You certainly can be hard on people.

Mikhail (*spreading his arms*). There you are!

Sintsov. What am I to tell the delegates?

Mikhail. Let them wait. You can go.

              Sintsov goes off unhurriedly.

Polina. That clerk has an interesting face. How long has he been with us?

Mikhail. About a year, I believe.

Polina. He gives the impression of being a decent sort. Who is he?

Mikhail (*with a shrug*). He gets forty rubles a month. (*Glances at his watch, looks around with a sigh, and notices Pologhy.*) Are you looking for me?

Pologhy. I'm waiting to see Zakhar Ivanovich.

Mikhail. Why?

Pologhy. On account of a violation of property rights.

Mikhail (*to Polina*). There—I present to you—another of our new employees—a man with an urge for truck-gardening. He's firmly convinced that everything on this earth has been created for the sole purpose of infringing on his interests. Everything interferes with him—the sun, England, new machines, frogs—

Pologhy (smiling). Frogs, when they croak, permit me to say, interfere with everybody.

Mikhail. You'd better go back to the office. You have a strange habit of dropping your work to come and make complaints. I don't like it. You may go.

Pologhy bows and walks off. Polina, smiling, watches him through her lorgnette.

Polina. You *are* strict. He's funny, though. You know, in Russia people are more diverse than in other countries.

Mikhail. Say more perverse—viciously so—and I'll agree with you. I've had people taking orders from me for fifteen years. I know what they are—those kind Russian people so painted up in the priestly literature—

Polina. Priestly?

Mikhail. Of course. All those priests' sons, the Chernishevskys, the Dobrolyubovs, the Zlatovratskys, the Uspenskys— (*Looks at his watch.*) Zakhar Ivanovich is a long time coming out.

Polina. Do you know what he's doing? He and your brother are finishing last night's chess game.

Mikhail. And down there they're planning to quit work after dinner. Believe me, Russia will never make good. That's a fact. It's a land of anarchism. There's an ingrained distaste for work and an utter incapacity for order. Respect for the law is absent.

Polina. But that's natural. How can you have respect for the law in a country where there is no law? Just between ourselves, hasn't our government—   *Agrafena goes off.*

Mikhail. Well, of course. I make no excuses for anybody—including the government. You take the Anglo-Saxons—

Zakhar Bardin and Nikolay Skrobotov stroll on.
There's no better material for building a state. The Englishman walks before the law like a trained horse in the circus. He has the sense of legality in his bones, in his muscles— Good morning, Zakhar Ivanovich. Hello, Nikolay. Permit me to inform you of the latest result of your liberal policy toward the workers. They demand the instant dismissal of Dichkov, failing which they'll stop work after dinner. Yes. What have you to say?

Zakhar (rubbing his brow). I? H'm! Dichkov, you say? The fellow who uses his fists—and annoys the girls? Why, of course, we must fire Dichkov. That'll be only just and proper.

Mikhail (getting excited). Come, come, my esteemed partner, let's talk seriously. We're discussing business, not justice. Justice is for Nikolay to look after. And I may say once again—justice as you understand it is ruinous for the business.

Zakhar. How so, my friend? You're talking in paradoxes.

Polina. Discussing business in my presence—first thing in the morning?

Mikhail. A thousand apologies. Still I'll continue. I regard this conversation as crucial. Before I went on my leave I held the plant like this—*(shows a closed fist)* and while I was here nobody dared to squeak! All those Sunday entertainments, lectures, and that sort of thing—these, you know, I never regarded as useful with men as they are. The raw Russian brain doesn't flare up with the fire of reason when a spark of knowledge falls upon it—it smolders and smokes.

Nikolay. One must speak calmly.

Mikhail (barely able to control himself). Thanks for the advice. It's very wise, but of no use to me. Your attitude toward the workers, Zakhar Ivanovich, has, in six months, loosened and shaken up the strong machinery built up by my labors over a period of eight years. I was respected, I was regarded as the master. Now it's clear to everybody that the firm has two masters, one kind, the other evil. The kind master is, of course, you—

Zakhar (embarrassed). Now, really—you mustn't say that.

Polina. You speak very strangely, Mikhail Vassilyevich.

Mikhail. I have reason for the way I speak. I've been placed in the most stupid position. Last time I told the workers I'd rather close the factory than fire Dichkov. They realized I'd do as I said, and calmed down. Last Friday, Zakhar Ivanovich, you said to a worker, Grekov, that Dichkov was a ruffian and you were going to fire him—

Zakhar (softly). But, my dear friend, if he punches people in the nose and that sort of thing? You must agree we can't tolerate that. After all, we're Europeans, we're civilized people.

Mikhail. Before everything else we're manufacturers. Workers punch one another in the nose every holiday—what business is that of ours? As to the necessity of teaching the workers good manners—that's a question you'll have to settle afterward. Right now a delegation of workers is waiting for you in the office. They will demand that you fire Dichkov. What do you propose to do?

Zakhar. But is Dichkov such a valuable man?

Nikolay (dryly). As I understand it, it's not a question here of a man but of a principle.

Mikhail. Precisely. The question is—who are the masters in the factory—we or the workers?

Zakhar (put out). Yes, I know. But—

Mikhail. If we give in to them, there's no telling what they'll demand next. They're an impudent lot. The Sunday schools and the rest have had their effect, and after six months the men look at me like a pack of hungry wolves, and already there are illicit handbills circulating among them. The smell of socialism is unmistakable.

Polina. Such a godforsaken place and all of a sudden—socialism. It's amusing—

Mikhail. You think so? My dear Polina Dmitriyevna, when children are small they're all amusing, but gradually they grow up, and one day we find ourselves face to face with full-blown blackguards.

Zakhar. What do you want to do then?

Mikhail. Close the factory. Let them starve a little—that'll cool them off.

> *Yakov rises, goes over to the table, downs a drink, and slowly walks off.*

Once the factory is closed, the women will swing into action. They'll cry, and on men intoxicated with dreams women's tears act like smelling salts—they sober them up.

Polina. You sound awfully cruel.

Mikhail. Life demands it.

Zakhar. Well, such a measure, you know—is it really necessary?

Mikhail. Can you suggest anything else?

Zakhar. Suppose I go talk to them, eh?

Mikhail. You'll give in to them, of course, and then my position will become impossible. You'll excuse me, but I'm hurt by your hesitation—very deeply. Quite apart from the harm it does.

Zakhar (hurriedly). But I'm not objecting, my friend. I'm

only thinking. You know, I'm more a landowner than an industrialist. All this is new to me—too complicated. One wants to be just. Peasants are easier, more agreeable than workers—I get on with them excellently. There are some very interesting individuals among the workers, but taken in the mass, I agree, they're unruly and dissolute.

Mikhail. Especially since you made them all kinds of promises.

Zakhar. Well, you see, right after you went away, there sprang up a kind of liveliness—I mean excitement—among them— Perhaps I behaved incautiously—but I had to calm them. There were articles about us in the newspapers—and very sharp ones, you know—

Mikhail (*impatiently*). It's seventeen minutes past ten now. The question must be settled. It boils down to this: either I close the factory, or I withdraw from the business. If we close down the factory, we'll suffer no losses—I've already seen to that. The urgent orders are ready for shipment, and our warehouses are pretty well filled too.

Zakhar. Y-yes. The question has to be settled now—I understand. What's your opinion, Nikolay Vassilyevich?

Nikolay. I think my brother is right. We have to adhere firmly to definite principles if we want to preserve culture.

Zakhar. That is, you also think we should close? Oh, the whole thing is such a nuisance! My dear Mikhail Vassilyevich, don't be annoyed with me—I'll give you my answer in—ten minutes. All right?

Mikhail. By all means.

Zakhar. Polina, I'll ask you to come with me.

Polina (*following her husband*). Good Lord! All this is so unpleasant.

Zakhar. The peasant has an inborn feeling of respect for the gentlefolk—   *The two go off.*

Mikhail (*between his teeth*). The jellyfish! He can say that after the peasant riots in the south! The fool!

Nikolay. Keep calm, Mikhail. Why lose control of yourself?

Mikhail. My nerves are shot, I don't mind saying. I go to the factory and I have to carry this— (*Pulls a revolver out of his pocket.*) I'm hated—thanks to this idiot. But I can't give up the business—you'd be the first to condemn me if I did. All our capital is tied up in it. If I leave, this bald-headed fool will ruin everything.

Nikolay (calmly). That's bad, if you don't exaggerate.

Sintsov appears.

Sintsov. The workers are asking you to come and see them.

Mikhail. Me? What's up?

Sintsov. They've heard the rumor that the factory is to be closed after dinner.

Mikhail. Now how do you like that! Where did they get it?

Nikolay. Probably Yakov Ivanovich told them.

Mikhail. Oh, hell! (*Gazes at Sintsov with an irritation which he cannot restrain.*) And why do you, especially, Mr. Sintsov, feel so concerned about it—coming here, inquiring?

Sintsov. I've been asked by the bookkeeper to come fetch you.

Mikhail. Have you? You have the strange habit of looking out from under your eyebrows and twisting your lips in a diabolical smile. What makes you so pleased, if I may ask?

Sintsov. I think that's my own affair.

Mikhail. And I think otherwise. I suggest that you show me more civility in the future. Yes. (*Sintsov looks intently at him.*) Well? What are you waiting for?   *Enter Tatyana, left.*

Tatyana. Oh, director— Are you in a hurry? (*Calls to Sintsov.*) Good morning, Matvey Nikolayevich!

Sintsov (amiably). Good morning. How are you feeling? Tired?

Tatyana. No, I'm not, thank you. Only, my hands are sore from rowing. Going back to your work? I'll walk with you as far as the gate. You know what I want to tell you?

Sintsov. Of course not.

Tatyana (walking beside Sintsov). In everything you said yesterday there was a lot of intelligence, but even more of— something emotional, deliberately slanted. Some speeches, I feel, are more convincing when they are not colored by emotion— (*Their conversation fades out.*)

Mikhail. There's a situation for you, if you please. Your employee, whom you've cut short for impertinence, permits himself, before your very eyes, to be familiar with the wife of your partner's brother. The brother's a drunkard, the wife an actress. What the devil did they come here for? Nobody knows.

Nikolay. A strange woman— Good looking, knows how to

dress, seductive—and seems to be on the way to having an affair with a pauper. It's bizarre but stupid.

Mikhail (ironically). There's democracy for you. She, if you please, is the daughter of a village schoolmarm and says she feels drawn to plain people. It must have been the devil prompted me to get mixed up with these landed gentry!

Nikolay. Well, you haven't done so badly. You're the head of the business.

Mikhail. I will be—but not yet.

Nikolay. I think she'd be an easy mark—seems very sensual.

Mikhail. Where's that liberal? Has he gone to bed? No, I insist, Russia's not capable of living growth. People have been given all sorts of new ideas, nobody can tell his proper place— they all wander, dream, talk— The government is a bunch of men who've taken leave of their senses—they're vengeful and stupid—understand nothing, are incompetent in everything—

Reënter Tatyana.

Tatyana. Shouting? Everybody's beginning to shout—I don't know why.   *Enter Agrafena.*

Agrafena. Zakhar Ivanovich asks you to come over, Mikhail Vassilyevich.

Mikhail. At last. (*He goes off.*)

Tatyana (seating herself at the table). What's he so excited about?

Nikolay. I don't think it's anything to interest you.

Tatyana (calmly). He reminds me of a policeman I once knew. In our theater in Kostroma we used to have a policeman —a tall fellow, with bulging eyes— He didn't walk, he ran— didn't just smoke, but practically choked on the fumes. One got the impression he wasn't so much just living as jumping and tumbling, trying to reach for something quick. Yet what he was after—he himself didn't know.

Nikolay. You think he didn't?

Tatyana. I'm sure of it. When a man has a clear objective, he proceeds toward it calmly. But this one hurried. And it was a peculiar kind of haste—it lashed him on from within—and he ran and ran, getting in everybody's way, including his own. He wasn't avaricious, greedy. He only wanted avidly to do all he had to do as quick as he could—he wanted to get all his duties out of the way—not overlooking the duty of taking bribes. Nor did he accept bribes—he grabbed them in a hurry, forgetting even to say thank you. One day he got himself run over by some horses and was killed.

Nikolay. Are you suggesting that my brother's energy is aimless?

Tatyana. Did I suggest that? I didn't mean it. I just wanted to say that he reminds me of that policeman.

Nikolay. That's not very flattering to my brother.

Tatyana. I had no intention of speaking flatteringly of him.

Nikolay. You have an original way of being coquettish.

Tatyana. Have I?

Nikolay. But not a particularly gay way.

Tatyana (calmly). Are there any women who feel gay with you?

Nikolay. Well, really!   *Enter Polina.*

Polina. Today nothing seems to go right in this house. Nobody comes to breakfast, everybody's irritable—as if they didn't have enough sleep. Nadya left with Cleopatra Petrovna early this morning to pick mushrooms in the woods. And I asked her yesterday not to. Oh, God! It's getting so hard to go on living.

Tatyana. You eat too much.

Polina. Why this tone, Tanya? Your attitude to other people really isn't normal.

Tatyana. Isn't it?

Polina. It's easy to be calm when you don't have anything and are free. But when you're the source from which a thousand people get their daily bread, it's no joke.

Tatyana. Then drop it, don't feed them, let them live as they please. Give them everything you have—the factory, the land —and stop worrying.

Nikolay (lighting a cigarette). From what play is that?

Polina. Why do you talk that way, Tanya? I don't understand you. You ought to see how upset Zakhar is. We've decided to close the factory for a while—until the workers calm down. But you must realize with what a heavy heart one makes such a decision. Hundreds of people will be left without work. And they have children—it's terrible.

Tatyana. Then don't close the factory, if it's so terrible. What's the sense of making things unpleasant for yourself?

Polina. Oh, Tanya, you irritate me. If we don't close, the workers will go out on strike, and that will be even worse.

Tatyana. How exactly will it be worse?

Polina. In every way. We can't give in to all their demands, surely. And after all, it's not their own demands—they've simply been taught by socialists, and they just shout what they're told. (*With feeling.*) I don't understand it. Abroad socialism is in its proper place and acts openly. But here in Russia it's being whispered to the workers from around the corners by people who don't seem to understand that in a monarchist state it's utterly out of place. We need a parliament and not that sort of thing at all. What's your opinion, Nikolay Vassilyevich?

Nikolay (*with a curt laugh*). I see it somewhat differently. Socialism is a very dangerous phenomenon. And a country which lacks an independent, or what one might call a racial, philosophy, and where everything is caught on the wing as it comes from outside—such a country is bound to provide suitable soil for socialism. We're a people of extremes—that's our disease.

Polina. That's very true. We are people of extremes.

Tatyana. Particularly you and your husband. Or our assistant district attorney for that matter—

Polina. You don't know it, Tanya, but in our province Zakhar is looked upon as a Red.

Tatyana. I think he turns red only from shame, and not very often at that—

Polina. Good heavens, Tanya! How can you say that?

Tatyana. Why, is it anything offensive? I didn't know. As I see your life, it strikes me as an amateur performance—the parts are badly cast, there are no players of talent, the acting is terrible—and you can't make out what the script is all about.

Nikolay. There's some truth in what you say. And everybody complains— Oh, what a dull play!

Tatyana. Yes, we're spoiling the play. It seems to me, the extras and the stage hands are beginning to realize that. One day they'll drive us off the stage.   *The General and Kon come on.*

Nikolay. I say! So that's the way you look at things!

General (*shouting*). Polina! Some milk for the General— some cold milk. (*To Nikolay.*) Ah, here you are—the coffin of laws! My delightful niece, your hand! Kon, answer the question: What's a soldier?

Kon (in a bored tone). Whatever his superiors want him to be, Your Excellency.

General. Can a soldier turn into a fish?

Kon. A soldier must be able to do anything.

Tatyana. Dear Uncle, you entertained us with this scene yesterday. Must we have it every day?

Polina (sighing). Every day after the swim.

General. Yes, every day. And always different—without fail. This old clown must think up the questions and answers himself.

Tatyana. Do you find it amusing, Kon?

Kon. His Excellency does.

Tatyana. And you?

General. He, too.

Kon. I'm rather old for the circus—but you have to bear with it if you want to eat—

General. You sly rascal! About face—forward march!

Tatyana. Don't you find it boring to make a fool of an old man?

General. I'm an old man too. And you're pretty boring, yourself. An actress is supposed to make people laugh. And what do you do?

Polina. You know, Uncle—

General. I know nothing.

Polina. We're closing the factory.

General. Ah! Splendid! It whistles. Early in the morning you're fast asleep—when suddenly—whoo-oo-oo! Close it!

                                   Mikhail comes on quickly.

Mikhail. Nikolay! Come here a minute. Well, the factory's closed. But we have to take measures for any eventuality. Send a telegram to the lieutenant governor—describe the situation briefly and ask for troops. Sign my name.

Nikolay. He's a friend of mine, too.

Mikhail. I'll go tell these delegates— No, to hell with it! Don't mention the telegram to anybody. I'll announce it myself when necessary. All right?

Nikolay. Yes.

Mikhail. It's a wonderful feeling, you know, when you get something your own way. I'm older than you in years, my boy, but I'm younger in spirit—don't you think?

Nikolay. That's not youthfulness. I think it's just nerves.

Mikhail (with a chuckle). I'll show you what nerves I have. You'll see. *(Goes off laughing.)*

Polina. So they've decided, Nikolay Vassilyevich?

Nikolay (going off). I gather they have.

Polina. Oh, my God!

General. What have they decided?

Polina. To close the factory.

General. Oh, yes. Kon!

Kon. Yes, sir.

General. Put the fishing tackle in the boat.

Kon. It's already there.

General. I'd rather go fish and save my breath than stay here and be bored to death. *(Laughs.)* That was cleverly put, wasn't it?   *Nadya runs on.*
Ah, little moth! What's happened?

Nadya (happily). An adventure! *(She turns around and calls to Cleopatra and Grekov, who are right behind her.)* Come on, please! Grekov! Don't let him go, Cleopatra Petrovna! You know, Auntie, we were coming out of the woods, when suddenly three drunk workmen popped up—

Polina. There! Just as I've always told you.

Cleopatra. It was perfectly disgusting.

Nadya. Why disgusting? I thought it was funny. Three workmen, Auntie—they smile and say: "Our good dear ladies—"

Cleopatra. I'm going to ask my husband to fire them.

Grekov (smiling). On what grounds?

General (to Nadya). Who's this raggle-taggle individual?

Nadya. He saved us, grandpa, don't you see?

General. I don't see a thing.

Cleopatra (to Nadya). You're making a mess of your story.

Nadya. I'm not.

Polina. But I can't make head or tail of it, Nadya.

Nadya. It's because you won't let me tell it to you properly. They come up to us and say, "Ladies, let's you and us sing songs."

Polina. What insolence!

Nadya. Not at all. "We know," they say, "you have very good voices. Of course, we're a bit drunk, but we're better men when we're drunk"— That's true, Auntie. Drunk they don't look as grim as they always do—

Cleopatra. Fortunately for us, this young man—

Nadya. I can tell it better than you. Cleopatra Petrovna began to lay into them—it was quite unnecessary, I assure you. Then one of them, such a tall, thin fellow—

Cleopatra (threateningly). I know him!

Nadya. He took her by the arm and said in such a sad voice: "You're a beautiful, educated woman, and it's a pleasure to look at you. And you're bawling us out. Have we done anything wrong to you?" He spoke very well, right from the heart. But the other one, he really was bitter. He said to the first: "What's the good of talking to them? Do you think they can understand anything? They're just like wild animals." That's what we are —wild animals—she and me. (*She laughs.*)

Tatyana (sarcastically). You seem to be pleased with the title?

Polina. I told you, Nadya— You run around everywhere—

Grekov (to Nadya). May I go?

Nadya. Oh, no. Please stay. Will you have tea? Or milk? Will you?

The General laughs. Cleopatra shrugs her shoulders. Tatyana stares at Grekov, humming to herself. Polina, her head bowed, carefully dries some spoons with a towel.

Grekov (smiling). No, thank you.

Nadya (persuasively). Please, don't be shy. They're all kind people, I assure you.

Polina (protestingly). Oh, Nadya!

Nadya (to Grekov). Don't go. I want to tell the rest of it—

Cleopatra (grumpily). In short, this young man appeared just in time and persuaded his drunken comrades to leave us alone —and I asked him to see us home. That's all.

Nadya. Oh, my goodness! If it were all the way you tell it— everybody would die of boredom.

General. How do you like that?

Nadya (to Grekov). Sit down, please. Auntie, do ask him to sit down. Why are you all so sour?

Polina (sitting, to Grekov). I thank you, young man.

Grekov. Don't mention it.

Polina (more dryly). It was very kind of you to defend the women.

Grekov (*calmly*). They needed no defense—nobody was harming them.

Nadya. Oh, Auntie! How can you talk like that?

Polina. I'll ask you not to teach me—

Nadya. But won't you understand—nobody defended us. He simply said to them: "Leave them alone, boys, you're not being polite." They were awfully glad to see him—they shouted: "Come with us, Grekov, you're a clever fellow!" And he is very clever, Auntie—you must excuse me, Grekov, but it's true!

Grekov (*smiling*). You're putting me in an awkward position.

Nadya. Not I, Grekov—they're the ones who are doing it.

Polina. Look Nadya. You know I don't understand such raptures. All this is too funny for words. Let's have no more of it.

Nadya (*excitedly*). Then laugh! Why do you all sit there like owls? Laugh!

Cleopatra. Nadya has a knack for turning every trivial incident into a noisy and rapturous story. This is particularly fitting right now, before the eyes of—a stranger who, as you see, is laughing at her.

Nadya (*to Grekov*). Are you laughing at me? Why?

Grekov (*simply*). I'm not laughing at you. I'm admiring you.

Polina (*amazed*). What's that? Uncle—

Cleopatra (*snickering*). There you are!

General. Well, that's enough! One can have too much of a good thing. Here, young man, take this and go.

Grekov (*turning away*). No, thanks. It's not necessary.

Nadya (*covering her face with her hands*). Oh, why?

General (*stopping Grekov*). Wait. This is ten rubles.

Grekov (*calmly*). What of it?

                              For a second everybody is silent.

General (*embarrassed*). Eh—what are you?

Grekov. A worker.

General. A blacksmith?

Grekov. A mechanic.

General (*sternly*). It's the same thing. And why don't you take the money?

Grekov. I don't want it.

General (*with annoyance*). What kind of comedy is this? What *do* you want?

Grekov. Nothing.

General. Perhaps you want to ask for the hand of the young lady? Do you? (*He laughs loudly. The others look embarrassed.*)

Nadya. Oh, what are you doing!

Polina. Uncle, please—

Grekov (*to the General, calmly*). How old are you?

General (*startled*). What did you say?

Grekov (*in the same tone*). How old are you?

General (*glancing around*). What's all this? I'm sixty-one. Well?

Grekov (*walking off*). At that age one ought to be more intelligent.

General. What? I? More intelligent?

Nadya (*running after Grekov*). Oh, please—don't be angry. He's an old man. And they're all kind people, really they are.

General. What the devil!

Grekov. You don't have to worry. It's all very natural.

Nadya. It's the heat. It's made them ill tempered. And I told the story so badly—

Grekov (*smiling*). No matter how you might tell it to them, they wouldn't understand—believe me.   *The two disappear.*

General (*enraged*). He dared—to say that—to me?

Tatyana. You made a mistake in thrusting your money—

Polina. Oh, Nadya, that girl!

Cleopatra. My, my! What a proud Spaniard! Well, I'll ask my husband to have him—

General. A whelp!

Polina. Nadya is impossible. She's gone with him. How she worries me!

Cleopatra. They're getting more and more out of hand every day. These socialists of yours—

Polina. What makes you think he's a socialist?

Cleopatra. I can see through them. All decent workers are socialists.

General. I'll tell Zakhar—to kick this sniveling youth out of the factory this very day.

Tatyana. The factory is closed down.

General. Kick him out anyway!

Polina. Tanya! Go call Nadya—do me a favor. Tell her I'm astounded—   *Tatyana goes off.*

General. The brute! How old are you, eh?

Cleopatra. Those drunks were booing us—and you're chummy with them—organize lectures— What good is it?

Polina. Yes, it's true. Can you imagine? Last Thursday I was driving to the village—suddenly they began booing! Booing even at me—how do you like that! Apart from the rudeness of it, it could have frightened the horses.

Cleopatra (censoriously). Zakhar Ivanovich is much to blame for that. He underestimates the distance between himself and these people, as my husband puts it.

Polina. He's soft-hearted—he wants to be kind to everybody. He's convinced that kind relations with the people are more profitable to both sides. The peasants bear out his view very well. They rent land, pay their dues, and everything goes on excellently. But then—   *Tatyana and Nadya return.* Nadya, my dear, do you understand how unseemly it is—

Nadya (heatedly). It's you—it's you who are unseemly! You've gone crazy because of the heat—you're sick and spiteful, and don't understand a thing. And you, grandpa—oh, how stupid you are.

General (incensed). I? Stupid? Another one?

Nadya. Why did you say that—about asking for my hand? Aren't you ashamed of yourself?

General. Ashamed? Well, I never. Thank you. That's enough for today. (*Goes off, shouting.*) Kon! The devil take all your relatives, where have you got stuck with your idiotic feet, donkey, blockhead?!

Nadya. And you, Auntie—you who have lived abroad, who talk about politics. Not to have invited a man to sit down—not to have offered him a cup of tea!

Polina (rises and throws down a spoon). It's intolerable—such talk from you!

Nadya. And you, too, Cleopatra Petrovna—on the way home you were so nice and polite to him—but as soon as you got here—

Cleopatra. What am I supposed to do? Kiss him? I'm sorry, he needed a wash. Nor am I prepared to listen to your lectures. You see, Polina Dmitriyevna? Here is democracy for you—or what do you call it—humanism! So far it all falls on my husband's shoulders—but it'll fall on yours too, mark my word!

Polina. Cleopatra Petrovna, I apologize to you for Nadya.

Cleopatra. That's unnecessary. Nor does it matter about Nadya. The trouble is not with her alone. Everybody is to blame. (*She goes off.*)

Polina. Listen to me, Nadya. When your dying mother asked me to take care of you, to bring you up—

Nadya. Don't mention my mother. You always wrong her.

Polina (startled). Nadya, are you ill? Think what you're saying. I'm her sister. I know more about her than you do.

Nadya (with tears in her eyes, which she doesn't attempt to check). You don't know anything. The poor are no relatives to the rich. My mother was poor—and kind. You don't understand poor people. You don't understand even Aunt Tanya.

Polina. I must ask you to leave me, Nadya. Go, please.

Nadya. I will go. But I'm still right—not you! (*She goes off.*)

Polina. Ah—my God! A healthy girl, and suddenly such a fit, such hysterics. You'll forgive my saying so, Tanya, but I see your influence in this—I do. You talk to her about everything as if she were an adult. You take her into the company of employees. Those office clerks—those queer fellows from among the workers—it's absurd! And then—going out boating with those men—

Tatyana. Calm yourself—have something to drink. You must agree you behaved toward that workman—rather unintelligently. Surely, he wouldn't have broken the chair, if you'd asked him to take a seat.

Polina. No, you're wrong. Nobody can say that I treat the workers badly. But everything must have its limit, my dear.

Yakov appears in the rear.

Tatyana. Another thing—I don't take Nadya anywhere. She goes there herself—and I don't think she should be interfered with in that.

Polina. She goes herself! As if she understood where she's going. *Yakov comes on slowly.*

Yakov (sitting down). Well, there'll be a riot at the factory.

Polina (wearily). Oh, stop it, Yakov Ivanovich.

Yakov. Yes, there will be—there will be a riot. They'll set fire to the works and roast us all—like pigs.

Tatyana (with annoyance). You seem to have been drinking already.

Yakov. By this time I've always been drinking. I just saw

Cleopatra—she's a no-account. Not because she has lots of lovers
—but because in her breast, instead of a soul, there sits an old,
vicious dog.

Polina (rising). Oh, God! Oh, God! Everything was going so
well, and all of a sudden— (*She begins walking in the garden.*)

Yakov. A small dog, with a mangy coat— Greedy— It sits and
bares its teeth— Has satisfied its hunger—eaten everything—
but wants something more— Yet it doesn't know what it wants
—and is restless—

Tatyana. Keep quiet, Yakov. Your brother is coming.

Yakov. I don't want my brother. Tanya, I realize it's impossible for you to love me any more. All the same, it hurts me.
Yes, it hurts me, but doesn't stop me from loving you.

Tatyana. You ought to cool yourself off. Go take a dip in the
river.   *Zakhar comes on.*

Zakhar (as he approaches). Have they announced the closing
of the factory?

Tatyana. I don't know.

Yakov. They haven't announced it, but the workers know it.

Zakhar. How do they? Who told them?

Yakov. I did. I just went there and told them.

Polina (coming up). Why?

Yakov (with a shrug). Because. It's of interest to them. I tell
them everything, if they listen to me. They like me, I think. It
pleases them to see the brother of their boss a drunkard. In their
eyes that probably makes me a living example of the idea of
equality.

Zakhar. H'm—you visit the factory pretty frequently, Yakov
—of course, I have nothing against that. But Mikhail Vassilyevich says that talking to the workers, you sometimes criticize the order of things in the factory.

Yakov. He's a liar. I don't understand anything about orders
or disorders.

Zakhar. He also says that sometimes you bring vodka with
you.

Yakov. He lies again. I don't bring it, but send for it, and not
sometimes, but always. You understand yourself that without
vodka I'm of no interest to them.

Zakhar. But, Yakov, think, you're the owner's brother—

Yakov. That's not my only defect—

Zakhar (offended). Well, I'll say no more. An atmosphere of hostility is being created around me which I can't understand.

Polina. Yes, that's true. You should have heard what Nadya was saying here. *Pologhy rushes on.*

Pologhy. Excuse me! The director—Mikhail Vassilyevich—has just been—killed!

Zakhar. What?

Polina. You don't mean—?

Pologhy. Yes, killed—fell to the floor—shot down—

Zakhar. Who shot him?

Pologhy. The workers.

Polina. Have they caught them?

Zakhar. Is the doctor there?

Pologhy. I don't know.

Polina. Yakov Ivanovich, go right over, please!

Yakov (spreading his arms). Go where?

Polina. How did it happen?

Pologhy. Mikhail Vassilyevich got upset—and kicked a worker in the stomach—

Yakov. They're coming here.

Hubbub. Mikhail Skrobotov is led on, supported under the arms by his brother Nikolay and Levshin, a somewhat bald-headed, middle-aged workman. Walking behind them are a few clerks and workers, also a Police Sergeant.

Mikhail (exhaustedly). Leave me—lay me down—

Nikolay. Did you see who shot you?

Mikhail. I'm tired—very tired.

Nikolay (insistently). Did you notice who fired the shot?

Mikhail. It hurts— Some man with red hair— Lay me down — Some man with red hair—

Mikhail is placed on the turf seat.

Nikolay (to the Police Sergeant). Did you hear? A man with red hair—

Police Sergeant. Yes, sir.

Mikhail. Ah, it makes no difference now—

Levshin. Rest, Mikhail Vassilyevich, it's all right. Oh, human affairs—kopeck affairs. We get ruined for a kopeck— It's a mother to us, and it's our death—

Nikolay. Sergeant, ask all who aren't needed here to leave.

Police Sergeant (in a low voice). On your way, fellows. There's nothing for you here.

Zakhar (quietly). But where's the doctor?

Nikolay. Misha! Misha! (*He bends over his brother. The others follow suit.*) I think—he's dead—he is.

Zakhar. It can't be. He's just fainted.

Nikolay (slowly, in a low voice). Do you understand, Zakhar Ivanovich? He's dead.

Zakhar. But—you may be mistaken.

Nikolay. No, I'm not. And it's you who placed him in the line of fire.

Zakhar (aghast). I?

Tatyana. How cruel—and stupid!

Nikolay (moving toward Zakhar menacingly). Yes, you.

> *Police Inspector comes on the run.*

Police Inspector. Where's Mr. Skrobotov? Is he seriously wounded?

Levshin. He's dead. He was always hurrying everybody, and now—there he is—

Nikolay (to the Police Inspector). He said before he died he had been shot by a man with red hair—

Police Inspector. A man with red hair?

Nikolay. Yes. Take the necessary measures immediately.

Police Inspector (to the Police Sergeant). Round up all the red-headed men at once.

Police Sergeant. Yes, sir.

Police Inspector. Every one of them.

> *The Police Sergeant leaves. Cleopatra comes on, running.*

Cleopatra. Where is he? Misha! What is it? A faint? Nikolay Vassilyevich, is this a faint? (*Nikolay turns his head away.*) Is he dead?

Levshin. He's found his rest. He threatened to use a pistol. And the pistol, you see, turned against him.

Nikolay (bitterly, in a low voice, to Levshin). You get out of here. (*To the Police Inspector.*) Take him away.

> *Nadya comes on.*

Cleopatra. Well, when is the doctor coming?

Police Inspector (to Levshin, in a low voice). Get going.

Levshin (quietly). I'm going. Why push?

Cleopatra (in a low voice). They've killed him?

Polina (to Cleopatra). My dear—

Cleopatra (bitterly, in a low voice). Go away! It's your doing —yours!

Zakhar (looking depressed). I understand, of course—you're stunned— But why say such things? Why?

Polina (with tears in her eyes). You can't imagine, my dear, how terrible it is!

Tatyana (to Polina). You'd better get out of here—

Cleopatra. It's you who killed him with your cursed flabbiness.

Nikolay (dryly). Calm down, Cleopatra. Zakhar Ivanovich no doubt realizes his guilt before us.

Zakhar (depressed). My friends—I don't understand. What in the world are you saying? How can you make such accusations?

Polina. How horrible! My God, and so pitiless!

Cleopatra. So they were pitiless? You set the workers against him, you destroyed his influence among them— They had feared him, had trembled before him—and now you have it—they've killed him. You're responsible for that, yes you are! His blood is on your hands!

Nikolay. Enough, Cleopatra—don't shout.

Cleopatra (to Polina). You're crying? Let his blood run from your eyes!

Police Sergeant (coming on, to the Inspector). Sir.

Police Inspector. Not so loud.

Police Sergeant. We've got all the redheads.

> *The General comes into the garden, rear. He is pushing Kon in front of him and laughing boisterously.*

Nikolay. Quiet!

Cleopatra. What do you say, murderers?

CURTAIN

ACT II

*The same setting. It is a moonlit night. Thick, heavy shadows
lie on the ground. On the table, scattered in disorder, are numerous cucumbers and eggs, a quantity of bread, several bottles
of beer. Shaded candles light the table.* AGRAFENA *is washing
dishes.* YAGODIN *is seated on a chair, holding a stick in his hand
and smoking.* TATYANA, NADYA, *and* LEVSHIN *are standing at
left. All talk in subdued voices and seem to be straining to hear
something. The general mood is one of anxious waiting.*

Levshin (to Nadya). All that's human on this earth is poisoned by copper, dear Miss. That's why your young heart feels
bored. All humanity is bound up with the copper kopeck, but
you're still free, and so there's no place for you among the
humans. On this earth the kopeck jingles to every man: love me
as you love yourself. That doesn't concern you. The little bird
neither sows, nor reaps.

Yagodin (to Agrafena). Levshin has started teaching the
masters too. A queer fellow.

Agrafena. Well, he speaks the truth. A little truth won't do
the masters any harm.

Nadya. Do you have a very hard life, Levshin?

Levshin. Not very. You see, I have no children. My woman
—my wife, that is—is with me, but all my children are dead.

Nadya. Aunt Tanya! Why is it, when there's somebody dead
in the house, everybody speaks low?

Tatyana. I don't know.

Levshin (smiling). It's because, Miss, we're all to blame before the dead, in all sorts of ways.

Nadya. But Levshin, it isn't always that somebody—gets
killed, as he was. People talk low however a man dies.

Levshin. We kill everybody, my dear. Some with bullets, some with words, and everybody with our deeds. We drive people into their graves, and neither see it nor feel it. But when we throw a man right into the arms of death, we begin to get some glimmering of our guilt before him. We feel sorry for him, ashamed before him, and are frightened in our hearts. For we too are being driven out of life, we too are being readied for the grave—

Nadya. Y-yes—that's frightening.

Levshin. Don't worry. It's frightening today, but it'll be all gone tomorrow. Again people will be pushing each other around— Somebody who's been pushed too much will fall, and everybody will be quiet for a minute, a bit uncomfortable. But they'll sigh and pretty soon they'll start it all over again—their accustomed way. Poor muddled people! Now you, Miss—you don't feel guilty—dead folks don't bother you, you can talk out loud even when you're near them—

Tatyana. What's to be done to make life different? Do you know?

Levshin (mysteriously). We have to destroy the kopeck— bury it. Once it's gone, why quarrel, why squeeze each other?

Tatyana. Is that all?

Levshin. That'll be plenty for a start.

Tatyana. Care for a stroll in the garden, Nadya?

Nadya (pensively). All right—

The two withdraw to the rear of the garden. Levshin moves up to the table. The General, Kon, and Pologhy appear near the tent.

Yagodin. You don't mind scattering seed even on a stone, Levshin. You're queer.

Levshin. Why?

Yagodin. You're wasting your time. Do you think they'll understand? The worker's heart will, but it won't suit the master's.

Levshin. She's a nice lass. Grekov was telling me about her.

Agrafena. Will you have more tea?

Levshin. That I will.

The three at the table fall silent. The General's rich voice is heard. The white dresses of Nadya and Tatyana are seen gleaming through the trees.

General. Or you can stretch a line across the road—so it can't be seen. A man is walking along and suddenly—plop!

Pologhy. It's pleasant to see a man fall, Your Excellency.

Yagodin. Do you hear?

Levshin. I hear—

Kon. Nothing of that sort can be done today—there's a dead man in the house. When there's a dead man you can't joke.

General. I take no lessons from you. When you die I'll dance.

Tatyana and Nadya come down toward the table.

Levshin. The man's in his second childhood.

Agrafena (walking off to the house). He's a great one at practical jokes—

Tatyana (sitting down at the table). Tell me, Levshin, are you a socialist?

Levshin (simply). Me? No. Yagodin and I, we're both weavers.

Tatyana. Do you know any socialists? Have you heard of them?

Levshin. We've heard. Know them—we don't. But we've heard of them, oh, yes!

Tatyana. Do you know Sintsov, the office clerk?

Levshin. We know him. We know everybody in the office.

Tatyana. Have you talked to him?

Yagodin (uneasily). What can we talk about? They're above, we're below. When we come to the office they tell us what the director told them to say—and that's all. There's all our acquaintance.

Nadya. You seem to be afraid of us, Levshin? You don't have to be—we're merely interested—

Levshin. We're not afraid. We've done nothing wrong. They've called us here to watch the place, and we've come. Some men down there got bitter in their hearts and now they're saying: We'll set fire to the factory and everything—there'll be nothing left but embers. But we're against mischief. We mustn't burn anything. Why burn? We built it all ourselves—with our fathers and grandfathers—and all of a sudden we have to burn it! Oh, no!

Tatyana. Perhaps you think we're asking you questions for some evil purpose?

Yagodin. Why? We want no evil.

Levshin. The way we look at it is like this: what's been made with your hands is sacred. Man's work has to be valued fairly, there's no question about that, but burn it—no! But our folks don't think—they love fire. And they're bitter. The director was very stern with us when he lived—not that I want to speak ill of him. He waved his pistol—threatened—

Nadya. And Uncle? Is he better?

Yagodin. Who, Zakhar Ivanovich?

Nadya. Yes. Is he kind? Or does he—treat you badly too?

Levshin. We don't say that.

Yagodin. They're all the same to us—the stern and the kind ones.

Levshin (amiably). The stern one is a master, and the kind one is a master. Disease doesn't pick and choose between people.

Yagodin (listlessly). Of course Zakhar Ivanovich is a good-hearted man—

Nadya. Then he's better than Skrobotov?

Yagodin (quietly). Skrobotov is dead.

Levshin. Your uncle, Miss, is a fine man—to look at. Only that doesn't make our lot any easier.

Tatyana (with irritation). Come on, Nadya. They don't want to understand us—you can see it.

Nadya (quietly). Yes.

> *The two go off in silence. Levshin looks after them, then glances at Yagodin—they both smile.*

Yagodin. By heaven, they do tear at your soul.

Levshin. You see, they're interested to know—

Yagodin. And maybe they think we'll blab out something—

Levshin. The young miss is a good girl. It's a pity she's rich.

Yagodin. We must tell Sintsov the madam has been asking questions.

Levshin. We will. And we'll tell Grekov too.

Yagodin. I wonder what's going on at the factory. They have to give in to our demands.

Levshin. They'll give in. Later they'll take it all back.

Yagodin. Out of our hides—

Levshin. Naturally.

Yagodin. Y-yes. Ah, I feel sleepy.

Levshin. Hold on. Here comes the General.

> *The General comes on. Pologhy walks deferentially beside him, with Kon behind. Suddenly Pologhy grasps the General by the elbow.*

General. What's that?

Pologhy. A hole in the ground.

General. Ah! What's this on the table? Muck, it looks like to me! Were you eating this?

Yagodin. Yes, sir. Your granddaughter ate with us too.

General. Well, so you're guarding the house, eh?

Yagodin. Yes, sir—we're keeping watch.

General. Good for you! I'll tell the governor about you. How many of you here?

Levshin. Two.

General. Fool! I can count up to two. How many of you altogether?

Yagodin. About thirty.

General. Have you firearms?

Levshin (*to Yagodin*). Where's your pistol?

Yagodin. Here it is.

General. Don't take it by the muzzle—damn fool! Kon, teach these idiots how to handle firearms. (*To Levshin.*) Have you got a revolver?

Levshin. No, I haven't.

General. Well, will you shoot if the mutineers come?

Levshin. They won't come, Your Excellency. They got worked up, but it's all over now.

General. What if they do come?

Levshin. They feel sore on account of the closing of the factory. Some of them have children—

General. Don't give me that stuff! I'm asking—are you going to shoot?

Levshin. Why, Your Excellency, we're ready. If there's any shooting to be done, we'll do it—why not? Only we don't know how to shoot, and we haven't anything to shoot with. If we had rifles—or guns—

General. Kon, go teach them. Go that way, to the river.

Kon (*sullenly*). I beg to inform Your Excellency, it's night now—and there'll be excitement if we start shooting—people will come to see what it's about. However, I'll do whatever you say.

General. Hold off till tomorrow.

Levshin. And tomorrow it'll be all quiet. The factory will open—

General. Who'll open it?

Levshin. Zakhar Ivanovich. He's having a talk with the workers right now.

General. Damn it! I'd close that factory for good—to hell with that early morning whistle!

Yagodin. A later hour would suit us better too.

General. And I'd starve all of you to death. A lesson to you—not to mutiny!

Levshin. Why, Your Excellency, we don't mutiny.

General. Silence! What are you hanging around here for? You must walk along the wall. And if anybody tries to get over —shoot! I'll answer for you.

Levshin. Come on, Yagodin. Don't forget your pistol.

                              Levshin and Yagodin go off.

General (after them). Pistol! Stupid asses! Can't even call the thing by its right name!

Pologhy. If I may take the liberty, Your Excellency, these people are all coarse and brutal. I'll cite my own case. Having a plot of land, I grow vegetables on it, doing all the work with my own hands—

General. That's to your credit.

Pologhy. I work during my free time—

General. Everybody must work.

                    Tatyana and Nadya are approaching.

Tatyana (from a distance). Why are you shouting?

General. They annoy me. (*To Pologhy.*) Well?

Pologhy. But almost every night the workers purloin the fruits of my labor—

General. They steal?

Pologhy. Exactly. I try to secure the protection of the law, but same is represented here by the Police Inspector, a person indifferent to the sufferings of the population—

Tatyana (to Pologhy). Listen, Mr. Pologhy, why do you speak in such a stupid language?

Pologhy (embarrassed). I? I'm sorry. But I went to a high school for three years and I read the newspaper daily.

Tatyana. Oh, I see—

Nadya. You're very funny, Pologhy.

Pologhy. If it pleases you, I'm very glad. A man has to be pleasant—

General. I love fishing. Do you?

Pologhy. I haven't tried, Your Excellency.

General (with a shrug). A strange answer.

Tatyana. What haven't you tried—to fish or to love?

Pologhy (embarrassed). The first.

Tatyana. And the second?

Pologhy. I've tried the second.

Tatyana. Are you married?

Pologhy. I only dream of that. But my salary being only twenty-five rubles a month, I can't nerve myself to it.

> *Nikolay and Cleopatra come on in great haste.*

Nikolay (bitterly). It's something incredible! Utter chaos!

Cleopatra. How dare he? How could he?

General. What's happened?

Cleopatra. Your nephew's a jellyfish! He agreed to all the demands of the mutineers, the murderers of my husband.

Nadya (quietly). Surely they're not all murderers.

Cleopatra. It's an insult to the dead man—and to me. To open the factory before the man who was killed by these scoundrels for closing it has been buried—why, it's an outrage!

Nadya. But Uncle is afraid they'll burn down everything—

Cleopatra. You're a child—and ought to keep silent.

Nikolay. And the speech that young whippersnapper made! It was an unmistakable preaching of socialism.

Cleopatra. A nobody, an office clerk, orders everything about, offers advice—he even had the effrontery to say that the crime was provoked by my husband himself.

Nikolay (jotting something down in his notebook). This man is a suspicious character—he's too clever for an office clerk.

Tatyana. Are you talking about Sintsov?

Nikolay. Precisely.

Cleopatra. I feel as if someone had spat in my face.

Pologhy (to Nikolay). Permit me to remark: when reading newspapers, Mr. Sintsov always discusses politics and talks most unfavorably of the authorities.

Tatyana (to Nikolay). Do you find it interesting to listen to this?

Nikolay (challengingly). I do. You think you can embarrass me?

Tatyana. I think Mr. Pologhy doesn't belong here.

ENEMIES109

Pologhy (embarrassed). Please forgive me—I'll go! (*He goes off quickly.*)

Nadya. What's going on?

General. I'm too old for this business. A murder, a mutiny! Zakhar should have foreseen all this when he invited me here—

Zakhar comes on, looking excited but pleased. He notices Nikolay and stops in embarrassment, adjusting his spectacles.

Listen, my dear nephew—eh—do you realize what you're doing?

Zakhar. Just a moment, Uncle. Nikolay Vassilyevich!

Nikolay. Yes.

Zakhar. The workers are terribly worked up. Fearing they might wreck the factory—I satisfied their demand that work be resumed—and also about Dichkov. I laid down one condition—that they hand over the criminal, and they've already started a search for him—

Nikolay (dryly). They don't have to worry about that. We'll find the murderer without their aid.

Zakhar. I feel it'd be better if they would do it themselves—yes. We've decided to open tomorrow noon—

Nikolay. Who are we?

Zakhar. I—

Nikolay. I see. Thank you for the information. It seems to me, though, that after my brother's death his rights have passed on to me and his wife, and if I'm not mistaken, you had to consult us, and not make a decision on your own.

Zakhar. But I asked you to meet me. Sintsov took my message to you—you refused to come.

Nikolay. You must agree it's difficult for me to consider business matters on the day of my brother's death.

Zakhar. But you did go to the factory?

Nikolay. Yes, I went there—listened to the speeches— What of it?

Zakhar. But you must understand—your brother, it turns out, sent a telegram to the city asking for soldiers. The reply has arrived—the soldiers will be here tomorrow before noon—

General. Ah, soldiers! That's better! You can't fool around with soldiers!

Nikolay. That was a wise step—

Zakhar. I don't know. The soldiers will come—the excitement among the workers will rise— God knows what might happen if the factory weren't reopened. I believe I acted wisely. The possibility of a sanguinary conflict has now been removed—

Nikolay. I see it differently. You shouldn't have yielded to these—people, if only out of respect for the memory of the murdered man.

Zakhar. Oh, my God—but you're ignoring the possibility of a tragedy.

Nikolay. I'm not concerned with that.

Zakhar. Maybe. But what about me? I shall have to live with the workers. And if their blood is shed— Besides, they could have wrecked the factory!

Nikolay. I don't believe it.

General. Neither do I.

Zakhar (depressed). So you condemn my action?

Nikolay. I certainly do.

Zakhar (with sincere feeling). Why—why must we be enemies? You know all I want is to avoid what might happen if— I mean, I want no shedding of blood. Is a peaceful, reasonable course of life impossible? You look at me with hatred in your eyes, the workers with suspicion. Yet I want to do good, nothing but good.

Nadya (with tears in her eyes). Don't get upset, Uncle. He doesn't understand. Oh, Nikolay Vassilyevich, how can you fail to understand? You're so clever—why don't you believe my uncle?

Nikolay. You'll pardon me, Zakhar Ivanovich, I'm going. I can't engage in a business conversation with children participating. (*He goes off.*)

Zakhar. You see, Nadya—

Nadya (taking him by the arm). Never mind him. You know the main thing is to have the workers satisfied—there are so many of them, and we're only a few.

Zakhar. Wait—I have to say something to you. I'm very displeased with you, yes, I am.

General. So am I.

Zakhar. You sympathize with the workers. That's natural at your age, but one mustn't lose his sense of proportion, my dear. Now, this morning you brought that Grekov to the table. I

know him, he's a very intelligent fellow—but you shouldn't
have made a scene before your aunt because of him.

General. Give it to her.

Nadya. But you don't know what happened.

Zakhar. I know more than you do, believe me. Our masses
are crude, uncivilized—give them a finger and they'll grab an
arm—

Tatyana. Like a drowning man clutching at a straw.

Zakhar. There's a great deal of animal greed in them, my
friend, and what they need is not petting but educating. Please,
think this over.

General. Now I'll speak. You treat me outrageously, you impudent girl. I have to remind you that you'll be my equal some
forty years from now. At that time I will, perhaps, allow you
to talk to me as an equal. You understand? Kon!

Kon (back among the trees). Yes, sir.

General. Where's—what's his name?—that stick-in-the-mud?

Kon. Which stick-in-the-mud?

General. That sticky one. Or is it muggy, cloggy?

Kon. You mean Pologhy? I don't know.

General (walking toward the tent). Find him.

*Zakhar walks about hunched over, wiping his spectacles.
Nadya, seated on a chair, is absorbed in her thoughts.
Tatyana is watching the scene, standing.*

Tatyana. Is it known who killed Skrobotov?

Zakhar. They say they don't know but will find him. Of course
they know. *(Glancing around and lowering his voice.)* It was a
collective decision on their part—a plot! Truth to tell, he har-
assed them, even bullied them. There was in him that morbid
trait—a love of power. And so they—it's simply terrible.
They've killed a man, and they look at you with such clear
eyes as if they were completely unaware of their crime. They
did it with such a terrifying simplicity.

Tatyana. I've heard Skrobotov was going to shoot, but somebody snatched the revolver from him and—

Zakhar. That makes no difference. It was they who killed,
not he.

Nadya (to Zakhar). You ought to sit down—

Zakhar. Why did he call for soldiers? They learned about it—
they know everything—and that hastened his death. I had to

open the factory, of course—or I'd have spoiled my relations with them for a long time. And these are the times when one has to treat them with extra consideration and softness—for who knows how it'll all end? In such periods as ours a wise man has to have friends among the masses— (*Levshin is seen walking, rear.*) Who's that coming?

Levshin. It's us—patrolling.

Zakhar. Well, what do you say, Levshin? You people killed a man and now you're gentle and meek, eh?

Levshin. We're always meek, Zakhar Ivanovich.

Zakhar (*imposingly*). Yes. And kill meekly too? By the way, Levshin, you're preaching something, I hear, some new theory that says we need no money, no employers, and so forth. One can forgive—that is, understand that in Leo Tolstoy— But you'd better stop it, my friend. That kind of talk will do you no good.

> *Tatyana and Nadya walk off, right, where the voices of Sintsov and Yakov are heard. Yagodin emerges from among the trees.*

Levshin (*calmly*). And what kind of talk is it? I've lived and thought, so I say what I've learned.

Zakhar. Employers are not wild beasts—that's what you have to realize. You know, I'm not a hard man, I'm always ready to help you. I wish well—

Levshin (*with a sigh*). Of course, nobody wishes himself ill.

Zakhar. No, you have to understand—I wish you well.

Levshin. We understand.

Zakhar (*after a glance at Levshin*). No, you don't. You're strange people. One moment you're like wild animals, another like children.

> *He goes off. Levshin looks after him, leaning on his stick.*

Yagodin (*coming up*). Has he given you another sermon?

Levshin. A Chinaman. A regular Chinaman. What was he saying? The man simply can't understand anything except himself.

Yagodin. He wishes well, he said.

Levshin. That's it.

Yagodin. Let's go—here they come.

> *The two withdraw to the rear. Tatyana, Nadya, Yakov, Sintsov come on, right.*

Nadya. We're walking, spinning around—as if in a dream.

Tatyana. Will you have something to eat, Matvey Niko-layevich?

Sintsov. Better give me some tea. I've talked so much today I have a sore throat.

Nadya. Aren't you afraid of anything?

Sintsov (seating himself at the table). I? No, not a thing.

Nadya. And I'm frightened. Suddenly everything's got all tangled up, and now I don't understand any more which people are good and which are bad.

Sintsov (smiling). It'll get untangled. Only you mustn't be afraid to think. Think fearlessly, to the end. There's nothing to fear anyway.

Tatyana. Do you think everything has quieted down?

Sintsov. I do. The workers seldom win their battles, and even small victories give them great satisfaction.

Nadya. Do you like them?

Sintsov. That's not the word. I've lived with them a long time, I know them, I see their strength, I have faith in their intelligence—

Tatyana. Faith in the future belonging to them, too?

Sintsov. In that too.

Nadya. The future—that's one thing I just can't visualize.

Tatyana (with a chuckle). They're very sly, these prole-tarians of ours. Nadya and I tried to talk to them—it was a stupid attempt.

Nadya. I even felt hurt. The old man spoke as if we two were some kind of evil characters, something like spies. There's an-other fellow here, Grekov—he looks upon people differently. But the old man only smiles—and in a peculiar way as though he were sorry for us—as though we were ill.

Tatyana. Don't drink so much, Yakov. It's not pleasant to watch.

Yakov. What else can I do?

Sintsov. Is there really nothing?

Yakov. I have an abhorrence—an unconquerable abhorrence of business activity and business in general. You see, I'm a man of the third group—

Sintsov. How so?

Yakov. It's like this. Men can be divided into three groups:

some work all their lives, others are able to lay aside money, and still others will neither work for bread alone—since there's no sense to it—nor put away money—since that's a stupid and rather unseemly occupation. Now I'm one of the third group. It includes all the loafers, tramps, monks, beggars, and other hangers-on of this world.

Nadya. You're being dull, Uncle. And you're not that sort of man at all. You're just sweet and kind.

Yakov. In other words, no good for anything. I realized that when I was still at school. People are divided into three groups from their teens.

Tatyana. Nadya is right, Yakov—this is all very dull.

Yakov. I agree. Matvey Nikolayevich, do you think life has a face?

Sintsov. Possibly.

Yakov. Well, it has. Its face is always young. Not so very long ago life regarded me with indifference, but now it looks sternly at me and asks: "What sort of man are you? Where is it you're going?" (*He is frightened at something, wants to smile, but his lips tremble, refuse to obey him, and his face is twisted into a sorry grimace.*)

Tatyana. Now drop that, please, Yakov. The district attorney's down there, walking this way. I'd like you not to talk while he's here.

Yakov. All right.

Nadya (*quietly*). Everybody's expecting something to happen—and they all feel scared. Why do they forbid me to meet the workers? It's stupid.   *Nikolay walks up.*

Nikolay. May I ask for a glass of tea?

Tatyana. Certainly. Here you are.

There is silence for a few seconds. Nikolay stands, stirring his tea.

Nadya. I would like to know why the workers don't believe my uncle and generally—

Nikolay. They believe only those who orate to them on the theme "Proletarians of the world, unite!" They believe that!

Nadya (*with a shrug of her shoulders, quietly*). When I hear these words—this call to all parts of the world—I feel as if we were all outsiders unnecessary on this earth—

Nikolay (*with growing agitation*). Of course! Every person of culture must be feeling like that. Soon, I'm sure, another call will ring out over the earth: "Culture-loving people of the world, unite!" It's time we shouted this. The barbarian is coming to trample thousands of years of human effort under foot. He's on the march, driven by greed—

Yakov. With his soul in his belly, his hungry belly. It's a spectacle to make one thirsty. (*Pours himself some beer.*)

Nikolay. The crowd is marching, driven by greed and organized by the unity of its desire—to fill its stomachs!

Tatyana (*reflectively*). The crowd— Everywhere there's a crowd—in the theater—in church—

Nikolay. What can these people bring with them? Nothing but destruction. And, mind you, in this country the destruction will be more terrifying than anywhere.

Tatyana. When I hear anybody talk of the workers as forward-looking people, I feel strange—it's so far removed from the way I see them.

Nikolay. And you, Mr. Sintsov, you, of course, disagree with us?

Sintsov (*calmly*). I do.

Nadya. But don't you remember, Aunt Tanya, how the old man spoke of the kopeck? It seems awfully simple.

Nikolay. And what are the reasons for your disagreement, Mr. Sintsov?

Sintsov. I think differently.

Nikolay. A perfectly reasonable answer. But, perhaps, you'll acquaint us with your views?

Sintsov. No, I'm not in the mood.

Nikolay. I'm extremely sorry to hear that. I bear up in the hope that when we meet again your mood will have changed. Yakov Ivanovich, if you don't mind, I'll ask you to walk home with me. My nerves are in such a bad state—

Yakov (*rising with difficulty*). Certainly—certainly. (*The two go off.*)

Tatyana. This district attorney is a most objectionable person. It goes against my grain to have to agree with him.

Nadya (*rising*). Why do you?

Sintsov (*with a chuckle*). Yes, why do you, Tatyana Pavlovna?

Tatyana. Because I feel as he does.

Sintsov (to Tatyana). You think as he does, but feel differently. You want to understand things, he doesn't bother—he has no need to.

Tatyana. He's probably very cruel.   *Nadya goes off.*

Sintsov. I think so. Up in town he's in charge of prosecution in political cases, and he treats the prisoners abominably.

Tatyana. Incidentally, he was jotting down something about you in his notebook.

Sintsov (with a smile). No doubt. He has talks with Pologhy —and all in all—he's quite industrious. Tatyana Pavlovna, I'd like to ask you to do something for me.

Tatyana. By all means. If I can, I'll be happy to, I assure you.

Sintsov. Thank you. I suppose the secret police have been called up.

Tatyana. Yes, they have been.

Sintsov. That means they'll be searching houses. Could you help me to hide certain things?

Tatyana. You think they'll search your home?

Sintsov. I'm almost sure of it.

Tatyana. And they may arrest you?

Sintsov. I don't think so. What have I done? Made speeches? But Zakhar Ivanovich knows that in those speeches I appealed to the workers to preserve order—

Tatyana. And your past—is it spotless?

Sintsov. I have no past. Well, will you help me? I wouldn't trouble you, but I think everybody else who could hide these things will have their homes searched tomorrow. (*Laughs quietly.*)

Tatyana (with embarrassment). I'll be frank with you. My position in the house doesn't permit me to regard the room I've been given as my own.

Sintsov. Then you can't? Oh, well—

Tatyana. Don't be displeased with me.

Sintsov. Oh, no! Your refusal is understandable—

Tatyana. But wait, I'll talk to Nadya—

She goes off. Sintsov drums on the table with his fingers as he looks after her. Cautious steps are heard.

Sintsov (in a low voice). Who's there?   *Grekov comes on.*

Grekov. It's me. Are you alone?

Sintsov. Yes. There are some people walking around over there. What's doing at the factory?

Grekov (with a chuckle). Well, they decided to find the man who fired the shot. Now the authorities are investigating. Some shout, "The socialists killed him." In short, people are trying to save their filthy skins.

Sintsov. Do you know who did it?

Grekov. Akimov.

Sintsov. No, really? I never would have suspected. Such a nice sensible fellow.

Grekov. He has a hot temper. He wants to give himself up. And he has a wife, a baby—they're expecting another. I just spoke to Levshin. Full of high-flown ideas, that one—says we've got to get some smaller fry to take the blame.

Sintsov. He's queer. But damn, it's annoying. (*There is a pause.*) Look, Grekov. You'll have to bury everything in the ground. We have no other place to hide it.

Grekov. I've found a place. The telegrapher has agreed to take everything. You know, Matvey Nikolayevich, you ought to get away from here.

Sintsov. No, I won't go.

Grekov. They'll arrest you.

Sintsov. Maybe. But if I leave, it'll make a bad impression on the workers.

Grekov. That's true. But I feel sorry for you—

Sintsov. Nonsense. The man to be sorry for is Akimov.

Grekov. Yes. And we can't help him either. He wants to confess. You know, it's funny to see you as the head of the patrol guarding the chief's property.

Sintsov (smiling). What can you do? My men seem to be asleep?

Grekov. No. They're standing in groups, talking, arguing. What a fine night!

Sintsov. I wouldn't be staying here either, but I'm waiting for somebody. You're going to be arrested too. I'm sure of it.

Grekov. So am I. Well, I'm off. (*Goes off.*)

Sintsov. Good-by.   *Tatyana comes on.*
Don't trouble yourself, Tatyana Pavlovna. Everything has been fixed. Good-by.

Tatyana. I feel very sorry about it, really.

Sintsov. Good night.

> *He goes off. Tatyana walks about slowly, her eyes fixed on the toes of her shoes. Yakov comes on.*

Yakov. Why don't you go to bed?

Tatyana. I don't want to. I think I'll go away from here.

Yakov. You do? There's no place *I* can go. I've already gone past all the continents and islands.

Tatyana. It's depressing here. Everything is rocking on its foundations—it makes your head swim. You have to tell lies, and I dislike that.

Yakov. H'm—you dislike that—to my regret—yes, to my regret—

Tatyana (speaking to herself). But a moment ago I lied. Of course Nadya could have agreed to hide those things—only I have no right to push her onto such a path—

Yakov. Who are you talking about?

Tatyana. I? It's nothing. How strange everything's become. Just a little while ago life was clear, one had definite desires—

Yakov (quietly). Alas, talented drunkards, handsome idlers, and other specialists of gay living no longer arouse interest. So long as we stood outside the tiresome hurly-burly of existence, we were admired. But the hurly-burly is growing more and more dramatic. Somebody is already shouting: "Hey you, comedians and entertainers, get off the stage!" But the stage—that's your province, Tanya.

Tatyana (with disquiet). My province? I thought that as an actress I had solid ground under my feet—that I could reach the heights— *(Wearily yet forcefully.)* I feel uncomfortable, awkward in front of people who stare at me and say with cold eyes, "We know all that. It's old and boring." I feel weak, disarmed in front of them—I can't lay hold of them, arouse them. I want to tremble with fear or joy, I want to speak words charged with fire, passion, wrath—words that are sharp like knives, that burn like torches— I want to toss them lavishly, to strike awe in people! Let the people flare up, shout, rush out. But I can't find such words. Instead I toss them beautiful words, like flowers, words that are full of hope, happiness, love! They all cry—and I with them—we cry such fine tears. They applaud me, smother me with flowers, carry me in their arms. For a moment I reign over the people. In that moment is life—all life packed in one minute! But living words—I can't find.

Yakov. We all know how to live only in moments—

Tatyana. Everything that's best is always in a single moment. How I long for different, more responsive, people—for a different, less trivial, life, a life in which art would be a necessity to all and at all times. How I long not to feel myself unnecessary, superfluous— *Yakov gazes into the darkness, his eyes wide.* Why do you drink so much? It's killing you. You used to be handsome—

Yakov. Drop it—

Tatyana. Do you realize how my heart aches?

Yakov (with a kind of horror). No matter how drunk I may be—I understand everything—that's the hell of it! My brain works on and on, always with devilish insistence. And staring at me I keep seeing a broad, dirty face with enormous eyes which ask me, "Well?" You understand, just the one word, "Well?" *Polina runs on.*

Polina. Tanya! Please, Tanya, go in there. I beg of you. It's Cleopatra—she's gone mad! She's insulting everybody— Maybe you can calm her down.

Tatyana (wearily). Oh, leave me alone with your squabbles! Hurry up and finish each other off, and stop rushing about, stop getting under other people's feet.

Polina (frightened). Tanya! What's happened to you?

Tatyana. What do you want? Tell me.

Polina. But look at her—here she comes.

Zakhar (off stage). I'm asking you, keep quiet.

Cleopatra (off). You're the one who ought to keep quiet in front of me!

Polina. She'll make a disturbance here—and the workers are right over there—it's terrible! Tanya, please— *Zakhar comes on with Cleopatra at his heels.*

Zakhar. For God's sake—I think I'm going mad.

Cleopatra. You won't run away from me—I'll make you listen. You've been playing up to the workers, you want their respect, and you toss them the life of a man like a chunk of meat to vicious dogs. You are humanitarians at other people's expense, at the cost of their blood.

Zakhar. What on earth is she talking about?

Yakov (to Tatyana). You'd better go. (*He leaves.*)

Polina. Madam, we are decent people and cannot permit a woman with a reputation like yours to shout at us.

Zakhar (alarmed). Keep quiet, Polina—for God's sake!

Cleopatra. What makes you think you're decent? Because you prattle about politics? About the sufferings of the people? About progress and humaneness? Is that it?

Tatyana. Cleopatra Petrovna! That's enough!

Cleopatra. I'm not talking to you. You're an outsider here, it's none of your business. My husband was an honest—an upright man. He knew the people better than you. He didn't prattle the way you do. And you, with your vile stupidities, betrayed him—killed him!

Tatyana (to Polina and Zakhar). Will you go, please?

Cleopatra. I'll go myself! I hate you—all of you! (*She goes off.*)

Zakhar. Has anybody ever seen such a crazy female?

Polina (with tears in her eyes). We must leave everything— we must go away. Such insults—

Zakhar. What's got into her? I could understand, if she had been in love with her husband, lived happily with him. But she changes her lovers twice a year—and she shouts!

Polina. We must sell the factory.

Zakhar (with annoyance). Leave, sell—that's no answer. We must think it over—and think well. Now I was just talking with Nikolay Vassilyevich—that female broke in and interrupted us—

Polina. He hates us, this Nikolay Vassilyevich—he's full of venom.

Zakhar (calming down). He's been too embittered and shaken up by what's happened, but he's a man of intelligence, and there's no reason for him to hate us. Right now, with Mikhail's death, there are very practical interests that bind us together —yes.

Polina. I distrust him and I'm afraid of him. He'll cheat you.

Zakhar. Those are little things, Polina. The man has sound judgment. The fact is I chose a questionable position in my relations with the workers—that much has to be admitted. This evening, when I spoke to them— Oh, how hostile these people are, Polina—

Polina. I've been telling you that. They're enemies, always.
*Tatyana walks off, laughing quietly. Polina looks at her
and continues in a deliberately louder tone.*
Everybody is our enemy. Everybody envies us—and pounces on
us because of that.
Zakhar (pacing with quick steps). Yes, there's some truth in
that too, of course. Nikolay Vassilyevich says—it's not a war of
classes, but a war of races, a struggle between the high race
and the low race. That's obviously crude—far-fetched. But when
you begin to think that we, the people of culture, have created
the sciences, arts, and so forth— H'm, equality, physiological
equality—that's all very well. But first you have to be human,
become civilized—after that we can talk of equality.
Polina (intently). That's a new line of thought for you—
Zakhar. It's still too sketchy, not fully thought out. I must get
my own ideas straight—that's what I've got to do.
Polina (taking him by the arm). You're too soft-hearted, my
friend—that's the cause of your troubles.
Zakhar. We know too little and every so often we get a surprise. For example, Sintsov—he surprised me at first, then won
my regard with his great simplicity, his extraordinarily clear
logic. It turns out he's a socialist—that's where the simplicity
and logic come from.
Polina. Yes, he attracts one's attention—such an unpleasant
face. But you ought to get a little rest—come along, dear.
Zakhar (following her). And that workman, Grekov. He's so
terribly cocky. Nikolay Vassilyevich and I were just recalling
his speech. He's barely out of his teens, but how he spoke, with
what arrogance!
*They go off. There are a few moments of quiet. Strains of
a choral song can be heard in the distance. Yagodin, Levshin, and Ryabtsov come on. Ryabtsov is a young fellow
with a good-natured, round face, and a habit of tossing
back his head. The three workmen stop under the trees.*
Levshin (quietly and mysteriously). You and I and all of us,
Pavel, are comrades in this business.
Ryabtsov. I know—
Levshin. It's a common business, a human business. Today,
my boy, every good soul is worth a lot. People are lifting their

minds, listening, reading, thinking— Those who are beginning to understand things are worth a great deal.

Yagodin. That's true, Pavel.

Ryabtsov. I know. I'm ready to go.

Levshin. A man mustn't rush into anything without thinking. You have to understand first. You're young, and this thing means Siberia.

Ryabtsov. It's all right. I'll run away.

Yagodin. It may not be Siberia. For Siberia you're too tender in years, Pavel.

Levshin. We'll say Siberia. In this business the more frightening it is the better. If a man isn't afraid of Siberia, he's made up his mind once and for all.

Ryabtsov. I've made up my mind.

Yagodin. Don't be in a hurry. Think it over.

Ryabtsov. What is there to think about? We killed a man, so somebody has to suffer for it.

Levshin. Truly spoken. Somebody has to. And if one doesn't take it on himself, many others will be bothered—some of the better men among us, men who are more important to our common cause than you are, Pavel.

Ryabtsov. Why, of course, that's just how I feel. I may be young, but I understand we have to hold fast to one another, like a chain.

Levshin (with a sigh). That's it.

Yagodin (smiling). Yes, once we join hands, close in, and give a good push, it's all over for the other party.

Ryabtsov. That's right. No need to talk about it. I'm single, so it's up to me to do it. Only it does turn my stomach to think that it has to be done for the blood of—

Levshin. It's for your comrades, not for anybody's blood.

Ryabtsov. I mean he was such a rotten man—so vicious—

Levshin. It's the vicious one that has to be killed. The kind one will die by himself—he's no trouble to others.

Ryabtsov. Well, is this all?

Yagodin. This is all, Pavel. Tomorrow, then, you'll go and tell them?

Ryabtsov. Why put it off till tomorrow? I said I'm going now.

Levshin. No, you'd better tell them tomorrow. Night is like a mother—it's a kind counselor.

Ryabtsov. That's true enough. All the same, I'm going now.

Levshin. God be with you!

Yagodin. Go, Pavel. And don't let anything stop you.

   Ryabtsov goes off unhurriedly. Yagodin turns his stick over, looking at it intently. Levshin gazes into the sky.

Levshin (quietly). Fine people are growing up today.

Yagodin. Good weather, good crop.

Levshin. If it goes on this way, we'll get our lives straightened out yet.

Yagodin (sadly). I feel sorry for the boy.

Levshin (quietly). Don't you think I am? A fine prospect, having to go to jail, and for something not so very good at that. He has one consolation, though—he's ruining his life for his comrades.

Yagodin. Yes—

Levshin. We'd better not talk about that. Ah, I wish Andrey hadn't pressed that trigger. What can you do by killing? Nothing. You kill one dog, the master buys another—that's all there is to it.

Yagodin (sadly). What a lot of our kind get ruined—

Levshin. Come on, watchman. We've got to guard the master's chattels. (*They start off.*) Oh, Lord!

Yagodin. What's the matter?

Levshin. I'm feeling low. If we could only hurry up and get life straightened out.

CURTAIN

ACT III

A large room in the BARDINS' *house. The rear wall has four windows and a door leading to the veranda. Through the windows can be seen soldiers, gendarmes (members of the secret police), and a group of workers including* LEVSHIN *and* GREKOV. *The room has an uninhabited look: the furniture is sparse and old and consists of odd pieces; the wallpaper hangs loose here and there. A big table stands along the right wall. There is a double door in this wall, and another in the left wall.*

KON *is moving chairs, angrily setting them around the table.* AGRAFENA *is sweeping the floor.*

Agrafena. You have no business being angry with me—

Kon. I'm not angry. I don't give a damn for anybody— I'll be dead soon, thank God. My heart often misses a beat.

Agrafena. We'll all be dead—that's nothing to brag about.

Kon. Well, I've had enough of this—I'm sick of it. At sixty-five nothing but dirty tricks, like nuts to crack—I've no teeth for them. They've rounded up a crowd of people—keep them soaking in the rain—

        Enter, left, Captain Boboyedov and Nikolay.

Boboyedov (cheerfully). Ah, here's the conference room—excellent! So you're to participate in your official capacity?

Nikolay. That's right. Call the Corporal, Kon.

Boboyedov. And this is how we're to serve up this dish? In the center that—what's his name?

Nikolay. Sintsov.

Boboyedov. Sintsov—a touching sight. And around him workers of the world? Fine. It warms the cockles of your heart. Our host, incidentally, is a charming man—very charming. We thought differently of him in our department. I know his sister-in-law—she played at Voronezh—an excellent actress, I must say.   *Kvach enters from veranda.*

Well, how is it, Kvach?

Kvach. We've searched everybody, sir.

Boboyedov. Yes. And what?

Kvach. We've found nothing—they must have hidden it. I wish to report, sir—the Police Inspector is in a hurry and is doing his job carelessly.

Boboyedov. Well, of course. The police are always like that. Has anything been found in the houses of the arrested men?

Kvach. Yes, at Levshin's, behind the icons.

Boboyedov. Take everything to my room.

Kvach. Yes, sir. The young gendarme, sir, who's joined recently—the one from the dragoons—

Boboyedov. What about him?

Kvach. He too is careless in his duties.

Boboyedov. Well, you'd better handle him yourself. You can go.   *Kvach leaves.*
This Kvach is a character, you know. Nothing much to look at and even a bit stupid, you'd think. But he can smell things out like a dog.

Nikolay. You ought to take notice of that office clerk, Bogdan Denisovich.

Boboyedov. Oh, certainly, certainly. We'll put the screws on him.

Nikolay. I'm talking about Pologhy, not Sintsov. I think he can be useful in the future.

Boboyedov. You mean the man we had a talk with? Of course, we'll take care of him.

Nikolay walks to the table and carefully lays out papers on it. Enter Cleopatra, right.

Cleopatra (at the threshold). Will you have more tea, Captain?

Boboyedov. Thank you. I shall be glad to. It's beautiful here. A delightful spot. By the way, I know Madame Lugovaya. She played at Voronezh, didn't she?

Cleopatra. I believe she did. And how are you making out with your house-to-house search? Have you found anything?

Boboyedov (gallantly). Everything, everything. You don't have to worry. Even when there's nothing in the place something is always—found.

Cleopatra. My late husband thought very little of all these secret handbills. He used to say, paper doesn't make a revolution—

Boboyedov. H'm—that's not altogether true.

Cleopatra. He called the handbills instructions to fools from the secret office of plain idiots.

Boboyedov. That's neat, though also wrong.

Cleopatra. And now from papers they've passed to deeds.

Boboyedov. Rest assured they'll be severely punished—most severely.

Cleopatra. That gives me great comfort. Your presence here has instantly made me feel relieved—more free.

Boboyedov. It's our duty to bring cheer to society.

Cleopatra. And it's such a pleasure to see a contented, healthy man—it's such a rare sight.

Boboyedov. Oh, in our force we have only picked men.

Cleopatra. Let's go into the dining room.

Boboyedov (following her). Delighted. Tell me, where's Madame Lugovaya playing this season?

Cleopatra. I don't know.

   They go off. Tatyana and Nadya enter from the veranda.

Nadya (excitedly). Did you notice the look the old man—Levshin—gave us?

Tatyana. I did.

Nadya. Oh, it's all so bad, so shameful! Nikolay Vassilyevich, what's the reason for all this? Why have they been arrested?

Nikolay (dryly). There are more than enough reasons for their arrests. And I'll also ask you not to walk across the veranda while those men are there.

Nadya. We won't.

Tatyana (staring at Nikolay). Is Sintsov under arrest too?

Nikolay. Mr. Sintsov is under arrest too.

Nadya (pacing the room). Seventeen men. Out there, outside the gate, their wives are crying—and the soldiers shove them around, laugh at them. Tell the soldiers to behave decently.

Nikolay. I have nothing to do with that. The soldiers are under the command of Lieutenant Strepetov.

Nadya. I'll go ask him—

   She goes out through the door, right. Tatyana walks up to to the table, smiling.

Tatyana. Now then, you cemetery of laws, as the General calls you—

Nikolay. The General doesn't strike me as a man of wit. I wouldn't repeat his smart sayings.

Tatyana. I made a mistake—he calls you the coffin of laws. Does it annoy you?

Nikolay. I'm just not in the mood for joking.

Tatyana. You're not as serious as all that?

Nikolay. May I remind you—my brother was killed yesterday.

Tatyana. How does that affect *you?*

Nikolay. What do you mean?

Tatyana (with a little laugh). Let's not put on an act. You're not sorry for your brother. You're not sorry for anybody—just as I'm not. Death, or rather the suddenness of death, upsets everybody. But I assure you, never for a single instant were you sorry for your brother with true human compassion—you don't have it in you.

Nikolay (with an effort). That's very interesting. But what do you want of me?

Tatyana. Have you noticed that you and I are kindred spirits? No? That's a pity. I'm an actress, a cold creature anxious only for one thing—to play a good part. You too want to play a good part and you too are without a soul. Tell me, you want to be a full-fledged district attorney, don't you?

Nikolay (in a low voice). I want you to end this conversation—

Tatyana (pauses, then laughs). No, I've no gift for diplomacy. I had a definite object in mind when I set out to talk to you— I wanted to be extra nice to you—fascinating. But as soon as I saw you I began to make impertinent remarks. You always stir up a desire in me to heap words on you that hurt—whether you be walking or sitting, talking or denouncing people in silence. Oh, yes, I wanted to ask you for something—

Nikolay (with a curt laugh). I can guess what it is.

Tatyana. Probably. But it's useless to ask for it now, I suppose?

Nikolay. Now or earlier—it doesn't make any difference. Mr. Sintsov is compromised too much.

Tatyana. It gives you a certain pleasure to tell me this, doesn't it?

Nikolay. I won't deny it—it does.

Tatyana (with a sigh). You see how alike we are! I too am very petty and spiteful. Tell me, is Sintsov entirely in your hands—in nobody else's but yours?

Nikolay. Of course.

Tatyana. What if I ask you to release him?

Nikolay. It'll be futile.

Tatyana. Even if I make a very special appeal?

Nikolay. Even so. You surprise me, really.

Tatyana. Do I? Why?

Nikolay. You're beautiful—you're unquestionably a woman of an original turn of mind—one senses character in you. You have innumerable opportunities to make a luxurious, beautiful life for yourself—and you occupy yourself with a nonentity. Eccentricity is a disease. Every intelligent man must regard you with indignation. Anyone who prizes womanhood, who loves beauty, will never forgive you such eccentric conduct!

Tatyana. So I'm condemned—alas! And Sintsov, too?

Nikolay. The gentleman will go to jail tonight.

Tatyana. Is that settled?

Nikolay. Yes.

Tatyana. And no concessions to please a lady? I don't believe it. If I wanted it very much, you would let Sintsov go.

Nikolay (in a tight voice). Try it—just try.

Tatyana. I can't—bring myself to it. Still, tell me the truth—it's not difficult to tell the truth once—would you have released him?

Nikolay (after a pause). I don't know.

Tatyana. I do. (*After a pause, with a sigh.*) What rotters both of us are!

Nikolay. There are things, you know, which even a woman can't be forgiven.

Tatyana (casually). Oh, fiddlesticks! We're alone—nobody can hear us. After all, I have the right to tell you and myself that we're both—

Nikolay. Please—I don't want to listen to you.

Tatyana (insistently and calmly). All the same, you set the value of your principles below that of a woman's kiss.

Nikolay. I've told you I don't want to listen to you.

Tatyana (calmly). Then go. I'm not holding you, am I?

Nikolay hurries off. Tatyana wraps herself in her shawl and, standing in the middle of the room, gazes out at the veranda. Enter, left, Nadya and the Lieutenant.

Lieutenant. The soldier never hurts a woman, I give you my word of honor. To him a woman is something sacred.

Nadya. You'll see for yourself.

Lieutenant. It's impossible. The army is the only place where a woman is still treated with chivalry.

They walk across and out the door, left. Enter Polina, Zakhar, and Yakov.

Zakhar. You see, Yakov—

Polina. But think, what else could be done?

Zakhar. We have to face the facts, the necessities of the situation—

Tatyana. What's this?

Yakov. He's raking me over the coals—

Polina. Such extraordinary cruelty! Everybody's pouncing on us. Even Yakov Ivanovich, who's always so gentle. But was it we who called the soldiers? Nor did anybody invite the gendarmes. They always come by themselves.

Zakhar. To accuse us of these arrests—

Yakov. I'm not accusing you—

Zakhar. You don't say it in so many words, but I feel it—

Yakov (to Tatyana). I was sitting. Zakhar walked up to me and said, "How are you feeling, old man?" And I said, "I'm disgusted, old man." That was all.

Zakhar. But you have to understand that socialistic propaganda, the way it's carried on in Russia, is impossible, is intolerable anywhere—

Polina. Take part in politics—yes, we all should—but what's that got to do with socialism? That's what Zakhar says. And he's right.

Yakov (dejectedly). Now what sort of a socialist is old Levshin? He's simply overworked and talks deliriously—from fatigue.

Zakhar. They're all delirious.

Polina. One must show some consideration for other people's feelings. It's been such torture for us.

Zakhar. You think it doesn't upset me to see a tribunal being set up in my house? But all this is Nikolay Vassilyevich's idea, and it would have been impossible to argue with him after such a tragedy.   *Cleopatra enters hurriedly.*

Cleopatra. Have you heard? The murderer has been found. They'll be bringing him in here pretty soon.

Yakov (muttering to himself). There it is—

Tatyana. Who is he?

Cleopatra. Some youngster. I'm glad. Probably, it's wrong from the humanitarian point of view, but I'm glad all the same. And seeing that he's a youngster, I'd have him flogged every day until the trial. Where's Nikolay Vassilyevich? Have you seen him?

She walks toward the door, left, as the General enters by the same door.

General (sullenly). Well, well—all standing around like wet hens.

Zakhar. It's an unpleasant situation, Uncle.

General. What? The gendarmes? Yes, this Captain is a regular bounder. I'd like to play a trick on him. Are they staying here for the night?

Polina. I don't think so. What for?

General. That's a pity. It would be a good idea to dump a bucket of cold water on him when he goes to sleep. They used to do that to lily-livered cadets in my school days. It's terribly funny when a naked man dripping with water starts jumping and yelling.

Cleopatra (standing at the door). God knows what you're saying, General. And what reasons have you? The Captain is a very decent man and wonderfully active. He came here and rounded up everybody. We have to appreciate that. (*She goes off.*)

General. H'm—in her eyes all men with long mustaches are decent. What I say is everybody must know his place. Decency is precisely that. (*Walks to the door, left.*) Hey, Kon! (*Exits.*)

Polina (in a low voice). She positively feels herself mistress here. Look how she behaves—so ill mannered—so rude!

Zakhar. I wish it would be all over soon. I want peace, rest, a normal life.   *Nadya rushes on.*

Nadya. Aunt Tanya, he's a fool, that Lieutenant. And he probably beats the soldiers. He shouts, makes terrifying faces— Uncle, something must be done to let the women see and talk

to their arrested husbands—five of them have wives. You go
tell the Captain—he's in charge here.

Zakhar. You see, Nadya—

Nadya. I see that you're not going. Go, please, tell him.
They're crying out there. Oh, do go.

Zakhar. I'm afraid it's useless. (*He goes off.*)

Polina. You, Nadya, are always disturbing everybody.

Nadya. It's you who are disturbing everybody.

Polina. We? Are you in your senses?

Nadya (*excitedly*). All of us—I, and you, and Uncle—it's we
who disturb everybody. We do nothing, and are responsible for
all that—the soldiers, the gendarmes, and everything. These
arrests too—and the women crying—it's all because of us!

Tatyana. Come here, Nadya.

Nadya (*walking over to her*). Here I am. Well?

Tatyana. Sit down and calm yourself. You don't understand
anything, nor can you do anything.

Nadya. And you can't even say anything. No, I don't want to
calm myself—I don't want to.

Polina. Your dead mother was right about you—you're an
impossible character.

Nadya. Yes, she was right. She worked and earned her bread.
And you—what work do you do? Whose bread do you eat?

Polina. There it goes! I must ask you to stop talking in this
tone, Nadya. What is all this shouting at your elders?

Nadya. You're no elders. Now, really, what sort of elders are
you? You're just old, that's all.

Polina. It's really your ideas, Tanya. And you must tell her
she's a stupid girl.

Tatyana. Did you hear? You're a stupid girl. (*She strokes
Nadya's shoulder.*)

Nadya. There you are. That's all you can say. That's all. You
can't even defend yourself— Extraordinary people! Really,
you're all unnecessary—unnecessary even here, in your own
house.

Polina (*sharply*). Do you realize what you're saying?

Nadya. Your house has been invaded by gendarmes, soldiers,
fools with mustaches, who give orders, drink tea, rattle their
sabers, clank their spurs, laugh—and seize people, shout at
them, threaten them, make women cry— And you? What say

have you got in all this? You've been simply pushed aside into the corners—

Polina. You're talking sheer nonsense. These people have come to defend us.

Nadya (sadly). Oh, Auntie! The soldiers can't defend anybody from stupidity—they just can't.

Polina (indignantly). What's that?

Nadya (stretching out her hands to Polina). Don't be angry with me! I said that meaning everybody. (*Polina hurries out of the room.*) There—she's run away. She'll complain to Uncle that I'm rude, unmanageable— Uncle will make a long speech—and all the flies will die of boredom.

Tatyana (reflectively). How are you going to live? I can't see it.

Nadya (drawing a circle around herself with her hands). Not like this. Never. I don't know what I'll do, but I'll never do things the way you do. I was just crossing the veranda with that officer—and Grekov is standing there smoking, and he gives me a look—and his eyes are laughing. Yet he knows he's going to be sent to jail, doesn't he? You see? The ones who live as they please aren't afraid of anything. They're jolly. I'm ashamed to look at Levshin and Grekov— I don't know the others, but these two—these I'll never forget. Here comes the fool with a mustache—ooh!   *Enter Boboyedov.*

Boboyedov. How frightening! Who is it you're trying to scare?

Nadya. I'm afraid of you. You will let the women see their husbands, won't you?

Boboyedov. No, I won't. I'm spiteful.

Nadya. Of course, seeing you're a gendarme. Why don't you want to let the women in?

Boboyedov (gallantly). Right now it's impossible. But later, before the men are taken away, I'll permit them to say good-by.

Nadya. Why is it impossible? It rests with you, doesn't it?

Boboyedov. Yes, with me, or rather with the law.

Nadya. Oh, bother the law! Let them in, I beg of you.

Boboyedov. The law is a bother, is it? So you too do not recognize laws? Dear me!

Nadya. Don't talk to me like that. I'm not a child.

Boboyedov. I don't believe it. Only children and revolutionists don't recognize laws.

Nadya. Then I'm a revolutionist.

Boboyedov (laughing). Oh, in that case I'll have to arrest you and send you to jail.

Nadya (wearily). Oh, please stop joking. Do let them in.

Boboyedov. I can't. The law!

Nadya. An idiotic law!

Boboyedov (seriously). H'm—you mustn't say that. If you're not a child, as you claim, you must know that laws are laid down by the supreme authorities, and that no state can exist without them.

Nadya (with feeling). Laws, authorities, state— Great heavens! But aren't they all for the people?

Boboyedov. H'm—I guess so. But first of all for maintaining order.

Nadya. But it's all worthless, if people are made to cry. Your authorities and your state—they are all unnecessary, if people cry. The state—what a stupid thing! What do I need it for? (*Walks toward the door.*) The state! You don't understand a thing, and still you talk. (*Goes off.*)

Boboyedov (somewhat nonplussed, to Tatyana). An original young lady. But a dangerous trend of mind. Her uncle, I believe, is a man of liberal views, isn't he?

Tatyana. You ought to know that better than I. I don't know what a man of liberal views means.

Boboyedov. Why, everybody knows that. A lack of respect for the authorities—and you have liberalism. You know, Madame Lugovaya, I saw you at Voronezh—yes. I greatly enjoyed your acting—it was so subtle, so extraordinarily subtle. You may have noticed, I always had a seat next to the lieutenant governor's. I was an adjutant at our local headquarters then.

Tatyana. I don't remember. It's possible. There are gendarmes in every town, aren't there?

Boboyedov. I should say there are. In every town, absolutely. And I must tell you that we, the administration, more than anybody else, are the true connoisseurs of art. Perhaps, the merchant class too. For example, take the subscriptions for a gift to a favorite actor on his benefit night—on the subscription list you'll always find names of the officers of the gendarmerie. That's a tradition with us, so to speak. Where will you be playing this coming season?

Tatyana. I haven't decided yet. But, of course, it'll have to be in a town which has true connoisseurs of art. That can't be avoided, can it?

Boboyedov (*missing the point*). Oh, of course. They exist in every town, absolutely. After all, people are getting more cultured—

Kvach (*speaking from the veranda*). Sir, the man who fired the shot is being brought here. What are your orders?

Boboyedov. Bring him in—and all the rest of them, too. Call the assistant district attorney. (*To Tatyana.*) Pardon me. I have to attend to my business for a little while.

Tatyana. Are you going to question them?

Boboyedov (*gallantly*). Just scratch the surface, by way of making their acquaintance. A little roll call, so to speak.

Tatyana. May I hear it?

Boboyedov. H'm—as a rule we don't allow it—in political cases. But this is a criminal case, we're not in our office, and I'm anxious to do something that will give you pleasure.

Tatyana. I'll keep out of sight. I'll watch from over there.

Boboyedov. Excellent. I'm very happy to be able to repay you in some little way for all the pleasure I had in watching you on the stage. I only have to get some papers.

> *He goes off. Two middle-aged workers bring Ryabtsov in. Walking alongside them and casting glances at Ryabtsov is Kon. Following them are Levshin, Yagodin, Grekov, and several other workers. A few gendarmes bring up the procession.*

Ryabtsov (*angrily*). Why did you tie my hands? Untie them, will you?

Levshin. Untie his hands, fellows. Why hurt the man's feelings?

Yagodin. He won't run away.

First Worker. That's the rule. The law says to tie them up.

Ryabtsov. I don't like it. Take it off.

Second Worker (*to Kvach*). Officer, do you mind? He's a quiet fellow. We can't understand ourselves how he did it.

Kvach. You may untie him. It's all right.

Kon (*suddenly*). You've made a mistake seizing him. At the time of the shooting down there he was on the river—I saw him, and so did the General. (*To Ryabtsov.*) Why do you keep mum, you fool? Tell them it wasn't you who fired. Why don't you speak up?

Ryabtsov (*firmly*). No, it was me.

Levshin. He ought to know, officer.

Ryabtsov. I did it.

Kon (*shouting*). You lie, you dirty troublemaker—

                  Enter Boboyedov and Nikolay Skrobotov.

Why, that very hour you were boating on the river and singing songs.

Ryabtsov (*calmly*). I did that—afterward.

Boboyedov. This one?

Kvach. Yes, sir.

Kon. No, he didn't.

Boboyedov. What's that? Take the old man away, Kvach. Who's he?

Kvach. He's with the General, sir.

Nikolay (*regarding Ryabtsov closely*). Just a moment, Bogdan Denisovich. Leave him alone, Kvach.

Kon. Keep your hands off! I'm a soldier myself.

Boboyedov. Stop it, Kvach.

Nikolay (*to Ryabtsov*). Did *you* kill the director?

Ryabtsov. I did.

Nikolay. Why?

Ryabtsov. He bullied us.

Nikolay. What's your name?

Ryabtsov. Pavel Ryabtsov.

Nikolay. All right. Kon, what were you saying?

Kon (*excited*). He's not the killer. He was out boating on the river at the time. I'll take an oath on it. The General and I saw him. The General even said: It would be a fine thing, he said, if we could upset the boat and make him take a dip—yes. You damn puppy! What are you up to?

Nikolay. What makes you so certain, Kon, that he was on the river at the moment the murder was committed?

Kon. You couldn't get from the factory to the spot he was in even in an hour.

Ryabtsov. I ran.

Kon. He was rowing and singing songs. After you've killed a man, you don't sing.

Nikolay (*to Ryabtsov*). You know that the law punishes

severely anyone who commits perjury and attempts to screen a criminal—you know that, don't you?

Ryabtsov. It's all the same to me.

Nikolay. All right. So it was you who killed the director?

Ryabtsov. Yes, it was me

Boboyedov. What a wild cub!

Kon. Liar.

Levshin. You keep out of this, my friend. You're an outsider here.

Nikolay. What's that?

Levshin. I say he's an outsider here but keeps butting in.

Nikolay. And you are not an outsider? Are you connected with this murder?

Levshin (laughing). Me? Why, sir, I once killed a hare with a stick, and I was miserable afterward.

Nikolay. Then hold your tongue! (*To Ryabtsov.*) Where's the revolver with which you fired the shot?

Ryabtsov. I don't know.

Nikolay. What was it like? Describe it.

Ryabtsov (baffled). What was it like? The kind they usually are—an ordinary one.

Kon (jubilantly). Oh, the son of a bitch! He didn't even see the revolver.

Nikolay. How big was it? (*Holds his hands to show the length of a foot.*) So big? Yes?

Ryabtsov. Yes—a little smaller.

Nikolay (to Boboyedov). Bogdan Denisovich, come here please. (*Lowering his voice.*) There's some dirty work here. The boy requires sterner treatment. Let's leave him until the court investigator comes over.

Boboyedov. But he's confessing his crime—what more do you want?

Nikolay (impressively). You and I have a suspicion that this boy is not the actual murderer, but a dummy, you follow me?

Yakov, drunk, enters cautiously by the door near Tatyana and looks on in silence. Now and then his head drops helplessly as if he were dozing off. Tossing his head back, he gazes about with frightened eyes.

Boboyedov (not getting the point). Oh, I see—yes, yes. Imagine that.

Nikolay. It's a plot—a joint crime.

Boboyedov. What a blackguard, eh?

Nikolay. Let the Corporal take him away for the present—and keep him completely isolated. I'm going to leave you for a minute. Kon, I want you to come with me. Where's the General?

Kon. He's digging worms.   *Nikolay and Kon go off.*

Boboyedov. Take this fellow away, Kvach. And keep a close watch on him—understand?

Kvach. Yes, sir. Come along, young man.

Levshin (affectionately). Good-by, Pavel. Good-by, son.

Yagodin (grimly). Good-by, Pavel, my boy.

Ryabtsov. Good-by. It's all right.

Boboyedov (to Levshin). Do you know him, old man?

Levshin. Naturally. We work together.

Boboyedov. What's your name?

Levshin. Yefim Levshin.

Boboyedov (to Tatyana, in a low voice). Just watch this. I want you, Levshin, to tell me the truth—you're a sensible old man, so you realize you must speak only the truth to a representative of the authorities—

Levshin. Why tell lies?

Boboyedov (highly pleased). Good. Now tell me honestly, what have you got hidden behind the icons in your house? Tell the truth.

Levshin (calmly). I haven't got anything.

Boboyedov. Is that the truth?

Levshin. It must be.

Boboyedov. Oh, Levshin, you ought to be ashamed of yourself. You've turned bald, and your hair is gray, and still you lie like a boy. Don't you realize that the authorities know not only what you do but even what you think? That's bad, Levshin. Now what's this I'm holding in my hand?

Levshin. I can't see very well—my eyesight isn't too good.

Boboyedov. I'll tell you—these are pamphlets forbidden by the government, which call upon people to rise against their sovereign. These pamphlets were found behind the icons in your house. Well?

Levshin (calmly). I see.

Boboyedov. Do you admit they are yours?

Levshin. Maybe they are mine. They all look alike.

Boboyedov. Then why do you, at your age, tell lies?

Levshin. Why, sir, I told you the absolute truth. You asked me what was behind the icons. And if you're asking me that, then there's nothing there—it's been taken out. And that's what I told you. There's nothing there. There was no call to shame me. I didn't deserve it.

Boboyedov (abashed). Oh, so? Well, let's have less of your talk—I'm not standing for any nonsense. Who gave you these pamphlets?

Levshin. Why should you know that? I won't tell you that. I don't even remember where they came from. No, you better not trouble yourself about that.

Boboyedov. Oh, so? All right. Alexey Grekov. Which one is Grekov?

Grekov. That's me.

Boboyedov. Did you come under investigation in connection with revolutionary propaganda among the workers at Smolensk?

Grekov. I did.

Boboyedov. Talents like these at such a young age? Glad to make your acquaintance. Oh, it's too stuffy here. Gendarmes, take the men out on the veranda. (*Checking the prisoners by the list in his hand.*) Vyrypayev, Yakov? I see. Svistov, Andrey?

The gendarmes lead the arrested men to the veranda.
Boboyedov, papers in hand, follows them.

Yakov (quietly). I like these men.

Tatyana. Yes. But why are they so simple? Why do they talk so simply, look at things so simply? Is it because they have no passion, no heroism in them?

Yakov. They have a calm faith in their rightness.

Tatyana. I'm sure they have passion—and I'm sure they have heroes. But at this point you get the feeling they despise everybody.

Yakov. Levshin is a fine fellow. What understanding eyes he has, so sad and so caressing! He seems to be saying, "Why all this? Why don't you step aside and give us freedom?"

Zakhar peeps in through the door.

Zakhar. These representatives of the law are amazingly stupid. They've set up a tribunal here—Nikolay struts about with the air of a conqueror—

Yakov. What is it that bothers you, Zakhar—only the fact that all this business is taking place before your eyes?

Zakhar. Of course. They could have spared me this pleasure. Nadya has gone completely berserk. She's been making insolent remarks to Polina and me, she called Cleopatra a shark, and now she's rolling on the divan blubbering. God knows what's going on here.

Yakov (reflectively). As for me, Zakhar, I begin to get more and more disgusted with the meaning of what's going on.

Zakhar. Yes, I understand. But what can we do? If you're attacked, you have to defend yourself. I simply can't find a place for myself in this house—it's as though everything had been turned upside down. It's damp today, cold—this rain! Autumn is coming on early.

Zakhar goes off. Enter Nikolay and Cleopatra, both agitated.

Nikolay. I'm convinced now that he's been paid to do it.

Cleopatra. They couldn't have thought it up themselves. You have to look for the hand of a clever man here.

Nikolay. You mean Sintsov?

Cleopatra. Who else? Here's Captain Boboyedov—

Boboyedov (from the veranda). At your service.

Nikolay. I'm thoroughly convinced now that the boy has been bribed. (*He continues in a whisper.*)

Boboyedov (in a low voice). Oh? H'mm—

Cleopatra (to Boboyedov). You do see, don't you?

Boboyedov. Y-yes— What scoundrels!

Continuing this conversation, Nikolay and Boboyedov disappear into the next room. Cleopatra, glancing around, notices Tatyana.

Cleopatra. Oh, you're here?

Tatyana. Has anything new happened?

Cleopatra. I don't think it will interest you. Have you heard about Sintsov?

Tatyana. I know all that.   *Yakov leaves the room.*

Cleopatra (challengingly). Yes, he's under arrest. I'm glad all these weeds have been pulled up out of the factory at last. Aren't you glad?

Tatyana. I doubt whether you care much how I feel.

Cleopatra (with malicious joy). You rather liked this Sintsov. (*As she stares at Tatyana, her face grows softer.*) What a strange look you have. Your face seems to be worn out too. What's the matter?

Tatyana. It's probably the weather.

Cleopatra (going over to her). Look—perhaps it's stupid, but I'm a forthright person. I've lived through a lot of things. I've felt a lot too—and that's made me bitter. I know only a woman can be a friend to another woman—

Tatyana. Did you want to ask me something?

Cleopatra. To tell you, not ask. I like you. You're so free, always so smartly dressed—and you hold your own so well with men. I envy you the way you talk and walk. But at times I don't like you—even hate you.

Tatyana. That's interesting. Why?

Cleopatra. Who are you, anyway?

Tatyana. What do you mean?

Cleopatra. I can't make you out. I want to see everybody completely defined. I like to know what a person wants. In my opinion, people who don't have a clear idea of what they want are dangerous. They can't be trusted.

Tatyana. Such strange talk. Why do I need to know your opinions?

Cleopatra (intensely, in a tone tinged with alarm). We all need to live closely, like one family, so we can trust one another. You see they're beginning to kill us, to rob us. Have you noticed what cutthroat faces those prisoners have? They know what they want—they certainly do. And they live like one family, they trust one another. I hate them. I fear them. Yet we all live fighting one another, without faith in anything, without any common ties, each going his own way. We rely on gendarmes and soldiers, they rely on themselves, and they're stronger than we are.

Tatyana. I, too, would like to ask you a straight question. Were you happy with your husband?

Cleopatra. Why do you want to know that?

Tatyana. I'm just curious.

Cleopatra (after a pause). No. He was always busy with outside things.   *Enter Polina.*

Polina. Have you heard? That clerk Sintsov has turned out to be a socialist. And Zakhar was always so open with him and even wanted to make him an assistant bookkeeper. Mere trifles, of course, but think how difficult life is becoming. Right beside you are people who are your enemies by conviction, but you fail to recognize them.

Tatyana. I'm glad I'm not rich.

Polina. I'd like to hear you say that when you're old. (*To Cleopatra, softly.*) Cleopatra Petrovna, your dressmaker wants you to try on your dress again. And they've also sent you some black crepe—

Cleopatra. I'm coming. My pulse has been fluttering. I dislike being ill.

Polina. I can give you some drops for the palpitations. They help.

Cleopatra. Thank you. (*She goes off.*)

Polina (*after her*). I'll be right with you. (*To Tatyana.*) One has to be gentle with her, it calms her. I'm glad you've had a talk with her. And generally speaking, I envy you, Tanya— you're always able to take up such a convenient middle position. Well, I'll go give her some drops.

> *Polina goes off. Tatyana looks out at the prisoners on the veranda. Yakov peeps through the door.*

Yakov (*with a broad smile*). You know, I was standing behind the door listening.

Tatyana (*distractedly*). They say it's not nice—to eavesdrop.

Yakov. It's not wise to listen to what people say in any case. You feel sorry for them. Now listen, Tanya, I'm going away.

Tatyana. Where to?

Yakov. Anywhere. I don't know myself yet. Good-by.

Tatyana (*gently*). Good-by. Write to me.

Yakov. It's awfully unpleasant here.

Tatyana. When are you leaving?

Yakov (*with a strange smile*). Today. You ought to go too —eh?

Tatyana. Yes, I'll go. Why are you smiling?

Yakov. Oh—because. We may never meet again.

Tatyana. Nonsense.

Yakov. Well, forgive me. (*Tatyana kisses him on the forehead. He laughs quietly, pushing her away.*) You kissed me as if I were dead.

*He walks off slowly. Tatyana looks after him and makes a
movement to follow, but checks herself with a slight wave
of her hand. Nadya comes in, carrying an umbrella.*

Nadya. Please, come out with me into the garden, Auntie. I
have a headache. I've just been crying and crying—like a fool.
If I go alone, I'll start to cry again.

Tatyana. What's there to cry about, my girl? Nothing.

Nadya. It's so annoying. I can't understand a thing. Who's
in the right? Uncle says he is—but I don't feel it. Is Uncle kind?
I was sure he was. Now I don't know. When he talks to me I
begin to seem spiteful and stupid to myself. But when I begin
to think about him—and ask myself all sorts of questions—I
just feel lost.

Tatyana (*sadly*). If you start asking yourself questions, you'll
turn into a revolutionist—and be destroyed in this chaos, my
darling.

Nadya. One has to be something. (*Tatyana laughs quietly.*)
Why do you laugh? One has to be. One can't live and blink his
eyes, understanding nothing.

Tatyana. I laughed because everybody's been saying that
today—everybody all of a sudden.

*As they start to move off, the General and the Lieutenant
enter. The Lieutenant smartly makes way for the ladies.*

General. The mobilization is necessary, Lieutenant. It has a
double purpose. (*To Nadya and Tatyana.*) Where are you off
to?

Tatyana. For a stroll.

General. If you meet that clerk—what's his name? Lieutenant, what's the name of the man I introduced to you today?

Lieutenant. Polo—Pollute-sky, I think, Your Excellency.

General (*to Tatyana*). Send him over to me—I'll be in the
dining room drinking tea with cognac and with the Lieutenant— Ho-ho-ho! (*Looks around, covering his mouth with his
hand.*) Thank you, Lieutenant. You have a good memory. An
excellent thing to have. An officer must remember the name and
face of every man in his company. A soldier who's just been
drafted is a cunning animal—a cunning, lazy, and stupid animal.
The officer gets inside his soul and turns everything there the
way he wants—he makes an animal into a man who is intelligent and loyal to his duty—

Zakhar comes in, looking worried.

Zakhar. Have you seen Yakov, Uncle?

General. I haven't seen Yakov. Is there some tea in there?

Zakhar. Yes.

The General and the Lieutenant go off. Kon, looking angry and disheveled, enters from the veranda.

Have you seen my brother, Kon?

Kon (severely). No. I'm through telling people things. If I see a man, I won't say anything. I'll hold my tongue. No more. I've done enough talking in my life—   *Enter Polina.*

Polina. The peasants have just come. They're asking for more time to pay their rent.

Zakhar. What next! They certainly picked a moment—

Polina. They're complaining that the crops have been bad and they have no money.

Zakhar. They're always complaining. Have you run into Yakov anywhere?

Polina. No. What am I to tell them then?

Zakhar. The peasants? Let them go to the office. I don't want to see them.

Polina. But there's nobody in the office. You know yourself this house is in a state of complete anarchy. It's almost dinner time, but this Captain keeps asking for tea. The samovar has been in the dining room since morning, and all in all our life seems to have turned into some kind of a circus.

Zakhar. You know, Yakov has suddenly decided to go away somewhere.

Polina. You'll forgive me, but really I'm glad he's leaving.

Zakhar. Yes, of course. He's very irritating—talks awful nonsense. Just a few minutes ago he got hold of me and began asking if my revolver was any good for shooting crows. He went on very insolently and then walked off with the revolver— Always drunk—

From the veranda enter Sintsov, escorted by two gendarmes, and Kvach. Polina gives Sintsov a silent look through her lorgnette and walks off. Zakhar adjusts his spectacles with some embarrassment and moves aside.

Well, Mr. Sintsov—it's all so sad. I'm very, very sorry for you.

Sintsov (with a smile). Don't trouble—it's not worth it.

Zakhar. Yes, it is. People must feel sympathy for one another.

Even if a man I trust has not justified my trust, all the same, seeing him struck by misfortune, I deem it my duty to feel sympathy for him—yes. Good-by, Mr. Sintsov.

Sintsov. Good-by.

Zakhar. Have you any—grievances against me?

Sintsov. Not a thing.

Zakhar (abashed). That's fine. Good-by. Your salary will be forwarded to you—yes. (*Speaking to himself, as he walks off.*) But this is impossible. My house has been turned into an office of the secret police.

> *Sintsov half laughs. All this time Kvach has been regarding him intently, paying particular attention to his hands. Noticing this, Sintsov fixes Kvach with his eyes for a few seconds. Kvach chuckles.*

Sintsov. Well? What's the matter?

Kvach. Oh, it's nothing—nothing at all.   *Enter Boboyedov.*

Boboyedov. Mr. Sintsov, you will presently proceed to town.

Kvach (joyfully). Sir, he's not Mr. Sintsov at all, but quite a different article.

Boboyedov. What's that? Explain yourself.

Kvach. I know the gentleman. He used to be at the Bryansk works and his name there was Maxim Markov. We arrested him there two years ago, sir. On his left hand, on the thumb, he has no nail. I know. He must have escaped from some place if he's living under a different name.

Boboyedov (pleasantly surprised). Is this true, Mr. Sintsov?

Kvach. It's all true, sir.

Boboyedov. So you are not Sintsov, my—my!

Sintsov. Whoever I may be, you have to be civil with me—don't forget that.

Boboyedov. My, my! One can see at once one's dealing with a man who means business. Kvach, you'll take him to town yourself. And watch out!

Kvach. Yes, sir.

Boboyedov (happily). Well then, Mr. Sintsov, or whatever your name is, you're going to town. You, Kvach, will immediately make a report to the chief, telling all you know about him. The file on the old case is to be asked for immediately—however, I'll do that myself. Wait here, Kvach. (*Goes off hurriedly.*)

Kvach (*good-humoredly*). So we meet again?

Sintsov (*smiling*). Are you pleased?

Kvach. Of course, an old acquaintance.

Sintsov (*disdainfully*). It's time you gave up this business. You with your gray hairs, tracking down people like a hound. Don't you find it humiliating?

Kvach (*good-humoredly*). It's all right, I'm used to it. I've held this job for twenty-three years. And I'm not a hound. My superiors respect me—they've promised me a medal. I'll get it now.

Sintsov. For me?

Kvach. For you. Where did you escape from?

Sintsov. You'll find out in due time.

Kvach. We certainly will. Do you remember there used to be a man at the Bryansk works—he was dark and wore spectacles? Savitsky was his name, a teacher? He was arrested again recently too. Only he died in prison. He was very sick. There aren't very many of you, I must say.

Sintsov. There will be—you just wait.

Kvach. Oh? That's fine. The more political offenders there are, the better for us.

Sintsov. You'll be getting awards more often?

> *Boboyedov, the General, the Lieutenant, Cleopatra, and Nikolay appear at the door.*

Nikolay (*glancing at Sintsov*). I felt it. (*He disappears.*)

General. Fine specimen, isn't he?

Cleopatra. Now one can understand where it all came from.

Sintsov (*ironically*). Look here, monsieur gendarme, don't you think your behavior is stupid?

Boboyedov. Don't give me lessons!

Sintsov (*insistently*). Yes, I will give you lessons. Stop this idiotic show!

General. Well, I like that!

Boboyedov (*shouting*). Kvach, take him out.

Kvach. Yes, sir. (*Leads Sintsov off.*)

General. He must be a wild animal, eh? How he—roars, eh?

Cleopatra. I'm convinced he's at the bottom of everything.

Boboyedov. It's possible—very possible.

Lieutenant. He will be tried, I take it?

Boboyedov (*with a chuckle*). We eat them without any legal sauce—and it's a treat, I tell you.

General. That's clever. Like oysters— (*With a snap of his jaws.*) Op!   *Enter Kon.*

Boboyedov. Exactly. Well, Your Excellency, now we'll quickly sort out the game and you won't be bothered with this comedy any longer. Nikolay Vassilyevich, where are you?

All except Kon withdraw. The Police Inspector enters from the veranda.

Police Inspector (*to Kon*). Are the prisoners to be questioned here?

Kon (*sullenly*). I don't know. I don't know anything.

Police Inspector. Table—papers—it must be here. (*Calls out to the veranda.*) Bring them all in. (*To Kon.*) The dead man made a mistake. He said a red-haired man shot him, but it turns out it was a dark-haired one.

Kon (*muttering*). Live men too make mistakes.

The arrested men are brought in from the veranda.

Police Inspector. Let them stand here—in a line. You stand at the end, old man. You ought to be ashamed of yourself. Old buzzard!

Grekov. Why do you swear at people?

Levshin. Never mind, Alyosha. Let him—

Police Inspector (*threateningly*). Shut up, you there, or I'll—

Levshin. Never mind. That's the kind of job he has—hurting people.

The Bardin family and their guests return. Nikolay and Boboyedov seat themselves at the table. The General takes the armchair in the corner. The Lieutenant stands behind him. Cleopatra and Polina stand at the door, with Tatyana and Nadya behind them. Zakhar looks over their shoulders, with an expression of displeasure on his face. Pologhy appears from somewhere, sidling in cautiously, bows to Nikolay and Boboyedov, and stops in the middle of the room, not knowing what to do next. The General beckons to him with his finger, and Pologhy tiptoes over to the General and takes his stand beside him. The gendarmes bring Ryabtsov in.

Nikolay. Let's start. Pavel Ryabtsov.

Ryabtsov. Well?

Boboyedov. Not well, fool, but yes, sir.

Nikolay. So you insist that it was you who killed the director?

Ryabtsov. I said I did it, so what more is there to say?

Nikolay. Do you know Alexey Grekov?

Ryabtsov. Which one is he?

Nikolay. The one standing next to you.

Ryabtsov. He works in our factory.

Nikolay. Then you and he are acquaintances?

Ryabtsov. We're all acquaintances.

Nikolay. Of course. But you've visited his house, gone out for walks with him—in short, you know each other well, you're friends?

Ryabtsov. I walk with everybody. We're all friends.

Nikolay. Are you? I think you're lying. Mr. Pologhy, tell us —what are the relations between Ryabtsov and Grekov?

Pologhy. They are relations of close friendship. There are two cliques here. The young people are headed by Grekov, a young man who's extremely ill mannered toward anybody in a superior position. The middle-aged are led by Yefim Levshin, a man utterly fantastic in his speech and foxlike in his ways—

Nadya (quietly). Oh, what a beast!

Pologhy glances at her and looks questioningly at Nikolay. The latter also casts a glance in Nadya's direction.

Nikolay. Well, go on.

Pologhy (with a sigh). The link between them is Mr. Sintsov, who keeps on good terms with everybody. This person has little resemblance to an ordinary man with a normal mind. He reads different books and has his own opinion about everything. In his house, which is diagonally opposite mine and which has three rooms—

Nikolay. You don't have to go into all these details.

Pologhy. Please excuse me. Truth demands completeness of form. His house is visited by all kinds of people, including those who are present here, such as Grekov—

Nikolay. Is this true, Grekov?

Grekov (calmly). I'll ask you not to address any questions to me—I'm not going to answer them.

Nikolay. I'm sorry to hear that.

Nadya (loudly). Oh, good!

Cleopatra. This is outrageous!

Polina. Nadya, my dear—

Boboyedov. Sh-sh—   *There is a noise on the veranda.*

Nikolay. I consider the presence of outsiders here unnecessary.

General. H'm— Who are the outsiders?

Boboyedov. Kvach, go see what that noise is out there.

Kvach. A man is trying to break in, sir. He's throwing himself against the door and cursing, sir.

Nikolay. What does he want? Who is he?

Boboyedov. Go find out, Kvach.   *Kvach goes out.*

Pologhy. Do you want me to continue or shall I stop?

Nadya. Oh, the dirty rat!

Nikolay. Stop, please. I'll ask the outsiders to leave the room.

General. How am I to understand that?

Nadya (shouting defiantly). You're the outsiders here, not I. You're outsiders everywhere—I'm in my own home. It's I who can demand that you leave the room—

Zakhar (to Nadya, agitatedly). You'd better go. Immediately. Go on.

Nadya. Indeed? In that case I'm truly an outsider here. All right, I'll go. But I'll tell you first—

Polina. Stop her. She'll say something terrible!

Nikolay (to Boboyedov). Tell your men to shut the door.

Nadya. You're all miserable, wretched men, without any conscience or heart—   *Kvach returns.*

Kvach (joyfully). Sir, one more has been discovered.

Boboyedov. What?

Kvach. One more murderer has shown up.

    Enter Akimov. A redhaired fellow, with a big mustache, he proceeds unhurriedly to the table.

Nikolay (rising involuntarily). What do you want?

Akimov. I'm the one who killed the director.

Nikolay. You?

Akimov. I.

Cleopatra (quietly). Oh, you scum! So now your conscience is bothering you!

Polina. My God! What terrible people!

Tatyana (calmly). These people will win out in the end!

Akimov (sullenly). Well, here I am. Eat me up!

General confusion. Nikolay quickly whispers something to Boboyedov, who listens to him with a perplexed smile. The prisoners stand silent and motionless. Nadya, in the doorway, gazes at Akimov and cries. Polina and Zakhar converse in whispers. In the stillness Tatyana's low-pitched voice can be heard.

Tatyana (to Nadya). Don't cry. These people will win out in the end!

Nikolay. Well, Mr. Ryabtsov, what have you to say now?

Ryabtsov (embarrassedly). Why, nothing.

Akimov. Don't say anything, Pavel, keep quiet!

Levshin (joyfully). Ah, my dear boys!

Nikolay (banging his fist on the table). Quiet!

Akimov (calmly). Don't shout, mister! We're not shouting.

Nadya (to Akimov, in a loud voice). Listen to me, you didn't kill that man. It's they who kill everybody—they kill all life by their greed—by their cowardice! *(To all.)* It's you who are the criminals!

Levshin (with feeling). You're right, young lady. It's not the one that strikes who kills, but the one that plants bitter hatred. You're right, my dear. *(General confusion and hubbub.)* Ah, Akimov, you shouldn't have done it!

Boboyedov. Silence!

Nadya (to Akimov). Why did you do it? Why?

Levshin. Don't shout, sir. I'm an older man than you.

Akimov (to Nadya). You can't understand anything that's going on. You ought to leave us alone.

Cleopatra. And what saintly airs he put on, that vile old man!

Boboyedov. Kvach!

Levshin. Well, Akimov, why don't you talk? Tell them he put the pistol against your breast, and then you—why, then you turned it—

Boboyedov (to Nikolay). Do you hear how he's prompting him? Oh, you old liar!

Levshin. No, I'm not a liar—

Nikolay. Well, what do you say now, Ryabtsov?

Ryabtsov. Why, nothing.

Levshin. Just hold your tongue. They're cunning. They're better with words than we are.

Nikolay (to Boboyedov). Throw him out!

Levshin. You can't throw us out, oh, no! No more of that. We've lived long enough in dark lawlessness. We've caught fire now, and you'll never put that light out. No matter what you do, you'll never stamp us out with fear—never!

CURTAIN

THE ZYKOVS

ANTIPA ZYKOV, the principal character of this play, belongs to the type of Russian businessmen who owed their success in life to their masterful personalities. They were the Russian merchant adventurers who opened Siberia to economic development, organized shipping companies on the Volga, bought and sold large estates, and rose to be the financial and industrial princes of the country. There is nothing small about Antipa. He is the authentic possessor of "the Russian soul" with its intensity of feeling and its ability to swing from one extreme to another.

Antipa's young wife Pavla is far more uncommon as a character. The fact that she was brought up in a convent (a comparatively unusual experience for a Russian girl, for Russian convents did not have schools for children as Catholic convents have in other countries) is to be held largely responsible for her faith in love as the guiding principle of life. But she never realizes that love as conceived and practiced in the cloistered world of a convent is too weak and passive a thing to control the actions of people in the storm-tossed world of human passions. This collision between the convent love which insists on the *sentiment* of love and the worldly love which insists on *actions* expressive of love forms the basis of the play and, in a sense, reflects the political controversy between the followers of Leo Tolstoy who preached non-resistance to evil, and the believers in political action who regarded force as the proper weapon of love and goodness.

A. B.

THE ZYKOVS

Characters

Anna Markovna Tselovanyeva

Sophia Ivanovna, Antipa Zykov's sister, a widow

Palageya, a servant

Mikhail (Misha), Antipa Zykov's son

Shokhin, a forest warden

Antipa Ivanovich Zykov, a timber merchant

Pavla (Pasha), Anna Markovna Tselovanyeva's daughter

Vassily Pavlovich Muratov, a forester

Matvey Ilich Tarakanov, Antipa Zykov's bookkeeper

Styopka, a young girl

Gustav Yegorovich Hevern, Antipa Zykov's partner

ACT I

A drab-looking room in the unpretentious, lower-middle-class house of the TSELOVANYEVAS. *In the center of the room a table laid for tea. Against the wall, between the two doors leading to the kitchen and to* ANNA MARKOVNA'S *room respectively, another table, with wines and refreshments. Right, by the wall, a small harmonium, with framed photographs and two vases of dried flowers on top. On the wall above, numerous picture post-cards and a water-color portrait of* PAVLA *dressed as a convent choirgirl. Two windows look out onto the front garden and the street.*

ANNA MARKOVNA, *a neat, smooth-looking woman of over forty, is sitting at the tea table. She is noticeably agitated, often glances out the windows, listens, fidgets with the cups on the table.* SOPHIA, *an extinguished cigarette in her mouth, paces up and down the room absorbed in thought.*

    Anna Markovna (sighing). They're late.
    Sophia (glancing at her wristwatch). Yes.
    Anna Markovna. I'm surprised you've never remarried, Sophia Ivanovna.
    Sophia. I can't find a man after my heart. When I do, I'll marry.
    Anna Markovna. There are few interesting men in this back-water.
    Sophia. An interesting man could be found, but it's hard to meet a serious one.
    Anna Markovna. If I may say so, you're a woman of serious character yourself——like a man in that respect. You ought to get yourself a quiet husband.
    Sophia (answering somewhat unwillingly). What will he be good for if he's quiet? To catch mice?
    Anna Markovna smiles embarrassedly. She appears to be

*ill at ease with Sophia—does not know how to talk to her.
Sophia, her hands behind her back, gazes at her, frowning.*
Tell me, who spread the rumor about Pasha—that she's slightly
off?

*Anna Markovna (hurriedly, in a low voice, as she glances
about).* It was my late husband's doing—and I too kept it up,
so that people would leave her alone. Pasha has always been
too outspoken, saying everything she thinks. Naturally, nobody
likes that. You see? And then my husband had a suspicion that
Pasha wasn't his daughter—

Sophia. Really?

Anna Markovna. He certainly had. Everybody knows that.
He used to shout about it when he got drunk. He was jealous
of a man here—a sectarian—

Sophia. Shokhin's father?

Anna Markovna. You see, you know it too.

Sophia. In no connection with your name. I only know there
was a sectarian here who was persecuted.

Anna Markovna (with a sigh). Well, I don't know about no
connection. *(In a low voice.)* But, God, he was persecuted.
(With a quick glance at Sophia.) My husband would sometimes
stare at her for a while and then suddenly roar—This is not
my daughter! I'm a low fellow, and you—that's me—are a fool
—she's not my daughter!

Sophia. He rather liked dramatizing himself, didn't he?

Anna Markovna. God knows!

Sophia. Did he beat you?

Anna Markovna. Of course. But I didn't worry about myself.
It was Pasha that I was afraid for. Somehow I got around him
and hid her in a convent—you see I have nothing to hope for
except her.   *The servant Palageya appears at the kitchen door.*

Palageya. They're coming!

Anna Markovna. You gave me a fright, you devil! You'd
think it was enemies coming. What do you want?

Palageya. Shall I bring in the samovar?

Anna Markovna. You'll be told when necessary. Go away.

*Enter Mikhail. He is slightly tipsy, is sweltering from the
heat, and has a tired smile on his beardless face.*

Mikhail. Don't stop up the door, woman. Take away your
circumference.

He pinches the servant, making her scream, and laughs with a kind of whimpering laughter. Anna Markovna tightens her lips, looking offended. Sophia, standing near the harmonium, frowns at her nephew, as he walks to the table.

It's hot, my mother-in-law to be! And here you're busying yourselves with teapots, sugar bowls—

Anna Markovna. Our Palageya is a little stupid—

Mikhail. Who is?

Anna Markovna. The servant woman.

Mikhail. Oh, I see. Only she? I'll make a note of that.

He turns to the table with the refreshments. Sophia strikes a few low chords on the harmonium.

Anna Markovna (in a disturbed tone). Why do you want to make a note of it?

Sophia. He's joking, Anna Markovna.

Anna Markovna. Oh, I'm so bad at understanding things.

Palageya (from the kitchen). A man's just come on horseback.

Sophia. That's Shokhin. That's for me, Anna Markovna.

Shokhin appears at the door.

Shokhin. Shokhin has come.

Sophia (her manner strict). I would have gone out to see you, Yakov.

Shokhin (bowing). Never mind! Hello, everybody!

Anna Markovna (withdrawing to the window). Don't mind me—

Sophia (to Shokhin). Well?

Shokhin. He ordered me to tell you he would write to you.

Sophia. Nothing more?

Shokhin. No, that's all.

Sophia. Thank you.

She makes a note in a little notebook on her chatelaine. Mikhail, with a wink at Anna Markovna, pours Shokhin a glass of vodka. Shokhin downs it furtively and makes a wry face.

Mikhail. Why are you always so gloomy, Yakov?

Shokhin. I don't get paid enough. Sophia Ivanovna, I want to tell you something.

Sophia. What?

Shokhin (*moving toward her*). Yesterday the forester was telling our mechanic that all of us ought to be put on trial for the way we run our estate. Because of us, says he, the rivers are getting shallow and the land is being ruined—

Sophia. All right. You may go.

Mikhail. Go, slave!   *Shokhin goes off.*

Anna Markovna. Was he talking about the forester?

Sophia. Yes.

Anna Markovna. A hard customer, that one. He quarrels with everybody, takes everybody to court, but is always drunk himself and spends all his spare time playing cards. He's a single man, has a good job—why doesn't he get married? People don't care for family life nowadays.

Mikhail. Don't they? What about me? I'm getting married.

Anna Markovna. You are, of course—under your father's orders. (*The words have slipped off her tongue. Embarrassed, she mumbles something and goes into the kitchen quickly.*)

Sophia (*to Mikhail*). You behave atrociously.

Mikhail. Do I? I won't do it again— Do you like my fiancée?

Sophia. She's good looking, simple—trusting. Do you like her?

Mikhail. Well, yes, I'm even a bit sorry for her— What sort of a husband will I make her?

Sophia. Are you serious?

Mikhail. I don't know. I believe I am.

Sophia. That's fine. Perhaps she'll make you think about yourself. It's time you did.

Mikhail. I do nothing but that.

Sophia. You fool around too much, always playing—

Mikhail. That's human nature. Take my fiancée—she's playing too—at simplicity, kindness—

Sophia (*looking at him intently*). What do you mean? She's really trusting.

Mikhail. The cat too is trusting. But try and deceive a cat.

Sophia. What has deception got to do with it?

Mikhail. You know what? It'd be much better if father married her and I got my discharge papers!

Sophia. What utter nonsense!

Mikhail. Anyway, if he doesn't marry her now, he'll take her away from me later. She's trusting.

Sophia. Stop it. What disgusting ideas you get! (*She walks away from him, visibly agitated.*)

Mikhail (*pours a glass of wine, laughing quietly, and declaims*).

> Reflected in the water,
> A flower lured my hand;
> But all my fingers captured
> Was green and slimy sand.

Sophia. What does it mean?

Mikhail. Nothing at all, a mere jest.

Sophia. Watch out, Misha, life is a serious thing.

> *Enter from the hall Antipa Zykov and Pavla. Antipa is getting on toward fifty, with a black beard touched with gray, black eyebrows, and curly hair receding at the temples. Pavla wears a very simple blue dress without a waistline, like a vestment. Over her head and shoulders is a blue chiffon scarf.*

Pavla. I always speak the truth.

Antipa. Do you? We'll see.

Pavla. You will. Where's Mother?

Anna Markovna (*from the kitchen*). I'm coming.

> *Antipa proceeds to the table with the refreshments. Pavla, smiling, moves toward Sophia.*

Sophia. Tired?

Pavla. It's hot. I'm thirsty.

Sophia. Did you make your dress yourself?

Pavla. Yes. Why?

Sophia. It suits you.

Pavla. I like to be free—

Antipa (*to Mikhail*). Steady, you're drinking too much, you'll make a fool of yourself.

Mikhail. A man that's getting married must show himself from all sides.

> *Taking his son by the shoulder, Antipa whispers something to him with a stern face. Mikhail chuckles.*

Sophia (*to Pavla, in a low voice, suddenly*). Which is more handsome?

Pavla. The older one.

Antipa. Shut up!

Sophia (*quietly*). What's the matter with you, Antipa?

Antipa (embarrassedly). You must forgive me, Pavla Niko-layevna. That was for your own good.

Pavla. What is?

Antipa. It's like this— *Enter Anna Markovna carrying a pie.*

Anna Markovna. Come and have something to eat, ladies and gentlemen—please.

Pavla (to Antipa). You have to be kind, or I'll be afraid of you.

Antipa (smiling amiably). You're always harping on your favorite subject—kindness. Ah, my child— *(He says something to her in a low voice.)*

Mikhail (although tipsy, realizes he is superfluous here, and wanders about the room chuckling to himself. Speaks to Sophia as he passes her). This is like a chicken coop—no room to move about.

Anna Markovna (watches everybody excitedly, comes over to Sophia). Come to the table, please. Call everybody—they don't listen to me.

Sophia (reflectively). I like your daughter.

Anna Markovna. Oh? God grant you keep liking her! I wish you'd look after her, set her right about things—

Sophia. Yes, of course. We women always have to pull together.

Pavla (to Antipa, in a tone of surprise). What about people?

Antipa. What about them?

Pavla. What will they think?

Antipa (with feeling). I don't give a hang! Let them think what they please. People! What do I owe them? Only suffering and insults. Here's what's helped me to build my life—my own arm! What do I care about people? *(He gulps down some vodka and wipes his mouth with a napkin.)* Now, you're my future—daughter, let's say. You always say one must be gentle and kind. This is the fourth time I've seen you, and your talk is always the same. That's because you've lived in a convent, in purity. If you had to live with people, you'd sing a different tune, my dear! Sometimes it gets so you look at the town and wish to heaven you could set fire to it—

Pavla. Then I'd be burned in it too.

Antipa. Oh, I'd get you— No, you wouldn't be burned.

Anna Markovna. Why don't you drink or eat something, Mikhail Antipovich?

Mikhail. Father doesn't permit me to—

Antipa. What's that?

Mikhail. And my fiancée doesn't offer it to me.

Pavla (blushes and bows). Please come, I'll pour you—

Mikhail. And yourself.

Pavla. I don't like it—

Mikhail. And I like vodka very much.

Pavla. They say it's bad for one.

Mikhail. All of a sudden it's bad! Don't you believe it! Your health!

Antipa. Health! People today don't know what it is to be strong and healthy. Am I right, Anna Markovna?

Anna Markovna. I don't know. My Pasha—

Antipa. I'm not talking about her, of course. But take my son, if you like—he hasn't had much to drink, has he? But his eyes are bleary and his face looks stupid—

Sophia. Be more careful what you say.

Anna Markovna (alarmed). Your son is still young.

Antipa (to Sophia). What I say is true. Anna Markovna knows how people drank in the old days. Her old man used to lap it up for weeks on end. (*To Anna Markovna.*) As for being young, that's not very important, youth is temporary, it's a passing thing.

> *The atmosphere is tense, everybody is waiting for something, each observing the other. Sophia watches her brother and Pavla quite openly. Mikhail smokes, gazing at his father with dull drunken eyes. Pavla casts frightened glances here and there. Antipa is at the table with the refreshments. Pavla lifts the teapot off the samovar. Her mother fidgets around the table whispering to her: "Oh, Pasha dear, I'm frightened."*

Sophia (to Antipa). Aren't you drinking too much?

Antipa (sullenly). You don't know me, it seems—

Sophia. Still, you'd better watch your step—

Antipa. Keep out of this. I know what I'm doing.

Sophia. Are you sure? (*They eye each other.*) What are you up to?

Antipa. What sort of a match is he for her? He can't be changed, but she'll be ruined for nothing—

Sophia (*stepping back*). See here, you can't possibly do such a thing!

Antipa. Quiet. Don't give me ideas. You'll only make it worse.

Mikhail (*with a snicker*). Nothing merry about this betrothal. Everybody's whispering—

Antipa. It's your aunt—she's too serious. Ah, pity there aren't more people here.

Pavla. You see, you too need people.

Antipa. Caught me! You *are* stubborn in your thoughts, Pavla Nikolayevna. Well, that's how a woman should be—she must stick to her point against everybody.

Pavla. And a man?

Antipa. A man? He's different. He's wild. Let something cut him to the heart, and he'll rush against anything—like a bear against a spear. Life rates cheaper with him, it seems.

Anna Markovna. Have some tea, please.

Antipa. Something cold would be nice now.

Mikhail. My advice is champagne.

Antipa. The first sensible advice I've heard from you. Go find it.

Mikhail. That I can. (*Goes off to the kitchen on unsteady feet, calling out.*) Hey you, beautiful!

Antipa (*winking at Pavla*). You see? And I've had three times as much as he has. I'm like that in everything—bigger than other people.

Pavla. Why are you afraid then?

Antipa (*surprised*). Afraid? I don't get it.

   Sophia is talking animatedly in a low voice to Anna Markovna, but keeps an ear cocked to catch what her brother is saying.

Pavla (*noticing Sophia's attentiveness*). Then why do you try to make my fiancé look cheap?

Antipa. Make him look cheap? Why, I'm not forgetting he's my son!

Pavla (*lowering her voice*). Why do you look at me this way?

Antipa. We're going to be living under the same roof—so I want to know what you're like. Now, you were saying life in

a convent is quiet and fine. Our home too is like a convent.
Only Sophia kicks up dust now and then.

Pavla. You seem to be really kind, underneath.

Antipa. Oh, I don't know! Of course, others see us better
than we see ourselves. It amuses me, though, how you stick
to your line. No, I don't think I can boast of being kind. (*Flaring up.*) Perhaps there has been something kind and good in
my heart, but what can I do with it, where can I apply it? It
needs a place where it will fit, and there's no place for kindness
in life—no place, you understand, where you can squeeze in
the good part of your heart. It's no use giving it to a beggar—
he'll spend it all on drink! No, Pavla, I don't like people. There's
only one good man in my home, Tarakanov, he used to be an
assistant police chief in the country—

Sophia. Thank you.

Antipa. You? You keep quiet. You're a different sort, a
stranger. God alone knows what you are, sister. Are you kind?
We've been talking about kindness, and you are neither kind
nor cruel—

Sophia. It's a fine picture you draw of me.

Antipa. Not a bad one. Look, Anna Markovna—she's nearly
twenty years younger than me, but in time of trial I turn to her
like I would to a mother.

Sophia. What's come over you? It's strange— You're so
talkative.

Antipa. If I am, there must be a reason for it. Well—that
man Tarakanov—he was fired from his job for kindness—
honestly! He has brains, and knows a lot, but he's no good for
any work—just incapable. All he's good for is to be looked at—
as something curious, amusing— In the old days they would
have made him a court jester—

Sophia. You would say something like that! Why a jester?

Antipa. That's how I see him. As for you, Sophia, you no
longer belong in the Zykov nest. You were married to a nobleman for six years—you have some gentlefolk blood in you—

Sophia. You ought to stop talking, Antipa.

Antipa. No, wait. You're clever, and good at every kind of
business. But then you're a woman, free as a bird—you can
take off and fly away—no one can stop you. Now, I've been

left alone. And if a man doesn't always know what he's going to be tomorrow, a woman of your character certainly knows less —you can take that from me!

Anna Markovna. What about Mikhail Antipich?

Antipa (sullenly). My son? Well—I know little about him that's good, if I'm to speak the truth. And as we are after an honest deal here, we need the whole truth. Mikhail has little to show for himself. He writes verse, plays the guitar—left high school—through lack of ability—and ability is nothing but patience. Well, I can't brag about my patience either—

Pavla (deeply stirred). What do you think of me, then, if you speak like that about your son and my fiancé?

Antipa (in a low voice, as if to himself). The right question to ask—

Anna Markovna. My dear ones, please listen to me— I'm the mother—

Sophia (sternly). Have you considered well what you're doing?

Antipa (getting to his feet, impressively). I can't reason things out. Let others do it if they care. I only know what I want. Pavla Nikolayevna, come out with me for a minute—

The three women rise. Pavla, as if in a dream, goes into the room next to the kitchen. Antipa follows her, with a heavy, morose air. The door is left open, and one can hear Antipa say: "Sit down—wait, I must collect my thoughts."

Anna Markovna (sinking into a chair). My God! What does he want? How can such a thing be, Sophia Ivanovna?

Sophia (pacing the room agitatedly). Your daughter is a very intelligent girl—if I understand her well— (*Lights a cigarette and looks around for a place to throw the match.*)

Anna Markovna. Why, he's after her himself—

Sophia. One moment—

Antipa (in the other room). What sort of a husband will he make for you? You're the same age as he is, but you're more mature in your soul. Marry me! He's older than I am, he's soft. It's I who'll love you like a young man. I will! I'll dress you in brocade, in gold and silver. I've had a hard life, Pavla, and not of the right sort either. Help me to a different life—help me to find joy in something good, to lean my heart against something kind. Will you, Pavla?

Sophia (agitated). Do you hear? How well he speaks! People of his age love strongly—

Anna Markovna. I don't understand anything. O Mother of God all merciful! In you rests all my hope—have mercy on my child, keep her from sorrow— I've known sorrow enough for my daughter as well as myself.

Sophia. Try not to get excited. I'm as shocked as you are. Although it's in his character. Well, there's little one can do about it. Your daughter doesn't seem to object either.

Anna Markovna. I can't make any of you out. You came for the betrothal of your son and nephew, and all of a sudden— what's happened? (*Goes to the room where Pavla and Antipa are.*) I want to hear—I'm the mother—I can't permit—

Antipa (inside the other room). God has placed you in my path— Anna Markovna, listen—

> *The door closes. Sophia paces the room, biting her lips. Muratov's face pops up in the window—an ironical face, with pouches under the eyes, a pointed beard, and thin hair.*

Sophia (alone). Oh, my God!

Muratov. Greetings!

Sophia. Oh! How did you get here?

Muratov. Why? Your faithful attendant Shokhin told me you were here, so I deemed it my duty to pay my respects.

Sophia. Through the window?

Muratov. Well, you know we're plain folk.

Sophia. Who believe in the simple life?

Muratov. Is that irony! Yes, we believe in the simple life. And are you match-making?

Sophia. Is that public knowledge already?

Muratov. Certainly. It's also known that the bride-to-be is not all there—

Sophia. You've heard, of course, about my alleged love affair with you?

Muratov. I have. People anticipate events.

Sophia. Have you contradicted this rumor?

Muratov. Why should I? I'm proud of it.

Sophia. Did you by any chance originate it yourself?

Muratov. That is what's called hitting the nail on the head. But when I'm talked to like that, I become impertinent.

Sophia. I'd ask you, though, to leave the window.

Muratov. All right, I'll go. May I call on you Sunday?

Sophia. Please. But you may stay away too.

Muratov. I'd better come. My respects for the present, and wishing you all possible success—in every enterprise!

Sophia. Don't forget to get me copies of the inventory that I asked you for.

Muratov. I never forget anything—   *Mikhail returns.*

Mikhail. You can't get any champagne in this goddam neighborhood. Look who's here!

Muratov. What are you doing, bridegroom, running around loose?

Mikhail (waving his hand in dismissal). Be seeing you tonight.

Muratov. I hope so. You owe us a farewell stag party.

Mikhail. Certainly.   *Muratov disappears.* Where's everybody?

Sophia (watching him intently). In that room.

Mikhail. I'm being put out, is that it? I heard Father's oratory.

Sophia (almost contemptuously). It seems you'll be superfluous everywhere.

Mikhail. I told you it'd be better this way. But why did they disturb my peace and quiet? There goes the farewell party! You seem to be bored, Aunt Sonya?

Sophia. Yes, with all of you. And more than bored—I'm horrified.

   Reënter Pavla and Antipa with Anna Markovna, in tears, close behind.

Antipa (solemnly). Look, sister Sophia—we've decided— *(Catches at his heart with his hand.)*

Pavla. Sophia Ivanovna, please understand and forgive me.

Sophia (embracing her). I don't know what to say— I don't understand you—

Antipa. You mustn't feel hurt, Mikhail. You know, you're young, and there are many girls to choose from—

Mikhail. I'm very glad. Honestly, I am. Pavla Nikolayevna, I said that I'm very glad, but you mustn't be cross with me—I know I'm no match for you!

Antipa. There, Anna Markovna, you see, just as I told you.

Pavla (to Mikhail). We'll all live together like friends—

Mikhail (nodding). We certainly will—

Antipa. Anna Markovna, you mustn't worry. I swear to God, your daughter won't shed a single tear because of me.

Anna Markovna (going down on her knees before him). You once had a mother—she loved you. Think of your mother, kind sir! For your mother's sake, have pity on my daughter!

Antipa and Pavla try to raise her to her feet. Sophia has turned away toward the wall and wipes her eyes with a handkerchief. Mikhail, in a state of agitation, drinks one glass of vodka after another.

Pavla. Please don't worry, Mother dear. Everything will be all right.

Antipa. Ask for any pledge you want, I'll take any vow— only get up. I'll put twenty-five thousand rubles in her name in the bank—there!

Sophia. That'll do, my friends. Pour something, Misha! You and I, Anna Markovna, will be the matrons of honor, although I'm rather too young for such a bearded son. *(To Antipa.)* What's the matter with you? You're shaking as if you were on trial.

Anna Markovna. My dear people— *(She embraces her daughter and weeps silently.)*

Antipa. I feel like sitting down and keeping silent for a few moments, as one does before going on a long journey.

Sophia. Well, well. It's too close here. Pavla, take everybody out into the garden.

Pavla (to Antipa and her mother, as she takes them by their hands). Come along—

Antipa, Pavla, and Anna Markovna go off.

Mikhail. You asked for a drink—

Sophia. Not now—later. You poor boy! *(Puts her arms around his shoulders and strokes his head.)* How are you feeling?

Mikhail. I'm all right, Aunt Sonya— Honestly, I don't care.

Sophia. Let's go into the garden.

Mikhail. No, I won't go out there.

Sophia. Why not?

Mikhail. I don't want to.

Sophia (looking in his eyes, quietly). So you do care?

Mikhail (with a chuckle). I feel a little embarrassed for
Father. He's such a handsome man, so strong, so of a piece, like
cast metal. Strange to see him go after sweetmeats—
  Sophia (going off, with a smile). What can you do? A man
always hankers after a little happiness—just a little—

CURTAIN

ACT II

The garden of the ZYKOV *house, showing, left, the wide veranda
of the house. Opposite the veranda, seated at a table under a
linden tree, are* PAVLA, *doing some embroidery work;* MIKHAIL,
with a guitar; and TARAKANOV, *an old man with a long beard,
wearing a duck suit and looking odd and somewhat droll. Up-
stage, just beyond the end of the veranda,* ANNA MARKOVNA *is
making jam. With her is the young girl* STYOPKA.

  Tarakanov. This is all due to the convulsion of ideas so no
one knows his right place.
  Pavla (repeats pensively). Convulsion of ideas.
  Tarakanov. Exactly.
  Mikhail (strumming his guitar). Why don't you tell us some-
thing from life, Matvey Ilich, and skip the philosophy?
  Tarakanov. You can't do without philosophy, since every-
thing has its hidden meaning which we must know.
  Mikhail. Why must we?
  Tarakanov. What do you mean?
  Mikhail. Suppose I don't want to know anything?
  Tarakanov. You can't do that.
  Mikhail. But I don't want to.
  Tarakanov. That's just a whim of youth.
  Pavla. Don't argue, you two, and talk simply.

Tarakanov. Suppose you're told to get out of the way, and you don't understand it—

Mikhail. Well?

Tarakanov. Well—you'll be knocked down.

Mikhail. I can always get out of the way, Matvey Ilich, I'm too particular—

Pavla (*glancing at him*). Don't lose your tempers— That's when one's apt to make the most mistakes.

Tarakanov. I don't understand what being particular means.

Anna Markovna. For goodness' sake, stop spreading gloom! Pavla, would you like to taste the jam?

Pavla. No, thank you, not now. I'll have it with pancakes for supper if you order them for me.

Mikhail. Why only for you? I may like pancakes with jam too.

Pavla (*with a sigh*). Drinkers don't like sweets.

Mikhail. That's known as an aphorism.

Pavla. What is?

Mikhail. What you said.

Pavla. Why an aphorism?

Mikhail. Damned if I know.

Tarakanov. A strange man you are, Misha.

Mikhail. All humans are strange and defy understanding. You too are strange. You ought to be holding a government job, taking graft—instead you philosophize.

Tarakanov. I don't need graft. I'm a simple man.

Pavla. I've heard you have a son?

Tarakanov. I've renounced him.

Pavla. Completely? Why?

Tarakanov. Yes, completely—because he doesn't love Russia.

Pavla (*with a sigh*). I don't understand.

Mikhail. Matvey Ilich doesn't understand anything himself.

Anna Markovna. How they talk to old people today!

Mikhail. The old people admit themselves that they live in a convulsion of ideas. Consequently, they should wait before they start teaching others.

Anna Markovna. I teach? Get on with you!

    Goes off to the veranda. Styopka glances about and slips a few handfuls of sugar into her pocket.

Pavla (*disturbed*). Please, don't quarrel! Why do you?

Tarakanov. Mostly for distraction.

Mikhail. That's right.

Pavla. Sing your song about a girl, Misha.

Mikhail. I'm not in the mood.

Pavla. Oh, please, Misha—

Mikhail (*glancing at her*). Well, I must do as my parents tell me—

> *Tunes up his guitar. Tarakanov fills his pipe and lights it. Accompanying himself softly on the guitar, Mikhail declaims in recitative.*

> > In a field a girl is strolling,
> > I don't know who she is.
> > Is it her my heart's awaiting,
> > Bewitched with melancholy?

Tarakanov. Who is the girl?

Pavla (*with annoyance*). Don't interrupt. It's a dream.

Tarakanov (*sighing*). Then it's a girl in general. I understand. In that case the thing to do is to get married.

Pavla. Oh, please, don't interrupt.

> *During Mikhail's recitation Muratov has come out on the veranda. He is in riding clothes and carries a whip. Listening to Mikhail, he screws up his face ironically.*

Muratov (*coming down into the garden*). What a poetic scene! Making jam, reading sweet verse— How are you, Pavla Nikolayevna? You're getting prettier every day! Greetings, retired preacher of truth and goodness. Hello, Misha—

> *Greeted with silence, he sits down beside Pavla—she edges away from him. Tarakanov, after a silent exchange of nods with Muratov, goes off into the garden, casting sullen glances at the forester.*

I've walked right through the house—not a soul there!

Pavla. Aunt Sonya is in—

Muratov. Then I heard the soft sounds of a guitar. Whose verse did you read, Misha, your own?

Mikhail. Yes, why?

Muratov. Rather poor stuff. Still, even that's probably all right for home use.

Pavla. Shall I call Aunt Sonya?

Mikhail (*with a light laugh*). Stay where you are. I'll call her.

Pavla. Better I—

Muratov. Why better?

Pavla. I don't know. Well, let Misha go—

Mikhail goes into the house. Muratov picks up his guitar, and cocks his head toward Pavla.

Muratov. Fine fellows, army clerks. They're brave, and they're expert at paying court to ladies—don't you think so?

Pavla. I don't know any.

Muratov. Army clerks and also barbers are very fond of playing the guitar.

Pavla. Are they?

Muratov. You make a poor Eve—you lack curiosity. Aren't you interested to know why I've become such a frequent visitor here?

Pavla (embarrassed). No, I'm not interested.

Muratov. That's a pity. I wish you'd give it some thought.

Pavla. You're an old acquaintance of Aunt Sonya's—

Muratov. An old acquaintance I am. But my heart is young and it's drawn to one who's young, as you're drawn, for example, to Misha, a very stupid fellow—

Pavla (aroused). He's not stupid at all—

Muratov. I know him better than you do— We always drink together—

Pavla. And I'm not drawn to him either.

Muratov (singing in a low voice). "O husband old! O husband stern!"

Pavla (rising). That's not true!

Muratov. What's not true?

Pavla. Everything! Everything you're saying. And I don't want to listen to you! You deliberately—

Muratov. Deliberately what?

Pavla. I don't know how to put it. You make fun of me. (*Hurries away.*)

Muratov (taking out his cigarette case, follows her with his eyes, and sighs). Little fool!

With the tip of his whip Muratov strikes lightly on the strings of the guitar. Anna Markovna peers out from around the corner of the veranda and instantly withdraws. Out of the house comes Sophia—she stops on the upper step of the veranda and takes a deep breath.

Sophia. What a glorious day!

Muratov (rising and walking toward her). It's hot and dusty! How are you?

Sophia. What did you do to upset Pavla?

Muratov. I?

Sophia. Don't start play-acting. You know I won't believe you.

Muratov. She amuses me a great deal.

    Anna Markovna and Styopka appear at the outdoor stove. How soon do you think the idyl will turn into drama?

Sophia (sharply). Don't talk nonsense! Have you brought the papers at last?

Muratov. No. My office clerk is terribly lazy.

Sophia. You're not any too industrious yourself.

Muratov. I'm lazy on principle. Why on earth should I toil for savages who are incapable of appreciating my labors?

Sophia. You've said that before.

Muratov. That proves I'm serious.

Sophia. And not trying to say something original?

Muratov. I live among people who are dishonest, lazy, and uncivilized. I don't want to do anything for them—I see no sense to it. I hope I make myself clear?

Sophia. Clear enough, but hardly attractive.

    Anna Markovna takes Styopka by the ear and leads her away.

Muratov. I can't help it. Incidentally, that Hevern of yours—

Sophia. Let's not talk about him—

Muratov. Why not?

Sophia. I don't want to.

Muratov. You don't want *me* to talk about him?

Sophia. That's right.

Muratov. Oh, really? H'm! And I came here partly with the idea of telling you something about that gentleman.

Sophia. That gentleman has a name—Gustav Yegorovich. I have great respect for him.

Muratov. What if he turns out to be a crook?

Sophia (rising, in a firm voice, wrathfully). What do you want?

Muratov (a little frightened). Will you permit me—

Sophia. I've just told you how I regard this man—

Muratov. But surely you can make a mistake!

Sophia. I'll answer for my mistakes myself. Besides I'm just as good as you at sizing up people.

Muratov. Yet you don't sense my attitude toward you, do you?

Sophia. That's not true. (*With a laugh.*) I know you neither believe me, nor respect me—

Muratov (*with a sigh*). Oh, how mistaken you are!

Sophia. Please, no oh's! And I'm not mistaken. You see me as one of the merchant species who had a landowner for a husband and was corrupted and worn out by him—a rich woman and a cunning one, sinful in her thoughts, but cowardly —and stupid too. You're counting on my stupidity when you parade your cynicism before me, aren't you?

Muratov. I'm no cynic. I'm a skeptic, as all people of intelligence are.

Sophia. I well remember your first attempts—when my husband was still alive— (*With a sigh.*) If you'd only known how I needed sympathy then—a concern that was honest.

Muratov. I treated you with as much honesty as I was capable of.

Sophia. Well, you're not capable of much. And I rather liked you then. I believed you were a good man, an intelligent man—

Muratov. I was less intelligent then than I am now.

Sophia. I didn't give in to you, and for a time it kindled your pride, your obstinacy.

Muratov. Not obstinacy—passion!

Sophia. Oh, please! You and passion!

Muratov. Are we getting into a quarrel?

Sophia. I'm sorry. I've been letting myself go—

Muratov (*bowing*). That's all right. I'm prepared to go on listening to you. We've needed to have some such conversation as this!

Sophia. You think so? I agree.

Muratov (*glancing around*). Well, go ahead.

Sophia (*looking at him*). Once I nearly believed you—

Muratov. When was that?

Sophia. It makes no difference to you. (*Rises and walks to and fro.*)

Muratov (*after a pause*). It would be interesting to know what you think of me.

Sophia. Nothing good—I can tell you that.

Muratov. Well, let's have it. If it cuts to the heart—

Sophia. What then?

Muratov. I don't know. Something will happen.

Sophia (*after thinking it over*). You know, I've come to the conclusion that you use your supposed infatuation for me to cover up your laziness, to justify your trivial existence.

Muratov. Not bad for an opening—

Sophia. You're a very dishonest man—

Muratov (*rises, smiling*). Now, that's really—

Sophia (*coming close to him*). Yes, a dishonest man. An honest man wouldn't use everything without paying for what he takes—

Muratov. I don't recall taking anything from you—

Sophia. They say you're strict in applying the law. I believe you prosecute people only because you don't like people—because they bore you, and you take out your boredom on them with petty, bitter spite. You use the power that's been given you like a drunkard, or like my late husband who was a sick man—I can't speak well and the words that come to my tongue seem foreign to me— But I feel everything clearly and I'll tell you candidly—I feel very sorry for you—

Muratov. I offer no thanks—

Sophia. You live terribly—

Muratov. Do I?

Sophia. You love nobody and nothing—

Muratov. That's true. I don't like people—

Sophia. You don't love your work either.

Muratov. Nor my work. Preserve forests? No, that doesn't excite me. Next?

Sophia. But that's what you studied—to preserve forests.

Muratov. I certainly did.

Sophia. How do you explain it then!

Muratov. I made a mistake—the usual Russian mistake. The thing a Russian craves first of all is to get away from his native surroundings. Where he'll go and how he'll get there is immaterial. But that's what we Russians are: take it or leave it. Well, have you said all you wanted to say?

Sophia. Yes.

Muratov. What's the conclusion?

Sophia. You can draw it yourself.

Muratov. Perhaps you hope that after this philosophical argument I'll shoot myself? No, I won't. There are thousands of people like me, and life is our dish, madam. People like you can be counted on the fingers of one hand—and in this life you're completely superfluous. You can't even figure out what to do with yourselves. Formerly you usually took to revolution, but nobody needs a revolution today—so you can draw the moral yourself.

Sophia (smiling). I seem to have cut you to the heart, after all.

Muratov. To the heart? No.

Sophia. But we're through with our argument?

Muratov (frowning at her). You're cleverer than I thought. I'm surprised you're able to put up with all this—this vulgarity around you. (*Sighs.*) Still, there's something in my heart that impels me toward you—

Sophia. It's of no use either to you or to me—

Muratov. Your way of looking at people is much too simple, madam, much too elementary!

Sophia (heatedly). Oh, please, no more of that complexity of yours. You ought to be ashamed of it. It's nothing but a screen for your lying and licentiousness.

Muratov. You're losing your temper? Then I'm off. I like being angry myself. But it gives me little pleasure to see another person, particularly a woman, delight in pouring out ill temper. (*Goes off to the house unhurriedly, pausing on the veranda steps.*) In spite of everything I don't regard this as a quarrel— if you don't mind?

Sophia (in a low voice). As you please.

Muratov. I don't then. And so until our next meeting, a more pleasant one for me, I trust.

> *Goes off. Alone in the garden, Sophia moves about shrugging and smiling. From around the corner Styopka appears.*

Styopka. Sophia Ivanovna, Grandma has boxed my ears—

Sophia (without looking at the girl). What did you do?

Styopka. I took a little sugar—

Sophia. You should have asked permission—

Styopka. She would never have given it to me.

Sophia. You should have asked me.

Styopka. You were out.

Sophia. You should have waited until I returned.

Styopka. I might have done that. I'm a fool.

Sophia (stroking her head). You are a little fool.

Styopka. When shall I be clever?

Sophia. In due time. Have patience. Somebody's driven up. Go see who it is.

Styopka (running). Look—it's your German!

Sophia (smiles and peeps around the corner of the veranda). Anna Markovna, why are you hiding?

Anna Markovna (coming out). You were talking here—and my jam got boiling over. You pet that girl too much—she steals sugar—   *Pavla appears on the veranda.*

Pavla. Aunt Sonya, there's somebody to see you.

Sophia. I know, I'm coming. Why so sad?

Pavla. Misha was telling about his school days—

Anna Markovna. Oh-ho!

Sophia. I must have a cold snack ready. (*Goes into the house.*)

Anna Markovna. I begin to feel sorry, Pasha dear, we sold our little house.

Pavla. Oh, it's nothing, Mother.

Anna Markovna. Having one's own home is always something. (*Lowering her voice.*) Sophia raked the forester over the coals here. Such a brave woman. She must have made up her mind to marry the German—

Pavla (reflectively). She's awfully nice—

Anna Markovna. They're all nice—for themselves! And you, Pasha—you shouldn't spend so much time with Mikhail—

Pavla. Stop it, Mother. Why do you keep harping on it? It's so boring. You've become spiteful. Who are you vexed with? I really can't understand it.

Anna Markovna. There, there. You'd better look at yourself— see what you've come to look like now.

> She disappears around the corner. Pavla pushes the guitar
> away irritably. Shokhin, holding a package, comes down
> from the veranda.

Pavla. Who is it you want?

Shokhin. No one. I've brought sugar.

Pavla. Are you Shokhin?

Shokhin. That's right, Shokhin, the head forest warden.

Pavla (in a low voice). Did you kill a man?

Shokhin (not immediately). Y-yes.

Pavla. Oh, God! You poor soul—

Shokhin (quietly). I was acquitted.

Pavla. Does it make any difference? You wouldn't acquit yourself before your own conscience, would you? How did you—

Shokhin. With an ax—the butt end—

Pavla. Merciful God! I'm not asking about that—

Shokhin. Well—where shall I put this? (*Places the package on the table, and bursts out sharply and hurriedly.*) You know what they did in 1907? They would come to the forest and begin cutting down trees—

Pavla. And you went after them?

Shokhin. That's what I was hired for.

Pavla. Oh, my God! How can anybody kill people for that?

Shokhin. They've been killed for less—

Pavla (gazes at him and calls out in a pitiful, childish voice). Mother!

Shokhin (hurt, in a low voice). There's no call for that! I mean no harm—

> *There is a noise in the house. Shokhin glances around, and runs off. Enter Antipa, covered with dust and looking tired.*

Antipa (glancing around). Who ran away?

Pavla. Shokhin—

Antipa. Why?

Pavla. I don't know.

Antipa. Where's Mikhail?

Pavla. In his room, I suppose—

Antipa (comes down the steps and puts an arm around her shoulders). Why looking so sad?

Pavla. It's that Shokhin—

Antipa. What do you mean?

Pavla. He killed a man—

Antipa (gloomily). Yes, so he did—the fool! I hired a lawyer for him, got him off— Now he's as loyal to me as a dog. But if you want, I can fire him—

Pavla. Oh, no! He'll do the same thing to me—

Antipa. Don't be silly.

Pavla. Or somebody else— No, don't fire him.

Antipa. Oh, well. God, I look at you—and big words begin to stir in my heart—but I don't know how to speak them. If you'd only understand—without words!

Pavla (diffidently). I will—if you wait—

Antipa. I'm waiting. (*After a sigh.*) Mind though. I haven't too much time. I live in a hurry and I like everything to open to me at once.

Pavla. They're saying that you've changed—

Antipa (sullenly). I? How have I changed? For what reason?

Pavla. I don't know the reason—

Antipa. Who was saying that?

Pavla. People.

Antipa (scornfully). People! (*Whistles.*)

Pavla. They say you're neglecting your business—

Antipa. It's my business. I neglect it or not as I please. (*Looks intently at her and puts his arm around her.*) It's odd to hear it from you—a mere child, but you must talk about business!

Pavla (quietly, as she glances around). And they also say that Aunt Sonya is getting the whole business into her hands—

Antipa (flaring up, angrily). If I find out who says this, I'll break his neck. And don't you repeat these filthy stories—those are my orders—you hear me? Nobody will make me quarrel with my sister—not a chance! (*Gives her a slight push.*) Imagine, the gall of these people!

Pavla (her feelings hurt, walks off slowly). There you go— losing your temper— And you yourself say: Talk to me about everything you think—

Antipa (grabs her by the shoulder). Wait. Of course I want you to talk to me, talk about everything. You mustn't be offended with me. I was just annoyed. But you talk—only talk about your own ideas, not what other people say. They speak mostly from spite and envy. People are weak and miserable— that's why they're envious—

Pavla. Misha is weak, but he's not spiteful or envious—

Antipa (recoiling from her). What's that? Why do you talk about him?

Pavla. Because what you say about people is not true.

Antipa. Not true? Because my son is not— H'm, it's strange how one thing leads to another—

Pavla (uneasily). You mustn't think, please—

Antipa (fixing her with his eyes, hurriedly). Think what?

Pavla (embarrassed). What you talked about last Thursday. I'm not the least bit interested in him—

Antipa (embracing her again and looking in her eyes). I didn't mean that, I swear to God! I believe you. You gave me your answer, and that's that—thank you! I love you, Pavla—I love you so, with such force, it almost chokes me. Let's go to the pond—let's, I'll kiss you there—

Pavla (in a low voice). Oh, not in the daytime. It's not nice—

Antipa (leading her away). It will be nice! Come on, my dear—come on—my precious star from heaven—

They go off. Hevern steps out onto the veranda and follows them with screwed-up eyes. Styopka brings a silver pail with ice and wine bottles. Sophia comes out last.

Sophia. Well, go ahead—

Hevern. You're in too gay a mood today, and it disconcerts me.

Sophia. Really? Do you like melancholy women better?

Hevern. You know whom I like—

Sophia (smiling). If you had more money, I'd be more serious toward you—if you don't mind my saying so.

Hevern (with a slightly wry face). It's a very valuable trait you have—always to speak frankly. But I shall have more money. I'm already rich. I understand well that nowhere is it so necessary to be rich as in Russia, where only money gives one independence and esteem. And I know that at forty I shall have one hundred thousand rubles. I am thirty-four now.

Sophia. You bring too much arithmetic into life.

Hevern. Oh, that's necessary. One has to be able to count if only so that at fifty one doesn't marry a girl of twenty. That can never be a true match and can only do harm to one's business.

Sophia (coldly). You think so?

Hevern. I'm sure of it. Late marriages in Russia are always unsuccessful. When a man is in a hurry to get home, his business suffers; his impatience may also affect the interests of third parties.

Sophia. Such as mine, for instance.

Hevern. Yours too. As well as mine—

Mikhail comes out. He shakes hands with Hevern, pours himself a glass of wine, seats himself on the upper step and studies the wine against the light. Hevern looks at him from above, while Sophia, smoking, watches Hevern.

Hevern. Did you try to catch perch this morning, Misha?

Mikhail. I did.

Hevern. And were you successful?

Mikhail. I was.

Hevern. How many did you catch?

Mikhail. One.

Hevern. Was it big?

Mikhail. About a pound.

Hevern. That's bad. Nothing takes up so much time as fishing. (*To Sophia.*) Yesterday I talked with your marshal of nobility. He's a very strange character.

Sophia. Is he? In what way?

Hevern. Yes, he's a very strange character. He's been to other countries, is interested in art, has visited museums, and not once did he go to the Reichstag! He doesn't understand that socialism is a historical phenomenon, and laughs at what should be studied. The bare instinct of an individualist property owner cannot defeat socialism by its own force. To wage war successfully, you must know your enemy.

Sophia. Yes, it's necessary to know the strong and the weak points of the enemy. But I'm not interested in socialism either.

Hevern. Oh, it's not essential for a woman! Yes, a strange man, this marshal of nobility. He spoke of the honest services of the nobility on behalf of Russia with such fire—so beautifully. But if you offer him two and a half thousand rubles, he will put his conscience in his pocket—

Sophia (*laughing*). Why exactly two and a half thousand?

Hevern. Just an example.

Sophia. Did you offer that?

Hevern (*in a forbidding tone*). No, what for? (*To Mikhail.*) You live as friends with Pavla Nikolayevna, don't you?

Mikhail. She's a fine woman, honest and kind—ı

Hevern. Is she? That's very nice. But many Russians, it seems to me, are kind only because they're weak in character—isn't that so?

Mikhail. I don't know. You can judge it better as a foreigner.

Antipa and Pavla are approaching through the garden. They walk apart, looking subdued. Noticing them, the others remain silent.

Antipa (looking out of sorts and grumbling). When the heart doesn't flame but only smolders, that's not yet real life. Don't you be too rash with your thinking—

Pavla (wearily). One moment you say I'm stupid, another, I mustn't think—

Antipa (with annoyance). Don't you understand? I'm talking about different things— (*Noticing Mikhail, draws himself up and asks in a sharp tone.*) Is the report ready?

Mikhail. Not yet.

Antipa. Why not? Didn't I tell you—

Mikhail. The accounts for the summer house haven't come in yet.

Antipa. They haven't come in? That's a lie.

Sophia. Don't shout. I have the accounts. They have to be checked—

Antipa (coming onto the veranda). You always defend others —when it's not necessary. If they have to be checked, why doesn't he do it himself?

Sophia whispers something to him sternly, to which he answers with a growl.

Hevern (to Pavla). How are you?

Pavla. I'm quite well, thank you.

Hevern. I'm very glad.

Pavla. Are you serious?

Hevern. About what?

Pavla. Are you genuinely glad when people are well?

Hevern (surprised). Of course! Certainly. How else can I be? When everybody around me is well, I benefit by it—

Pavla. How simple and true that is—

Hevern. I love everything simple. It's simple things that are true!

Antipa (to Hevern). Let's go look at the plan—

Hevern. Certainly.

Antipa. You come with us, Mikhail—come on. We've bought the marshal's forest, Sophia—you know about it, don't you?

Sophia. No, I don't.

Antipa (to Hevern). Why didn't you inform our lady partner?

Hevern (frowning). I was sure—

Sophia (to Antipa). How much?

Antipa. Twenty-three—

Sophia. You didn't want to pay more than eighteen.

Antipa. I didn't want to, but I had to.

Sophia. Why?

Antipa. A new competitor turned up. I'll tell you more later. Let's go. Come along, Mikhail.

> *They go off, with Hevern bringing up the rear. Smoking thoughtfully, Sophia follows Hevern with her eyes. Pavla leans against the railing, her head bowed.*

Sophia. What makes you so sad?

Pavla. I'm tired.

Sophia. What did you talk about?

Pavla. The same as always— He keeps saying how much he loves me—as if I didn't know. But he goes on and on—

Sophia. Come over here, you—guileless soul!

Pavla. No, really. Suppose I do love—but one can't talk about it all the time.

Sophia (sadly). It's very bad, my child, if one can't talk about it all the time.

Pavla. And the men are all alike. How strangely he looks at you!

Sophia. Who?

Pavla. Gustav Yegorovich.

Sophia. Oh, he! That's the way he looks at everything. The true manager!

Pavla. Do you like him?

Sophia. He's all right—a strong gentleman. He ought to be a good traveling companion—you could never miss a train with him along.

Pavla. I don't understand. Are you joking?

Sophia. You don't understand many things, my friend—

Pavla (sorrowfully). That must be so. Nothing is turning out as I expected.

Sophia. Tell me—why did you marry my brother?

Pavla. I thought it would be different. You see, I'm terribly frightened of everything—always afraid something may happen. Until I was twelve Father had me scared. Then, five years in the convent. There, too, everybody lives in fear. At first we feared being robbed. During the disturbances we had Cossacks stationed with us, and they kept whistling every night. They used to get drunk and sing loud songs. They didn't show any respect for the nuns, and things weren't at all nice. Everybody broke the rules, and was bitter, and afraid of everybody else— of God, too, instead of loving him. So I said to myself—I must get myself under somebody's strong arm—I won't be able to live alone according to my own lights—

Sophia (reflectively). Did you think Antipa was strong?

Pavla. He said he was. Misha doesn't care for anything or anybody—he's a stranger to us all. And those who wanted to marry me before him—they were all after money—

Sophia (caressing her). And I thought badly of you at first— do you remember, Pavla?

Pavla. Yes. But I don't like anything bad—I'm afraid of it. You used to look at me with such forbidding eyes, I hid in the corners and cried. I wanted to come and say to you: I'm not bad, I'm not greedy, but I didn't have the courage.

Sophia. You poor little girl. May God be with you! You'll find it hard—

Pavla. I already find it hard. There's that Shokhin always around. He killed a man, and goes about as if it were nothing!

Sophia. Don't worry about him. He's no villain—he's a sufferer.

Pavla. And I hoped to live quietly, with everybody around me kind and smiling, believing that I wished evil to nobody—

Sophia. That they will not believe—no.

Pavla. But why won't they?

Sophia (rises and moves about). Just they won't believe it. You said it well—with everybody smiling—

Pavla. As before a festival—you've done everything, you're tired and ready, and are waiting for the holy day with quiet joy.

Sophia. The festival is still a long way off, my dear, and there's little that's ready for it.

Pavla. Oh, God! Aunt Sonya, teach me—

Sophia. What?

Pavla. Teach me how to live better with people.

Sophia. I don't know how myself. Life goes by in trivialities, as if in a mist—

Pavla. What's your heart's desire?

Sophia. Mine? (*She pauses, then speaks in a low voice, with great force.*) I want to let loose, go wild, commit all sins, all rules, muss everything up. Then, after rising above all men, I'll throw myself at their feet: Listen to me, dear people, I'll say, I'm not your ruler—I'm only a low sinner—lower than anybody—and there are no rulers over you, nor do you need any rulers—

Pavla (*in a quiet frightened tone*). Why that? What's the reason for it?

Sophia. So that people be freed of fear before one another. There's nobody to fear today. Yet everybody's frightened, dejected—everybody lives in fear. You see it yourself. Nobody has the courage to say what he means to the last syllable.

> *Antipa appears at the door and stands listening.*

Pavla. I don't understand it. Won't you ruin yourself that way?

Sophia. God ruined himself for the sake of man, Shokhin's father used to say.

Antipa. What's all this about?

Pavla. Oh!

Antipa (*coming up to her in a hurt tone*). What's frightened you? If you're not guilty, you've nothing to fear. What were you discussing?

Pavla. Oh, various things.

Antipa (*to Sophia, somewhat bluntly*). You should talk less.

> *Sophia moves about without looking at him, hiding her excitement.*

Pavla (*caressingly*). You should shout less. You always shout —there's no need of that—

Antipa (*softly*). That's not because of bad temper—it's just that I have a big voice. It'd be a good thing to have some tea, mistress, eh? Go fix it. Tell them to bring it here. And something sweet too. Run along, dear. (*Pavla goes in. After watching her out of sight, Antipa turns to his sister with resentment in his voice.*) You're spoiling her for me— (*Sophia walks past him in silence. He repeats insistently.*) You're spoiling my wife for me, I say.

Sophia (*suddenly, sharply*). Shut up.

Antipa (*recoiling*). Say—what's the matter?

Sophia. Well, do you find it restful and enjoyable to have a young wife?

Antipa (*slumping into a chair, quietly*). Has she been complaining?

Sophia (*recovering her self-control*). No. I assure you she hasn't. You must forgive me. I'm in a bad mood. Something's troubling me. Please forgive me.

Antipa (*quietly*). You frightened me. Lord have mercy on us! I love her so much—I can't tell you how much!

Sophia (*again moving about*). You're not any happier for it —neither you, nor she.

Antipa. Well—just wait a while! (*After a pause.*) Sonya!

Sophia. Yes?

Antipa. Tell me—how is she with Mikhail? Anything between them?

Sophia (*stopping in front of him*). Get that right out of your head—hear me? And don't encourage the thought in yourself or in anybody else? Where's Hevern?

Antipa (*waving his hand*). In there—up to his ears in plans. To the devil with him—I'm tired of him.

Sophia. You're becoming much too profitable a partner for him.

Antipa (*on the alert*). How so?

Sophia. Just so. Keep your eyes open.

Antipa (*smiling broadly*). Oh, that? And I thought something had gone wrong between you and him—

Sophia. You think what you shouldn't.

Antipa (*sighing*). You're hard to make out, Sonya.

Sophia. And you mustn't shout at Mikhail in Pavla's presence —understand?

Antipa. Well, well. The boy gets on my nerves—too much. What does he live for?

Sophia. You think about yourself.

Antipa (*reflectively*). I won't harm Pavla.

Sophia. Don't make fun of her mother.

Antipa. I dislike that woman.

Sophia (supporting herself against the railing). I feel tired—

Antipa (jumps to his feet and hurries to her). Anything wrong? Shall I get you some water?

Sophia (leaning on him). I'm not feeling well—

Antipa. Why? Good God! What's the matter, Sonya?

Sophia. Wait— Oh, my Lord—

Antipa (putting his arms around her). Ah, my clever little girl! Come, lie down, rest—

> *He leads her away. Tarakanov strolls on from the garden as Mikhail, appearing on the veranda, comes down to the table and pours himself some wine.*

Tarakanov. Is the German gone?

Mikhail. He's a Swede—or a Greek.

Tarakanov. It's the same thing, a stranger. Is he gone?

Mikhail. He's staying for supper.

Tarakanov. H'm! It's amazing!

Mikhail. What is?

Tarakanov. Doesn't anybody notice he smells like a crook?

Mikhail. Oh, well— With you everybody's a crook.

Tarakanov. Not everybody, but half the people are. Where's Sophia Ivanovna? She sees everything.

Mikhail. I don't know—I really don't know.

> *Mikhail sits down on the steps and lights a cigarette. Tarakanov goes off, mumbling to himself and gesticulating. Pavla comes out of the house. Smiling, she stops behind Mikhail and tickles his neck with the end of her scarf. Mikhail speaks without turning to look at her.*

Look out. If Father sees this, there'll be trouble.

Pavla (with a grimace). I can't even tease. I'm young and I'm bored—

Mikhail. Everybody's bored.

Pavla. There must be a gay life somewhere.

Mikhail. Try and find it.

Pavla. Let's go into the garden.

Mikhail. I have to get back to the office. I'll finish my cigarette and in I go to earn my bread with the sweat of my brow—

Pavla (coming down the steps). Then I'll go alone. I'll set off like this and walk on and on for a week or a month. Good-by. Will you be sorry for me?

Mikhail. I've been sorry for you for a long time.

Pavla. That's not true. I don't believe you. (*Goes off. Looking back, shakes her finger at him.*) That's not true.
  Mikhail follows her broodingly with his eyes, puts out his cigarette, and rises. Standing behind him is his father.
Antipa. Where are you going?
Mikhail. To the office.
Antipa. What did she mean by saying "That's not true"?
Mikhail. I don't know. I didn't catch it.
Antipa. You didn't? (*Frowns at his son, as if about to say something, but instead dismisses him with a wave of his hand.*) Run along.
  Hunched over, he slowly walks after Pavla. Anna Markovna peers from around the corner and shakes her fists at him.

CURTAIN

ACT III

Sophia's *study and office—a large room with a big desk, a fireplace right, and two doors left, one door leading to* Sophia's *bedroom, the other to the inner rooms. In the back wall there are two windows and a door opening out onto the veranda.*

Sophia, *holding some papers, is standing at the desk.* Muratov, *about to leave, is flicking a shabby old hat against his leg.*

A gray autumn day looks in the windows through the swaying bare branches of trees.

  Sophia (*with an air of absorption*). One more question.
  Muratov (*inclining his head*). A dozen, if you like.
  Sophia. Tell me simply and frankly—what's prompted you to collect these papers?
  Muratov. My sentiment—
  Sophia. We'll leave sentiment out of it.
  Muratov. What am I to tell you then? (*Shrugs and chuckles.*)

You're so sharp with me I can hardly stand it. I didn't even say what sentiment—

Sophia. Jealousy?

Muratov. It may surprise you, no!

Sophia. A desire to annoy me?

Muratov. Not that either. I'm afraid I can't explain it without making you angry with me. (*After a pause.*) No, you won't understand it. I don't quite understand it myself.

Sophia. Suppose you try.

Muratov (*sighing*). Well, there's a difference of opinion between us, isn't there? (*She nods, watching him closely.*) These papers are proof of the fact that I'm right and you're wrong.

Sophia (*with a sigh*). An evasive answer.

Muratov. Permit me to take my leave.

Sophia (*looking him over*). Good-by. Why are you so lightly dressed? There's a strong wind, and it's likely to rain.

Muratov (*laughing softly*). Don't worry.

Sophia. Why do you laugh?

Muratov. I've a reason—I have, my lady. Well, I'm going.

Sophia. Excuse my not seeing you off. You'll be stopping at the office? Please send Tarakanov over.

> *Muratov goes out. Sophia throws the papers on the desk, wipes her hands with a handkerchief, and presses her fingers to her eyes. Antipa enters through the garden door. He looks unhealthy, disheveled, wears a heavy jacket without a waistcoat, his shirt collar is unbuttoned, and his feet are in felt slippers. Sophia flares up.*

You should have asked whether you could come in.

Antipa (*indifferently*). Where do you get that? I'm no stranger.

Sophia. What do you want?

Antipa. Nothing. (*Looks around.*)

Sophia (*scrutinizing him. In a softer tone*). What's the idea of running around all mussed up like that?

Antipa (*lowering himself into a chair by the fireplace*). When I'm dead you'll dress me up.

Sophia. What on earth—

Antipa. I don't like these genteel old houses. They're not houses, they're coffins. They even have a peculiar odor of their own. I made a mistake in moving over to your place. I've cut myself off from everything.

Sophia. Stop it, please. I've no time to listen to such nonsense.

Enter Tarakanov. Sophia hands him a fat file from her desk.

Matvey Ilich, take out all accounts for the summer house and the Usek Company, please. Do it here right away—

She sits down at the desk and writes. Tarakanov makes room for himself at a little table by the fireplace and puts on his spectacles. Antipa watches him with a smile.

Antipa. What do the newspapers have to say?

Tarakanov. China's taking up arms—

Antipa. Against whom?

Tarakanov. Against us, at the instigation of the Germans.

Antipa. You have no love for the Germans, eh?

Tarakanov. None at all.

Antipa. Why not?

Tarakanov. Because they're more clever than we are.

Antipa. One should respect clever people.

Tarakanov. I do. But I don't like them.

Antipa. You're a queer fellow.

Tarakanov. In Russia everybody who has intelligence is queer.

Antipa. You're probably right there. (*After a pause.*) Although you don't have much intelligence either, but you're queer all the same.

Tarakanov. That's not true.

Antipa. Isn't it? Why did you take off your uniform, give up your job?

Tarakanov. I've been explaining that to you—

Antipa. You've been explaining all right, but you never explained it.

Tarakanov. It is said, turn away from evil and you'll create good—

Antipa (striking the arm of his chair with his hand). Fiddlesticks! Turning away from evil you'll create nothing! No, you have to step right into the evil, strike at its heart, knock it down, trample on it, destroy it root and branch, and not give in to it, let it get the upper hand of you. That's what you must do! Am I right, Sophia?

Sophia. You are. But you're interrupting me.

Tarakanov. That's mere shouting, words, drum-beating. You wait until some evil comes down on you with all its weight—you'll be doing your uttermost to break away from it.

Antipa. I? Not likely. I'm not that sort. I know what our life is—it's a fist fight. No, I won't run away.

Tarakanov. We'll see.

> *Styopka peers into the room from the doorway left.*

Styopka. Antipa Ivanovich, the peasants have come.

Antipa. What peasants?

Styopka. From Kamenskoye.

Antipa. I'll show those scoundrels!

Sophia. Not so fast. It's not their fault. I know it was Hevern's orders—

Antipa. His orders? Are you sure?

Sophia. I'm telling you.

Antipa (going off). The addleheaded German.

Tarakanov. Less addleheaded than any of us.

Styopka. Give me something to read, Sophia Ivanovna.

Sophia. Ask Misha.

Styopka. He chased me away. He's singing right into the young mistress' ear—

Sophia. What's that?

Styopka. They're sitting side by side on the sofa and he's singing a song to her.

Sophia. Well, you run along. And don't prattle about trivial things.

Styopka. I've spoken only to you. (*She goes off.*)

Tarakanov (muttering to himself). The young mistress. What sort of mistress is she?

Sophia. How long have you known Muratov?

Tarakanov. I? About ten years.

Sophia. And what do you think of him?

Tarakanov (looking at her over his spectacles). In the early days I thought quite well of him. He got up many useful things in his line, that's forestry, such as new plantings and that sort of thing. He allowed peasants to collect brushwood, and cleared and drained a lot of forest land. Then, suddenly, it was as if something knocked him on the head—and he's become a most unpleasant character. Our men are like that—as if made of

straw—they flare up and burn with lots of smoke, but give off
neither light nor warmth.

Sophia (listening attentively, her elbows on the desk). What
is it you find so unpleasant about him?

Tarakanov. What do I find? The same as everybody else does.
He has no love for anybody, ruffles everybody's temper, sets
one person against another, tells tales. Also is rather loose as
regards women. Yet he's a clever man—that's the strange part
of it—   *Enter Pavla.*

Pavla. May I come in?

Sophia. Of course.

Pavla. It's cold everywhere.

Sophia. Order them to make a fire.

Tarakanov (handing over a bunch of papers). Here are the
papers. May I go?

Sophia. Thank you. On your way send me Styopka, please.
And Misha, too.   *Tarakanov goes off.*

Pavla. Why all dressed up?

Sophia. I'm expecting a visitor.

Pavla. Well, Misha's written another poem.

Sophia. Any good?

Pavla. Yes. It's about pine trees.

Sophia. Has he been drinking?

Pavla (with a sigh). Since/morning.

                    Anna Markovna appears at the door.

Anna Markovna. Naturally, the boy has to drink himself unconscious.

Sophia. Why has he?

Anna Markovna. Because he's been wronged.

Sophia. Countless people are wronged.

Anna Markovna. And they all drink. What do you think
makes people drink? Your own father drank because he was
wronged. He was clever, but nobody recognized that. So he
began to prove his cleverness by playing rough tricks on others,
just as the forester has been doing. Of course, they took him to
court, but it only made him more vicious. How much does a
man need? A man's soul is like a child's, it's ever so touchy—
Oh, what did I came here for? Oh, yes. Did you give Styopka
a yellow ribbon, Sophia Ivanovna?

Sophia. Yes, why?

Anna Markovna. Then it's all right. You see, she stuck the ribbon in her mop and made eyes at herself in the mirror.

Pavla. Mother, stop that.

Anna Markovna. What do I care? All I say is—you must guard other people's things even more than your own.

Enter Styopka.

Here she is, our beauty—

Styopka. Did you call me?

Anna Markovna (going off). Of course they called you. What's life without you?

Sophia. Light the fire, child.

Styopka (running off). Lord, how the old lady hates me— she has an awful temper!

Sophia. A delightful girl—

Pavla. The only gay spirit in the house. Only she's terribly forward.

Sophia (walking over to Pavla). You should ask Antipa to take you to Moscow.

Pavla. What for?

Sophia. You'll see life in a big city.

Pavla (indifferently). All right, I'll ask him.

Sophia (placing her hand on Pavla's head). You have no desire to go there?

> *Mikhail comes in from the inner rooms, looks at them, and slips quietly into a chair. Almost screened by a drape, he sits there drowsing.*

Pavla. No. I'd like to fall asleep for a year or two, and when I wake up see everything changed—

Sophia. That's childish, Pavla. You have to learn how to build your own life. You can't wait for others to take care of your needs.

Pavla. Please don't be angry with me.

Sophia. You're young and have a kind heart. Are you sorry for other people, is that it?

Pavla. I know what you want to say. But really, Misha doesn't stir any feeling in me at all. I only like listening to him.

Sophia (starting back in surprise). I wasn't talking about that. But now that you've raised the subject, I must say this to you—you're not behaving yourself with him. He's not a child, and it may end badly for you.

Pavla. But I'm so bored, and he's so amusing. What am I to do?

Sophia. Go away with Antipa, and I'll take care of Mikhail myself.

Pavla. Perhaps it'll be better if I go with Mother?

Sophia. You find it hard being with your husband?

Without answering, Pavla presses herself close to the older woman. Sophia lifts the girl's head and gazes into her eyes.

I understand you, dear. I told you I also had a husband—

Styopka rushes in.

Styopka. Sophia Ivanovna! The German has arrived. He looks gorgeous!

Sophia. There— (*Passing her hand over Pavla's face.*) Now then, please leave me alone with him, Pavla—

Pavla (jumping to her feet). Oh, God, how I wish you—

Sophia. Thank you, dear. Ask him to come in, Styopka.

As Pavla goes off, Sophia covers the papers on the desk with a book, touches up her hair before the mirror, and then notices Mikhail sitting in a chair.

Misha! Have you been here long?

Mikhail. Yes.

Sophia. Did you hear what we said?

Mikhail. I heard something. The German has arrived. The nun was making up something.

Sophia. Making up?

Mikhail. Yes, of course. She's always making things up. She still lives as if she were playing with dolls. I'm a doll to her, and so is Father, and you. She'll be like that all her life—

Sophia. You know, there's probably truth in what you say.

Mikhail. Why did you want to see me?

Sophia. That's off for the present. You go now. I'll call later.

Mikhail (rising). Fine. You marry this German, Auntie, and send us all packing to hell—all of us including the romantic papa with his second youth—

Sophia. Do go, please.

Mikhail. Sh-sh! You must be in complete command of your feelings— (*To Hevern, who appears at the door.*) Welcome, you bearer of civilization and culture!

Hevern shakes hands with Mikhail silently, whereupon

Mikhail goes off. Hevern kisses Sophia's hand and follows her to the desk.

Hevern (he is attired in elegant formal dress with a diamond stickpin and diamond ring). You probably guess why I asked you to receive me today.

Sophia (sitting down). I believe I do.

Hevern. It's very gratifying to me.

Sophia. Yes?

Hevern. It makes so many explanations unnecessary. May I smoke?

Sophia. Certainly. *(Moves an ashtray and matches toward him.)*

Hevern. I'm a little excited—

Sophia. Will you have some water?

Hevern. No, thank you. My excitement is natural under the circumstances.

Sophia. You have quite an impressive look today.

Hevern. I wish my thoughts impressed you enough to win your confidence.

Sophia. Well, perhaps you'll tell me what they are.

Hevern. That's precisely the object of my visit. *(Lights his cigar.)* You know I have great respect for your ideas—they match my aims perfectly.

Sophia. I'm flattered to hear it.

Hevern (bowing). Yes. I'm quite sincere. You'll not deny me a knowledge of Russia and Russian people, of course— I'm a good observer, I've lived among Russians for eighteen years and I've studied them well. My conclusion is this—Russia suffers first of all from a lack of healthy people capable of pursuing clearly defined aims. Do you agree?

Sophia. Go on.

Hevern. Yes, you have few people confident of themselves, of their powers. You have too much metaphysics, too little mathematics—

Sophia. As you've said many times before.

Hevern. That's what I think! Now let's take you. You are a woman of intelligence and character.

Sophia. Thank you.

Hevern. It's true. I even think of you allegorically—Sophia Ivanovna is the new, spiritually healthy Russia who, under conditions worthy of her, can perform any task, can do a great amount of cultural work.

Sophia. You're overloading me with praise.

Hevern. I'm perfectly serious. Hence, the alliance with me which I'm proposing has a profound meaning. It's much more than a simple marriage. My energy and yours—why, it'll be colossal. When two strong personalities realize their aims—it's very important. Especially so for Russia in these days when, dismissing all those—dreams, she must at last turn to the simple business of life and get her feet firmly on the ground. Your brother is absorbed in his family life and neglects his business, as I've had occasion to point out to you more than once, in order to protect your interests—

Sophia. Is this your first declaration of love?

Hevern (*somewhat taken aback*). Pardon me—this is something different. I've spoken to you about my sentiments four times already.

Sophia. Four times? Are you sure?

Hevern. I am. I remember the occasions. The first time it was in the garden of the marshal of nobility, at his birthday party— it rained and you got your feet wet. The second time it was in this place, on a bench by the pond. You discomfited me then by saying jocularly that frogs too croak about love.

Sophia. I remember the third and fourth occasions.

Hevern. Of course, it's true about frogs, but if I may say so it was not an appropriate joke. When a man's heart craves—

Sophia. Let's end this conversation, Gustav Yegorovich.

Hevern (*startled*). Why?

Sophia. Does it need explaining?

Hevern (*rising, in an injured tone*). Of course it needs explaining when the other party does not understand. I'll regard it as an insult if you reject—

Sophia. So? Very well then— (*She rises and paces the room.*) You propose to me that together we start saving Russia—

Hevern. You're caricaturing my statement.

Sophia. Well, you propose something of the sort. I do not consider myself capable of such a difficult task. This is in the first place. In the second place, I can't consider you, either, as worthy of that role—

Hevern. What role?

Sophia. Say the role of a cultural worker—

Hevern (smiling). Really? Why?

Sophia. Because you are a petty plunderer.

Hevern (more surprised than injured). Pardon me! This— this I didn't expect. Nor do I understand it.

Sophia. I speak after long deliberation. Here on my desk I have documents which convict you of a series of dishonest actions—

Hevern (sitting down, sharply). There can be no such documents.

Sophia (standing at the desk, calmly and weightily). I have a copy of your agreement with the Buyanovo peasants. I'm acquainted with your deal with the marshal of nobility—

Hevern (shrugging). That was business.

Sophia (in a lower voice, with an effort). You're urging Tarakanov to prepare a false inventory—

Hevern. Tarakanov is mentally unbalanced.

Sophia (lowering her voice still more). And Shokhin, whom you tried to bribe—is he too mentally unbalanced?

Hevern. It's all been misrepresented.

Sophia. You've been dipping more and more and with increasing brazenness into my brother's pocket—is this activity, according to you, also necessary in Russia?

Hevern (wiping his face with a handkerchief). Will you let me explain it to you?

Sophia (walking about the room). Well, my dear sir, what explanations can there be? Everything is clear.

Hevern (carefully putting out his cigar). Then in your opinion I'm a dishonest man, unworthy of being your husband?

Sophia (stops surprised, and laughs). You are an extraordinarily naïve man, you know!

Hevern (smiling and spreading his hands). Well, if I went too far, I did so because I was convinced of your kindly interest in me.

Sophia. I don't follow.

Hevern. I believed that you regarded me as your friend, and regarded my business interests as yours.

Sophia. Oh, I see. Well, you were mistaken.

Hevern. Mistakes should be excused. I felt that seeing the

way your brother is running the business, rather than condemn
me you would approve my foresight—

Sophia (goes up to him and speaks in a quiet but firm voice).
Get out!

*Hevern, bristling, makes a move toward her; she picks up
something from the desk. For a few seconds they stand
staring at each other in silence.*

Hevern (stepping back). You are—a very ill-mannered
woman. You are ridiculous as well!

*He goes off, quickly, putting on his hat before he is out.
Sophia seats herself on the corner of the desk and covers
her eyes with one hand, while rubbing her knee hard with
the other. Styopka appears at the door.*

Styopka (looking at Sophia and sighing). Do you want me to
make a fire?

Sophia (in a low voice). No. Oh, all right, make it.

Styopka. Shokhin asks if you'll see him.

Sophia. Oh, let him wait.

Styopka. He has to go to the forest.

Sophia. Don't bother me! All right, call him in— Quick!

Styopka hurries off, brushing past Antipa in the doorway.

Antipa. What the devil's all the rush? Sonya, what's happened? The German banged into me in the drawing room,
hissing and looking green—and left without saying good-by.

Sophia (in a coarsely cynical tone). He's taken you for ten
thousand this year, my boy.

Antipa. Really? A smart fellow! Doesn't pass up any chances.
Oh, people! And Pavla says one should be kind—people, she
says, are longing to have a warm faith reposed in them.
Where's Pavla—do you know?

Sophia. You should go away somewhere—

Antipa. Indeed! Why should I?

Sophia (putting away the papers on the desk). You've grown
too lazy, Antipa. It's no pleasure even to look at you. And
please leave me now. Why are you running around loose all
day long?

Antipa (bluntly, going off). I'm looking for a place for myself—

Sophia paces the room, straightening up her hair. Styopka

*enters with a load of kindling. Shokhin appears at the door.
Sophia glances at him.*

Shokhin. Shokhin has come.

Sophia. Yes. What is it, Yakov? Quick.

Shokhin. Please discharge me. Let me go.

Sophia. All right. Wait—what's the idea?

Shokhin. There are reasons.

Sophia. Well—I'm very sorry.

Shokhin. I'm sorry too.

Sophia. Has anybody wronged you?

Shokhin. No.

Styopka. He's telling lies. That saintly one, the holy nun, does him wrong—

Shokhin. Tell her to get out—

Styopka. I'll go by myself. (*Runs off.*)

Shokhin. The reason is I can't stay on with the young mistress— I'm afraid of her.

Sophia. What?

Shokhin. She makes me feel uncomfortable—with that pitying look of hers. I can't bear it. Of course, I'm a guilty man. But to be tried every day, that's not justice, that's torture. Since she came into the family it's as if she's put sand in our machine. One doesn't feel right with her. Even you are worn out—

Sophia (*stares at him without listening and speaks quietly*). And such soft, gentle eyes—

Shokhin. Her eyes? Don't believe them. Believe her acts. And there'll be nothing good in what she will do.

Sophia. I wasn't speaking about her.

Shokhin. Those that are quiet—they crawl up close and sting without missing. The snake is quiet.

Sophia. That'll do, Yakov.

Shokhin. Don't believe the German either. He's a stranger and has no shame. As to that man I shot, I mean his wife and children—

Sophia. I'll see to that, don't you worry. But where will you go?

Shokhin. To the city. After that—I don't know.

Sophia. I'm sorry for you.

Shokhin. And I'm sorry for you. You're all alone here. The

boss is drunk without wine. May God grant you success in
everything. Good-by, Sophia Ivanovna.

Sophia. Good-by. (*She extends her hand to him. He takes
and holds it in his, staring at her with furrowed brow.*) Perhaps
you'll change your mind?

Shokhin. No. I'd better stay away till she's dead.

Sophia. She? Why should she die?

Shokhin. Why should she live? She has nothing to live for.
Good-by. (*Backs out of the room.*)

Sophia (*looks after him, rubs her eyes and mutters*). It's a
nightmare.

> *She sees Pavla and Mikhail reflected in the mirror as they
> pass outside the door, with Pavla snuggling playfully to
> his shoulder. In a frightened, quiet voice she calls out:
> "Pavla!" The two enter side by side, Mikhail smiling em-
> barrassedly.*

Mikhail. Oh, a fire! That's nice.

Pavla. Why do you look so glum? (*Puts her arms around
Sophia.*) Hear what Misha's written—

Sophia (*peering into her face*). Look, my child. Only recently, this very day, I spoke to you—

Mikhail. Oh, a serious talk!

Sophia. I'd like you to go out.

Mikhail (*sitting down on the floor by the fire*). No, I won't
go.

Sophia (*in a tired voice*). You seem determined to drive me
mad—really!   *Enter Anna Markovna.*

Anna Markovna (*to Sophia*). And I've been looking for you
everywhere. You shouldn't hide yourself, because Antipa Ivanovich is not quite in his senses today—bawls everybody out—

Sophia. Anna Markovna, I want to talk to them privately.

Anna Markovna (*in an injured tone*). All right, I'll go. Although I'm the mother— (*She goes off.*)

Mikhail. But really, there's nothing to talk about, Aunt Sonya
—there's nothing new. You'd better hear my poem.

Pavla (*gazing narrowly at Sophia and swaying on her feet*).
I don't want to talk about anything either—

Sophia (*looks them over and goes to the desk*). Very well.
Let's sit quietly, then, and calm down.

Pavla. Go on, Misha, read it.

Mikhail. I'm ready, Mother.

Pavla. Again? I thought I asked you not to call me that.

Mikhail. It's your legal rank.

Sophia (impatiently). Read, Mikhail.

Mikhail (smiling). All right. Let me think how it goes.

Pavla. I remember it.   *Anna Markovna appears at the door.*

Anna Markovna (in a loud whisper). Father's coming—stop it.

Sophia. Anna Markovna, you shouldn't—

Anna Markovna. I'm at fault again—

> *Pavla clings to Sophia. Mikhail, on the floor, frowns and moves into the shadow. Enter Antipa. He regards everybody with sullen eyes, his arms hanging at his sides, his fingers moving.*

Antipa. Why must you all stop? Suppose you *are* gathered in a room, reading verse, talking—why not? There's nothing wrong in that— *(Suddenly, with anguish.)* Stop being afraid of me, damn it. I'm a human being like everybody else!

Sophia. Not so loud, Antipa.

Antipa. Shut up. Why do you always stop me? Why does everybody run away from me? Am I a wild beast or what? It's when a man is left alone—naturally he becomes wild—

Mikhail. Father!

Antipa. Yes?

Mikhail. Give Shokhin a raise.

Antipa (slowly). What's this? Making fun of me?

Mikhail. No, no, honest to God! Just that it'll brighten him up.

Antipa. What's that, Sophia?

Sophia. Nothing, just Misha's fooling. Shokhin is leaving us.

Antipa. Is he? Where's he going?

Sophia. I don't know.

Pavla. I'm glad he's going. I'm afraid of him—

Antipa. You're afraid of everything. That's where you make a mistake— *(Pauses.)* So Yakov is leaving? Strange. What's prompted him?

Mikhail. I didn't know he was leaving.

Antipa. What do you know? The father sells lumber, and the son cooks up verse. It's pretty funny—

Mikhail. Here it comes—

Everybody falls silent. Pavla whispers something to Sophia.

Antipa. I thought it was bad manners to whisper.

Sophia (wearily). Why don't you do something? Even drink, if there's nothing else. Anna Markovna, make us some tea, will you?

Anna Markovna. It's too early for tea.

Sophia. I want you to check Hevern's account, Misha.

Mikhail. Right away?

Sophia. Yes.

Mikhail. You've thought this up to get rid of us all. You've taken the best room in the house and object when anybody else sits here.

Sophia. What utter nonsense!

Mikhail. It isn't nonsense.

Antipa (to Pavla). Why are you so quiet?

Anna Markovna. Now if you please. She whispered—it was wrong. She keeps quiet—it's wrong again.

Antipa. Woman, shut up!

Anna Markovna. Oh, my God! Pasha dear!

Antipa. What do you mean always stirring up trouble here?

Sophia. Get hold of yourself, Antipa!

Antipa. Keep quiet, sister. I see through everything. You're blind—

Pavla (quietly and very firmly). Antipa Ivanovich, I'll ask you not to shout at my mother!

Antipa. My shouting won't break her to pieces.

Pavla (moving closer to him). You are a bad and spiteful man. I don't love you—I'm afraid of you.

Antipa. In God's name, Pavla, what's come over you?

Sophia. Wait, listen, Pavla—

Pavla. No, you listen to me. I love Misha.

Mikhail. Oh, for God's sake! (*Shrinks deeper into the shadow.*) Don't believe her, Father. She's just making it up because she's bored.

Antipa sinks into a chair and stares at his wife in silence. He looks fearful.

Pavla (wincing). Well— Oh, God— Kill me—I don't care! I know Misha doesn't love me—I know that. What of it? I love him—he's better than anybody. Well—kill me!

Anna Markovna. Pasha dear, don't speak like that—

Sophia. Anna Markovna, please go.

Antipa. Oh, Pavla! Go! Go quick! Sister, lead her away—quick!

> *Sophia puts her arm around Pavla and leads her out. Anna Markovna follows them silently, like a shadow. Mikhail, sitting on the floor, presses close to the wall behind the fireplace. Antipa sits petrified, staring at the floor like a bull, muttering:*

That's how it is— That's how it is, brother— You're an old man —yes, you are—

> *Fidgets in his chair, pulls open his shirt collar, picks up a ruler from the desk, breaks it, throws the pieces into the fire. Picks up a book, glances at it, tosses it on the floor. Finds a small revolver, smiles, and, screwing up one eye, gazes into its barrel. A calm and serious expression settles on his face as he sits motionless, with his eyes closed, his right hand with the revolver resting on his knee, and his left hand grasping his beard. Mikhail rises, frightened, quietly moves over to him and grabs the revolver, but Antipa holds it fast in his hand as he jumps to his feet and speaks.*

You?

Mikhail. Listen to me, Father—

Antipa. Get out of here—quick.

Mikhail (moving toward the door). I'm not to blame. I want nothing. She said it herself. You heard her—

Antipa. It makes no difference—it's all the same—

Mikhail. I know these thoughts—

Antipa. What thoughts?

Mikhail (pointing at the revolver). These—

Antipa (throws the revolver on the floor, toward the door). Fool! You think I'll do that because of you? You drunkard! Get out!

Mikhail. Don't think badly of me. I know I'm a useless sick man. I feel ashamed in front of you—in front of everybody. I tell you honestly, I seek nothing from Pavla.

Antipa (in a rage). Get out, if you don't want me—to kill you! I'll forget you're my son— (*Suddenly rushes over and, grabbing Mikhail by the collar, shakes him.*) So that's what you're thinking in that filthy head?

Mikhail. It's you who are thinking that—

Antipa. I?

Mikhail. I'm older than you—inside. I've done nothing wrong.

Antipa. You've taken the heart out of me.   *Sophia runs in.*

Sophia. Let go! Let him go! Run, Misha!

Mikhail runs off, picking up the revolver on his way out.

Antipa (*his head bowed, puts his arm around Sophia's shoulder*). Sophia, dear—quick! Get them all out of the house— Hide her somewhere. Send Mikhail away. I'm afraid of what I may do, Sophia—a great sin is walking around me. Do something! My heart—is giving way— (*Sophia seats him in a chair and closes the door.*) That's killed me—

A shot is heard. Antipa jumps to his feet, stares at the floor, and stands speechless.

Sophia (*glances at the desk and dashes to the door*). He's taken the revolver from the desk!

Antipa (*staggering*). It's Misha—my son—

CURTAIN

ACT IV

The same room. ANTIPA *is sitting, as though drunk, in an armchair by the fireplace. Behind him* MURATOV *walks about quietly, smoking, thinking.*

Antipa. What's the doctor saying?

Muratov. How would I know? I just got here with him.

Antipa. Oh, yes.

Muratov (*throwing him a disturbed glance*). He probably hasn't had time to look him over yet.

Antipa. Sophia pushed me out of the room. (*After a pause.*) Why did you come?

Muratov. I've told you—the doctor was at my place when Shokhin drove up—

Antipa. Shokhin— He too killed a man.

Muratov. So I tagged along with the doctor, thinking I might be of some use.

Antipa. You?

Muratov. Why, yes.

Antipa. Where's Shokhin?

Muratov. He's been sent to town for dressings.

Antipa. So. You have an explanation for everything.

Muratov. There's nothing to explain here.

Antipa (*with a snicker*). Nothing, h'm. You haven't much love for me, have you, aristocrat?

Muratov (*stopping for a second*). This is hardly the time to talk about love.

Antipa (*repeating slowly*). Hardly the time to talk about love. What words! Now I'm not afraid to say that I don't love anybody— Except Sophia—I respect her very much. (*After a pause.*) To say "I love"—that's very dangerous. Is the doctor drunk?

Muratov. Not very. As usual.

Antipa. Won't he do some harm to Mikhail?

Muratov. No—you know he's a good doctor.

Antipa. Yes. He's a good man, too. Only you've made him a drunkard. You've corrupted everybody here—including Mikhail — You are a harmful person. Wait!

> *Rises from the chair in alarm. Enter Sophia.*

Sophia (*walking in hurriedly, her sleeves rolled up*). Well, the wound is not dangerous. Do you hear, Antipa?

Antipa. Not dangerous? Is that true?

Sophia. Of course it's true.

Antipa (*sinking into a chair*). Thank you.

Sophia (*walks off to her room, speaking to Muratov on the way*). Don't let him go anywhere.

Muratov (*nods to her, and turns to Antipa*). You see?

Antipa. What did she whisper to you?

> *Sophia returns, carrying some towels.*

Sophia. I told him that you shouldn't go out for a while.

Antipa. You should have told me, not him.

Sophia (going off). That's unimportant—

Muratov. Well, Misha will recover.

Antipa. And I'm mortally sick.

Muratov. Oh, that'll all pass.

Antipa. Yes—when we're dead. And don't you try to cheer me up—I don't want it. Nothing will console me.

> *Pauses. Muratov stops and looks at him out of the corner of his eye.*

You're a man of education, you know the laws of things. Explain this to me. I'm in good health—I'm greedy for work—Perhaps my troubles come because I'm so healthy. But my son is weak and indifferent to everything—why is this? What law is operating here?

Muratov (reluctantly and uncertainly). Well—one generation works, the other gets tired, or rather is born tired—

Antipa. I don't understand—

Muratov. The children apparently show the fatigue of their parents passed on in their blood—

Antipa. Generation—you talk in words that seem to hint at something—

Muratov. I've made no hints.

Antipa. Well, look—some work, others loaf themselves to death. It doesn't seem right.

Muratov. Did you drink much when you were young?

Antipa. I? No. My father did. My wife too had a weakness for it—she came of a drunken family. She was bored with our life, since I hardly ever stayed home. She always smelled of mint or dry tea leaves—she ate them to drown the smell of wine. As for Mikhail, he was spoiled by Sophia—he lived with her, as you know—she taught him to read books, to make up verse. The pendulum, he says, is like a poleax—it chops off the heads of the minutes—a funny idea, minutes with heads—something like ants, I suppose. And yet, who knows, there may be nothing funny about that.

> *He closes his eyes as if dozing off. Sophia appears at the door and makes signs to Muratov. Muratov glances at Antipa and goes over to her.*

Sophia. Misha wants to see him. I took Pavla out of the room.

But she may return. Go and keep her away. She mustn't meet
Antipa for the present—you understand.

Muratov. Of course. But you do waste yourself on trivialities
—it's really shocking.

Sophia. Well, run along.

Muratov. I obey. But think—does it suit one like you—

Sophia (dryly). Are you going?

> *Muratov bows and goes off. Sophia watches him in the
> mirror.*

Antipa (lifting his head slightly). What do you want him for?

Sophia. I don't want him.

Antipa. That's the girl. It's better to beg or steal than live
with the likes of him—

Sophia (coming up to him). Listen—

Antipa. Sonya, how can that be? Father worked, I worked,
we've accumulated enough for a thousand people, but we can
do nothing with it. What has all the struggle been for? Mikhail
is a dead soul. You are childless—

Sophia. Is this the time to talk about these things?

Antipa. How do you like that? And the forester said: "Is this
the time to talk about love?"

Sophia. You *would* find a man like that to discuss love with—
you funny fellow.

> *She puts her hand on his shoulder. He takes it in his own
> hand and looks at her fingers.*

Antipa. Your hand is small, but strong. Ah, you should have
been a wife to me, not a sister—

Sophia (withdrawing her hand). Look—Misha wants to see
you.

Antipa (recoils and half rises). Did he want it himself or did
you put it into his head?

Sophia. He wanted it himself.

Antipa. You swear?

Sophia. You'll have to take my word for it.

Antipa (getting to his feet). It'll be hard for me to see him.

Sophia. Let's go.

Antipa. It always made me feel uncomfortable to look at
him. And what wrong did I do him? He was tired of life, and
I wasn't. Is she there?

Sophia. No. She's not to blame for anything.

Antipa. I know. Her kind are always innocent. It's such as me that are always to blame. Sonya, what is she—who is she, this Pavla?

Sophia. It's too late to ask. She's just a young girl living in the dream of her youth—

Antipa. There's the happiness and rest I've found.

Sophia. You have to pay a stiff price for happiness.

Antipa. I only wanted a little.

Sophia. It always looks small while you hold it in your hands, but let it go, and you learn at once how big and precious it is. (*Hurriedly.*) That has nothing to do with your case.

Antipa. Never mind. I hoped there would be children.

Sophia. You've thought this up now.

Antipa. No, I did hope for it, looked forward to it. A childless wife—what joy is there in that?

> *Sophia wants to answer, but turns away with a wave of her hand.*

What's the matter?

Sophia. I'm waiting for you. Are you coming?

Antipa. I am. Tell me, Sonya, why have women always felt bored and sick to death in my company? They look as if they love you, but they never open their hearts. Why is that?

Sophia. Stop whining.

Antipa. I'm not whining. I used to be a handsome man—

Sophia. In the eyes of women you've always been only half a man—

Antipa. That's a lie.

Sophia. If you think it over, you'll find I'm right.

Antipa (*glancing at the clock on the wall*). And what shall I talk about to Mikhail?

Sophia. You'll have to find a subject.

Antipa. The pendulum is like a poleax— You see, I'm not sorry for him— I'm only ashamed for myself—sorry for myself —because I tortured myself for nothing.

> *Sophia is absorbed in thought.*

Well, let's go.

Sophia (*resolutely*). No. Don't go. It'll be better not to.

Antipa. But what will he think?

Sophia. I'll tell him you're not well—or have dozed off.

Antipa. But perhaps I'd better go?

Sophia (*sternly*). I said no.

Antipa. Then I'll drop in on him in an hour or so—when I feel calmer. My thoughts are all drunk, running wild now. A terrible turmoil is going on in my heart, Sonya.

Sophia. You talk too much! (*Hurries off.*)

Antipa (*walks about the room, then comes to the desk, looks through the papers and mumbles, pointing to the door*). You don't understand everything either, my friend. No. (*Reads one of the papers, throws it back, frowns, picks it up again and reads, muttering to himself.*) Yes— Oh, say! (*Chuckles.*) Ah, Sonya! So that's it!

> *Shokhin, carrying packages, enters cautiously. Noticing Antipa, he draws back.*

Who's there?

Shokhin. Shokhin has come—with dressings.

> *For a few seconds they gaze at each other in silence.*

Antipa. There, Yakov, I too have killed a man.

Shokhin. One can't help it here—

Antipa. And a son at that—

Shokhin. It's too crowded. You can't see who's who.

Antipa. I hear you're leaving.

Shokhin. Yes, but I'm not complaining.

Antipa. Let's go together.

Shokhin. Where to?

Antipa. Where were you going?

Shokhin. I don't know yet.

Antipa. Well, I'll go along with you.

Shokhin. If you really mean it, I'll wait for you. You'll hand over the business to Sophia Ivanovna, I take it?

Antipa. Why not? She'll manage it.

Shokhin. Of course.

Antipa. And we'll go to all the holy places.

Shokhin. I'm not very good at praying—

Antipa. Your father took care of that for you—

Shokhin. It seems so. Where do I put these?

Antipa. What is it? Dressings? Take them in there.

Shokhin. I'm a little afraid—

Antipa. And there was a time you were afraid of nothing.

Shokhin. Everything up to a point.

Antipa. It's hard to live with people, Yakov.

Shokhin. The trouble is, you don't see them as people—they're all either judges or defendants.

Antipa. So, it's settled—we're going?

Shokhin. Well, if you're serious, nothing binds me.

Styopka rushes in.

Styopka. What are you doing here, mister? Hand over the dressings, quick. (*She notices the master, screams, and disappears.*)

Antipa. See? That's how frightful I am.

Shokhin. She's stupid, but a good girl—

Antipa. Is it right to frighten the good ones?

Shokhin (going off). No sense in that.

Left alone, Antipa gazes for a few seconds at a portrait over Sophia's desk, turns down the light of the desk lamp, then turns it up again. Pavla runs in.

Pavla. Sophia Ivanovna— (*Noticing Antipa, draws back and stands with her head bowed.*)

Antipa (comes up to her slowly, touches her head with the palm of his hand and, thrusting it back, looks in her eyes). Well?

Pavla (quietly). Go ahead—beat me.

Antipa. You meek little viper—

Pavla. Don't torture me—beat me—

Antipa. What shall I beat you for? (*Raises his fist.*)

Pavla. Make it quick, O Lord!

Antipa. What shall I beat you for?

Pavla. I don't know—for being young—for having made a mistake, thinking you were different—for not loving you— (*Covers her face.*)

Antipa (grips her hands, draws them apart, and, continuing to hold them, speaks hoarsely). Go—off with you! What have you done to me?

Pavla (sinking onto the floor). I've done nothing—

Antipa releases her hands, and as she falls he slowly raises his foot as if about to kick her. Checking himself, he squats on the floor and, placing her head on his lap, strokes it, whispering.

Antipa. Don't be frightened, my child—I'm not going to touch you—wake up! My sweet child—

Sophia's and Muratov's voices are heard off stage.

Sophia. Stop talking nonsense.

Muratov. But what is going to happen to you?

Enter Sophia and Muratov.

Sophia (rushing over to her brother). What have you done?

Muratov (stepping back with fright). Devil take it—

Antipa. Quiet.

Sophia (feeling Pavla). Has she fainted?

Antipa. I don't know.

Muratov. I'll go call the doctor.

Sophia. Quick, he's in Tarakanov's cottage.

Pavla (comes to and looks around. Speaks first to Antipa). Go away, please. Sonya, take me away.

Antipa. All right. (*Withdraws into the shadow by the veranda door and stands with his back to the others.*)

Sophia. What's happened?

Pavla. He was going to beat me—

Sophia (to Antipa). Please leave the room.

Antipa. I don't want to.

Pavla (stands up, holding on to Sophia). Antipa Ivanovich— you know, I wanted to love you.

Antipa. Don't talk about it.

Pavla. I wanted you to be kinder.

Antipa. H'm—

Pavla. But you never have pity or love for anybody. Why don't you love your son? Why are you jealous of him, why do you drive him away from you? He's a poor sick boy—is that his fault?

Antipa. Is it my fault I'm in better health? Is it my fault I don't feel sorry for those who are good-for-nothing? I love business. I love work. On whose bones has this world been built? Whose sweat and blood have watered the earth? That hasn't been done by the likes of him and you. Can he take upon himself the work I do?

Sophia. That's enough—

Antipa. Hundreds of people live without want, hundreds have come up in the world, thanks to my work and my father's before me. What has he done? I did something wrong, but at least I'm always working toward some end. To listen to you kindhearted people, every kind of work is a sin against something. That's not true. My father used to say, if you don't kill poverty you don't wash away sin, and that's the truth.

Pavla. Nobody speaks well of you.

Antipa. What of it? Out of their envy they accuse me of being rich. I say everybody should be rich, everybody should have power, so no man would have to bow his head before others or wait on them. Let people live in independence, without envy, and they'll be good in themselves. Let them fail to reach this state, and they will be lost in their baseness. Those are Sophia's words, and true words they are.

> *Sophia regards her brother intently.*

Pavla. And how about Misha?

Antipa. There I can do nothing—it's not in my power. I have nothing to blame myself for as regards him. (*Lowering his voice.*) Perhaps I am to blame toward you— I mean, I saw you, you took my fancy—I felt I wanted to taste joy with you, to have some rest—or have I not earned a rest?

Pavla. Lord! Can't we live quietly and peacefully, loving one another—loving everybody?

> *Sophia moves away from her, preoccupied.*

We have to change our way of life.

Antipa (*glumly*). Well, begin—show the way—

Pavla. My dear ones, we cannot—we mustn't go on living like this, without love or pity for anyone. My dear people, can we really hate everybody? Oh, God! Oh, God! After all, there is something we all believe in, there is justice somewhere.

Antipa. It hasn't been made ready for you yet.

Pavla. But surely we must think of justice, look for it—

Sophia (*in a low voice*). You can't think up justice, you have to work it out. Work, that's what we have to do, Pasha, not just look for something. You find only what you've had and lost.

Antipa (*gloomily*). The peace of one's soul is lost.

Sophia. Peace is not justice.

Pavla (*wearily*). I don't understand you—I don't understand anything.

> *Enter Anna Markovna, leading Mikhail. A smile on his face, he walks with a fairly steady step, grasping Anna's shoulder with one hand and stretching the other out in a conciliatory gesture.*

Sophia (anxiously rushes up and helps support him). Why did you get up? You shouldn't have let him.

Anna Markovna. He said, Lead me—I want to see Father.

Mikhail. It's all right, Aunt Sonya.

Anna Markovna. He said, Father won't come to me.

Pavla. But don't you understand—

Anna Markovna. You understand a whole lot! That's right, scold your mother some more!

Mikhail. Just a moment— Don't shout. It's all my fault.

> *Sophia helps him to a chair.*

Antipa (goes over to his son, not looking straight at him, and speaking in a low voice). You shouldn't have done it. I'd have come over myself—a little later. I was about to do it, but— we've been talking here—

Mikhail. Listen, Father—

Sophia. It's bad for you to talk.

Mikhail. It's worse to keep silent.

Antipa. Did you hurt yourself very much?

Mikhail. You must forgive me, Father—

Antipa. Oh, well—forget it! We don't know who's to blame for that—

Mikhail. I know.

Pavla. Who is it then?

Anna Markovna. Who can it be if not the poor, defenseless folks?

Sophia. You mustn't say such things, Anna Markovna.

Anna Markovna. Don't you pick on me, my good woman.

Antipa. For Christ's sake keep quiet, you crow, or I'll—

Sophia. Stop it, Antipa.

Antipa (panting). Pff! What a pest!

Mikhail. Hold on, Father, don't excite yourself. There's nothing really terrible in all this—it's more funny than anything—

Antipa. You would say something like that! Oh, Mikhail—it's all wrong, I tell you—it's all wrong.

Mikhail. Don't let it upset you.

> *Muratov appears at the door and beckons to Sophia. She goes over. They talk agitatedly.*

Sophia. The doctor? Did he really?

Muratov. He did. Says it's all stuff and nonsense. He said the people here have gone bats from having nothing to do—and then he left.

Sophia. But we must have a doctor here. Please send Shokhin to bring him back at once—

> *Muratov makes a wry face and goes off.*

Antipa (to Mikhail). Well, what are you laughing at?

Mikhail. I feel I want to tell you something nice, Father, something right from the heart—

Antipa (embarrassed). Now, now—what's all this about? You keep quiet—rest.

Mikhail. You see, Father, I understand you— Sometimes, quietly, from a distance, I've even admired you. And to admire—that means to like.

Antipa (surprised and incredulous). Did you hear, Sophia? Listen to what he says—

Pavla (to Sophia). But it's bad for him to talk.

> *Sophia checks her with a movement of her head.*

Mikhail. You are an ax in the hand of God—in some great, creative hand— Both you and Aunt Sonya. She's even sharper than you are. Whereas I and all those like me—we're nothing but rust. What I want to say, Father—and I've been thinking it over a lot—is this—there are no useless people—only harmful people. So you mustn't torment yourself.

Antipa (is moved. Bending over, he kisses his son on the brow, then draws himself up). Well, God bless you, son. Thank you. It makes me feel well. May God help you for what you said. A father, Mikhail—a father is not just a lump of flesh either—he's a living being, with a soul—he too loves. How can a man not love? He can't help it—all the joys are in love—

Pavla (weeping quietly). Oh, dear, I don't understand—

Antipa (to Pavla triumphantly). You see? (To Mikhail.) Then, too, being your father, how well I know you. Why, before you were able to talk I was already anxious about you, son —I thought—a man will grow here who is the closest thing I have—he'll take upon himself my labors and my sins—he'll justify my whole life—

Mikhail (deeply stirred). I've nothing to take them with— Aunt Sonya, I want—

> *He faints. Sophia rushes to him. Pavla, frightened, jumps out of the way. Antipa goes down on his knees. Anna*

Markovna keeps to her daughter's side. Muratov appears at the door.

Pavla (in a loud whisper). He's died.

Sophia. Stop it.

Anna Markovna. They got him at last.

Antipa. What's the matter with him, Sophia? Where's the doctor?

Sophia. The doctor's left. Bring some water—

Pavla (excitedly). There. Couldn't they have gone to his room? Oh, the heartless people!

Muratov (in a low voice). You shouldn't make so much noise.

Pavla (angrily). Leave me alone. What do you want? I don't like you.

Muratov (bowing). That leaves me practically undisturbed.

Mikhail (coming to). Help me to—

Sophia (to Antipa and Muratov). Lift him.

Mikhail. It's all right. I can manage—

               Antipa and Muratov lead him out. He laughs.

So much attention— I'm honored!   *The three of them go off.*

Pavla (stopping Sophia). What am I to do? Tell me—

Sophia. Wait. I have to see about Misha.

Pavla. I feel I'm going to die too. Tell me, what am I to do? Where am I to go?

Sophia. Figure it out for yourself. You're no wife to Antipa, no sister to Mikhail—

Anna Markovna. I told you we shouldn't sell our home.

Pavla. Keep quiet, Mother.

Anna Markovna. Where will you hide yourself now?

Sophia. You talk a lot about love, Pavla, but you don't know how to love. When one loves somebody, everything is clear— where to go, what to do—it all takes care of itself and one doesn't have to ask anybody about anything.

Anna Markovna. Now you know, live as it pleases you. Yes, fine advice you're giving her—

Sophia. On a sunny day you don't ask why it's bright. The sun hasn't risen yet in your soul, Pavla.

Anna Markovna. Don't listen to these speeches, Pavla, don't listen to them.

Sophia. You do a great deal of harm to your daughter, Anna Markovna.

Anna Markovna. Of course, who could be more harmful than a mother? Oh, no, my good woman, permit me to say—

Sophia (turning toward the door). I know it's useless to discuss this with you—forgive me, it just slipped out— (*Goes off.*)

Anna Markovna. Run, run quick to your lover.

Pavla. It's not true. She hasn't a lover.

Anna Markovna (calmly). No matter. She will have one.

Pavla (walking about the room). The sun hasn't yet risen in my soul—

Anna Markovna. Just you believe everything she says! Don't think of the sun but of yourself—how to have a quiet and pleasant life. Everybody wants a pleasant life. You must leave that bandit, and that lady, too, is no companion for you—she's of the same thieving blood. And we are quiet people. You have your own money—twenty-five thousand—and there'll be more if you look for it. With his own money a person can live as he likes—a ruble that's your own is dearer than a brother— Then take me—what sort of life do I lead in this house? It's time for me to get a rest—I'm forty-one and what am I here?

Pavla. Oh, what you're saying has nothing to do with it. Oh, why did I leave the convent?

Anna Markovna. With your own capital you can live like a lady, even in a convent. You could take me with you. There's no friend more faithful than a mother—she understands everything—she'll cover up everything.

Pavla. Wait—somebody's coming.

Anna Markovna. Let's get away from here, shall we? The police may be here soon.

Pavla. The police?

Anna Markovna. Certainly. I've sent for them.

Enter Muratov.

Pavla. How is he?

Muratov. He's tired and has dozed off.

Pavla. He won't die?

Muratov. He will eventually—that's certain.

Pavla. But when? Not now?

Muratov. I don't know exactly when.

Anna Markovna. You shouldn't make fun of our simplicity, sir.

Pavla. Forget it, Mother. The wound isn't dangerous, is it?

Muratov. It was a small caliber revolver without much fire-power—the bullet grazed a rib and came out through his side—nothing dangerous in that.

Pavla. Thank God! Thank God! Vassily Pavlovich, I believe I was rude to you today—

Muratov. Don't worry about that. I know your Christian sentiments.

Pavla. I don't even remember what I said.

Muratov. I assure you it was nothing.

Anna Markovna. You're all mussed up, Pasha—

Pavla (glancing in the mirror). Heavens! Why didn't you tell me before?

Anna Markovna. I was too busy.

Pavla. Please excuse me, I have to leave you.

Muratov. By all means.

Pavla. So Misha will be up soon?

Muratov. I don't know. The doctor says his organism is worn out by too much drinking and dissolute living.

Pavla. Oh, such words—

Anna Markovna. You run along. These things are no concern of yours.

> *The two go off. Muratov sits down in the chair at the desk, bends over, and clasps his head in his hands. He looks deeply depressed. Enter Sophia. At the sight of Muratov her tired face becomes stern. Muratov lifts his head and sits up straight.*

Sophia. I suppose you're tired?

Muratov. And you?

Sophia. I am a little.

Muratov. You should rest. I'll be off in a moment. But before I go, may I ask you a question?

Sophia (after a pause). Go ahead.

Muratov. I want to apply for a transfer to the Vladykin forestry station. You know the forester there has committed suicide—

Sophia. Yes, I know.

Muratov. But should I decide to stay on here, could I count—

Sophia (banging the desk with something, resolutely). No.

Muratov. But let me finish—I wanted to ask if I could count on a change in your attitude toward me.

Sophia. I understood your question without hearing it all.

Muratov (*rises, smiling*). Shokhin killed a man, but really you treat him more kindly than you do me.

Sophia (*after a pause*). Possibly— Probably— What is Shokhin? He's an honest brute. He thought it was his duty to kill people who stole from his master. But he has realized what he did. He will not forgive himself for it as long as he lives. He regards people differently now. (*She sits down.*)

Muratov. You are wrong as always.

Sophia. In the past seven years, the Shokhins at your forestry station have killed and maimed several dozen men.

Muratov. Not as many as that—

Sophia. And how many more have been thrown into jail, how many families have been ruined for an armful of brushwood! Have you counted those?

Muratov. Of course not. Nor do I see what business you have with these statistics. Madam, this is all romanticism. How would you recommend dealing with thieves?

Sophia. I don't know, but not that way. They don't steal from us, for example.

Muratov. They don't? This, madam, is not a fact but only an appearance, as our doctor, another romantic like you, is fond of saying.

Sophia. We'll have to bring this argument to a close. It flares up every time we meet.

Muratov. You argue with me quite unnecessarily.

Sophia (*rising*). Now listen to me, Vassily Pavlovich. In my eyes you're worse than Shokhin—than any drunken peasant. A peasant can be made into a man. You are hopeless. It's not easy for me to say all this to you—

Muratov. Romanticism doesn't suit a business woman like you.

Sophia. No, it isn't easy, either, to see you as you are. An intelligent and educated man who has no love for people— no desire to work—that repels me— I saw the fire go out, I saw you go to pieces, debauch others—

Muratov. Five minutes ago, from another room, I overheard

Anna Markovna utter a wise thought—everybody, she said, wants a pleasant life. That is profoundly true. Those people, including your nephew, whom I've supposedly debauched— what are they worth? What difference does it make whether it is I who'll crush them, whether it'll be done by somebody else, or whether they will slowly crush one another?

Sophia. It is easy to be a Mephistopheles in a country town. You should try to be an honest man.

Muratov. Quite well said. But what is an honest man?

Sophia. We have nothing to talk about.

Muratov. In other words, you can't answer me. What a solitary person you are—alone and powerless!

Sophia. That's not true. There are people somewhere who feel about life as I do. After all, one can take into his soul only what exists in life—and nothing else. I have something in my soul that's good and radiant. It must therefore exist outside my soul too. I have faith in the possibility of a different life. Therefore, in other people too there is this gracious faith. There are many things I don't understand. My education is deficient. But I feel life is a blessing and people are good— And you always lie about people—and even about yourself.

Muratov. I always speak the truth.

Sophia. The truth of those who are lazy, self-centered, or injured in their feelings—it's something evil and decaying—a dying truth.

Muratov. Until today it has been regarded as immortal.

Sophia. No, there is another kind that lives and grows— There is another Russia, not the one in whose name you speak. You and I are strangers to each other. I'm no traveling companion for you, and now, I hope, we've closed the subject.

Muratov (taking his hat from the mantelpiece). Unfortunately. But I'm convinced that on the way to that other truth you'll break your neck. I say chuck these fantastic dreams and accept my hand, the hand of an interesting man—will you?

Sophia gazes at him in silence. Muratov moves toward the door.

Think it over. We could go abroad, to Paris—it's far more entertaining than your town Myamlin. You're young, beautiful. They know how to appreciate beautiful women in Europe— what innumerable pleasures are in store for you! And I'm not jealous—your little flirtations will even please me— We could make life burn bright. What do you say?

Sophia (winces and speaks quietly, with disgust). Please go.

Muratov. It makes me sad—

> *Antipa runs into him in the doorway.*

Antipa. Let me by, will you?

Muratov. Well, good-by. (*Goes off.*)

Antipa. Good-by. (*To Sophia.*) Has Mikhail gone to sleep? That was a good talk I had with him. (*Looks closely at her and glances at the door.*) Has that slimy devil upset you with something again? Why are you so nice to him?

Sophia. A long time ago—some six years back—I liked that man—

Antipa. You were young. Do you want me to go?

Sophia. Wait— It doesn't matter, do as you like.

Antipa (after a pause). Perhaps Mikhail will drink less now— what do you think, Sonya?

Sophia. What?

Antipa. Well, never mind. Think your own thoughts— I'll go.

Sophia. What did you ask?

Antipa. I said perhaps Misha will cut down on his drinking.

Sophia. I doubt it. Hardly. Don't bother him. Leave him to me.

Antipa. I'm ready to leave everything to you. But what about —her?

Sophia. Let her go.

Antipa (quietly). Where to?

Sophia. Anywhere she wants.

> *Antipa sits down, lapsing into silence. Sophia walks over to him.*

What else can you think of?

Antipa (sullenly). It's not the custom among our kind to divorce our wives.

Sophia. What sort of a wife is she to you? Your life will be torture with her.

Antipa. No, that's no good. I'd better go myself. I'll leave everything to you and go where my feet take me. I've nothing to live for now. Ah, it's a great pity you have no children.

Sophia (moves away from him coldly). Who made me marry a dying man?

Antipa. Well, I did. I know. But then it's made you rich, the first woman in the district, stronger than any of these twopenny-halfpenny gentlefolk. As for children, they come not only from husbands—

Sophia. Your kind consideration comes too late!

Antipa. Ah, Sonya, Sonya—

Sophia. What are you "ah-ing" about? You won't go anywhere. That's all nonsense.

Antipa (*reflectively*). I feel ashamed. It's all wrong—all wrong! I'm not afraid of sin, but I don't like misery. And it's grabbing hold of me, this misery. With misery you can neither live nor work.

Sophia. Forget it. One can't escape from oneself. I feel no better than you do, and my misery is more bitter than yours, but I don't hide myself away. If you only know how painful it is to lose respect for a man—how it breaks one's heart— If you only knew how eagerly I've looked for good men, what faith I've had in finding them. Well, I haven't found one yet. But I'll go on looking—I will.

Antipa. We're unlucky people, you and I, Sophia. We have only enemies around us.

Sophia. If they were only clever. A clever enemy is always a good teacher.

Antipa. What can he teach?

Sophia. How to resist. My husband, for example. He was an enemy to me, but I respect him—he taught me a lot! (*Comes up to Antipa and lays her hand on his head.*) Well, enough of that. We are alone now, just you and me, and we'll live alone. Who knows, good people may come along yet who will teach us and help us. After all, good people do exist, don't they?

Antipa (*reflectively*). If you don't show your own goodness, you won't find anything good. Those are your own words—

Sophia. Show it then. Pull yourself together. Remember—did you ever give in to anybody? Must you give in to misfortune? Of course you mustn't.

Antipa (*rises, throws back his shoulders, and looks at his sister, smiling*). You make everything so simple, Sophia. Where do you get it, God bless you. Let me embrace you, my only one

—thank you! (*They embrace. Antipa brushes away his tears.*)
Well, let's live, let's argue. Now I'll make things hum—it'll
shake the earth.

 Sophia. That's more like it! Now go. I have to be alone—go,
dear! We're friends—and I'm glad.

 Antipa. Don't speak or I'll cry.

        Shokhin appears in the doorway.

 Shokhin. The Chief of Police has come.

 Antipa (*angrily*). What? Why?

 Sophia. Who asked him to come?

 Shokhin. Anna Markovna sent Vassily for him.

 Antipa. I'll show her—

 Sophia. Stop. I'll see to it myself. Keep out of it, stay here.

 Antipa. No, I'll throw her out the window, together with her
daughter.   *Shokhin grins broadly.*

 Sophia. Shokhin, don't let him go. (*To Antipa.*) Do you
hear me? Sit quietly.

 Antipa (*rushing about the room*). They called the police—
I'll show them! Why are you grinning?

 Shokhin. No reason.

 Antipa. Better not be! Do you think I'm really going with
you? No, let others step out of it—I'll stay where I belong.
Frightening me with the police, eh? (*Stopping before Shokhin.*)
And you too. You can't go anywhere—forget it. You've committed a sin against the people and have to redeem it before
them.

 Shokhin. But I'm going to stay now—

 Antipa. That's fine. It's a shameful thing to keep knocking
around. Look how our mistress Sophia Ivanovna bears up, and
she's a woman.   *Pavla runs in.*

 Pavla. Antipa Ivanovich, there's a visitor there—

 Antipa (*checking her with a movement of his hand*). I know.
It's the police. You have nothing to fear—it was your mother
who sent for him. Go your own way. Leave us.

 Pavla (*alarmed*). Where shall I go?

 Antipa (*turning away from her*). It's up to you. Good-by.

 Pavla. But where can I go?

 Antipa. Your mother will show you. Good-by.

 Pavla goes off slowly as Shokhin makes way for her, bow-

ing his head. Antipa walks to the veranda door and stops there, his head pressed against the glass pane. Shokhin gives a heavy sigh. Without changing his position, in a low voice Antipa repeats:

Good-by.

CURTAIN